THE BRIEF COMPASS

THE BRIEF COMPASS

The Nineteenth-Century German Novelle

ROGER PAULIN

CLARENDON PRESS · OXFORD
1985

Oxford University Press, Walton Street, Oxford OX2 6DP
Oxford New York Toronto
Delhi Bombay Calcutta Madras Karachi
Kuala Lumpur Singapore Hong Kong Tokyo
Nairobi Dar es Salaam Cape Town
Melbourne Auckland
and associated companies in
Beirut Berlin Ibadan Mexico City Nicosia

Oxford is a trade mark of Oxford University Press

Published in the United States
by Oxford University Press, New York

© Roger Paulin 1985

All rights reserved. No part of this publication may be reproduced,
stored in a retrieval system, or transmitted, in any form or by any means,
electronic, mechanical, photocopying, recording, or otherwise, without
the prior permission of Oxford University Press

British Library Cataloguing in Publication Data

Paulin, Roger
 The brief compass: the nineteenth-century
German novelle.
 1. German fiction—19th century—History and criticism
 I. Title
 833'.009   PT763

ISBN 0-19-815810-6

Library of Congress Cataloging in Publication Data

Paulin, Roger.
 The brief compass.

 Bibliography: p.
 Includes index.
 1. German fiction—19th century—History and
criticism. 2. Short stories, German—History and
criticism. I. Title.
 PT763.P38   1985   833'.01'09   85-13596
ISBN 0-19-815810-6

Set by Wyvern Typesetting Ltd, Bristol
Printed and bound in
Great Britain by Biddles Ltd,
Guildford and King's Lynn

For Eric Herd

PREFACE

This book proceeds largely out of my practice and experience as a teacher of German. I hope that it will provide some new insights into a subject on which a great deal has already been written. Rather than retrace the steps of others or reiterate their arguments, my aim is to place the German Novelle more squarely into the context of nineteenth-century literature—not only in Germany—than I believe has hitherto been done. Through this approach and method I hope that readers may see unexpected aspects in the most familiar of texts and gain new insights into them.

The book also touches on my own research interests. When, nearly fifteen years ago, I wrote two review articles, about the literature on Gotthelf and on the later Tieck respectively, I was surprised at the extent to which older, prescriptive views of the Novelle withheld recognition from these two writers' talents; that their *œuvre* seemed to be reduced in interest to those works that suited a more stringent view of the Novelle—that is, *Die schwarze Spinne* and *Der blonde Eckbert*. There seemed to be little dialogue between those seeking to see Tieck or Gotthelf in their historical context and others striving to define or describe the Novelle. I am of course simplifying what is in reality a complex issue and a somewhat contentious debate. Yet it is my hope to be able to reconcile theory, practice and social context, as factors all equally worthy of investigation. In proceeding from my teaching experience, I have chosen as examples for my argument texts that are widely used in schools and universities in the English-speaking countries. I have, however, made a few tentative suggestions about extending this canon: perhaps to include, say, Wilhelm Hauff, and certainly Ferdinand von Saar. My main hope is that we may start to read German nineteenth-century prose fiction in its European context, noting that it has nothing to lose and everything to gain by this reference beyond its own confines. It is, after all, a European genre, not, as I shall be pointing out, a 'Deutsches Hausthier'.

Roger Paulin
June 1984
Trinity College, Cambridge

ACKNOWLEDGEMENTS

My colleagues in the Department of German, Elisabeth Stopp and Peter Hutchinson, kindly read the manuscript and made most helpful comments. Anthony Close of the Department of Spanish gave me useful guidance on the Romance literatures. My Trinity colleagues Marian Jeanneret and David Kelley gave of their time to listen and talk, passing on valuable points. I am grateful to Jim Reed of St John's College, Oxford, for his wonted clarity of judgement and good sense.

During the time of writing, my wife and family and I rediscovered the pleasures of reading stories to each other. And that, in the age of television, is surely something.

CONTENTS

Bibliographical Note — xiii

'*ein Deutsches Hausthier*'? Some preliminary remarks — 1

Chapter One
'*or avenne che . . .*': The Novelle from the Renaissance to 1790 — 11

Chapter Two
'*unterhaltend*' and '*befriedigend*': Goethe's renewal in 1795 — 20

Chapter Three
'*etwas muß geschehen*': The Romantics — 25

Chapter Four
'*moralische Erzählungen*': Heinrich von Kleist and the Novelle tradition — 37

Chapter Five
'*schildert Alles*': The Biedermeier Novelle — 58

Chapter Six
'*Freude an der Welt*': The Realist Novelle — 76

Chapter Seven
'*die Schwester des Dramas*': Shakespearean themes in the Novelle — 82

Chapter Eight
'*unerhörte Begebenheit*', '*Wendepunkt*', '*Falke*': Definitions in their context — 90

Chapter Nine
'*von ziemlich gleichem Werthe*': The case of Theodor Storm — 108

Appendix
Selected statements on the theory and practice of the
Novelle   129

Notes   152

Index of terms   165

Index of names   166

BIBLIOGRAPHICAL NOTE

The following texts, listed chronologically, have proved especially useful and represent a kind of basic bibliography. In the notes, certain abbreviations are used, as indicated here in square brackets.

Karl Konrad Polheim, 'Novellentheorie und Novellenforschung (1945–1963)', *Deutsche Vierteljahrsschrift f. Literaturwissenschaft und Geistesgeschichte* 38 (1964) 208*–316* [Polheim].
E. K. Bennett, *A History of the German* Novelle, revised and continued by H. M. Waidson (Cambridge 1965).
Theorie und Kritik der deutschen Novelle von Wieland bis Musil, ed. Karl Konrad Polheim, Deutsche Texte 13 (Tübingen 1970) [*Theorie und Kritik*].
Rolf Schröder, *Novelle und Novellentheorie in der frühen Biedermeierzeit*, Studien zur deutschen Literatur 20 (Tübingen 1970) [Schröder].
Novelle, ed. Josef Kunz, Wege der Forschung lv (Darmstadt 1973) [*Novelle*].
Realismus und Gründerzeit. Manifeste und Dokumente zur deutschen Literatur 1848–1880, ed. Max Bucher, Werner Hahl, Georg Jäger and Reinhard Wittmann, Epochen der deutschen Literatur. Materialienband, 2 vols (Stuttgart 1975–6) [*Realismus und Gründerzeit*].
Die romanische Novelle, ed. Wolfgang Eitel, Ars Interpretandi 7 (Darmstadt 1977) [*Die romanische Novelle*].
Martin Swales, *The German* Novelle (Princeton 1977).
Handbuch der deutschen Erzählung, ed. Karl Konrad Polheim (Düsseldorf 1981).

'*EIN DEUTSCHES HAUSTHIER*'?
SOME PRELIMINARY REMARKS

i. The Novelle and nineteenth-century literature

Like the griffin, the sphinx or the basilisk, the 'pure' Novelle in German literature is a creature of myth and imagination. Travellers from the realms of gold return wide-eyed with accounts, but sightings can have been few and authentication almost impossible. Like medieval cartographers, they fill in the blank spaces on the map of nineteenth-century literature with fabulous creatures; the ocean wastes or torrid tracts of the world of poetry are punctuated with critical terms like 'Begebenheit', 'Wendepunkt' or 'Falke'.

The literary historian who tackles the subject of the nineteenth-century Novelle in Germany may perhaps be permitted a little initial light-heartedness. For he will discover very soon that the subject has been conducted at all times with high seriousness, taxonomic scrupulousness and definitive prescriptiveness. The relatively narrow scope, the obligato accompaniment of theory to practice, the high expectations placed on this literary form—these are all factors which may help to explain both the seemingly disproportionate attention which the genre has received and the ever-continuing attempts to define its special properties.

It is not my concern to attempt yet another definition of the Novelle or to trace the development of 'Novellentheorie', although these questions cannot be idly brushed aside as irrelevant. Rather this study will seek to investigate *why* people wrote in this particular genre at a particular time and how it came about that theory and practice coincided or diverged, as the case may be. It will take very much to heart the statement made by Gottfried Keller in 1881, in a letter to Theodor Storm: 'Das Werden der Novelle, oder was man so nennt, ist ja noch immer im Fluß.'[1] For the Novelle, like any other literary genre, was subject to peculiar constraints and urges which are those of a particular historical situation; it did not emerge fresh and complete at one given moment, but evolved according to processes that are historical, intellectual and social.

All this means that we shall be concerned not just with the history of the Novelle over about eighty years, but also with the history of German literature during the same period. For, whatever one may say about attempts to prescribe what a Novelle should be, the besetting sin of some (but not all) kinds of older Germanist 'Novellenforschung' has been their unwillingness to look at the wider context. Romance studies, to their credit, have nearly always done this, and my study will owe much to what they have been able to show in this respect. If the historical context matters, then we might as well begin with the position in European literature in the nineteenth century. For, unless the Novelle is one of those peculiarly German phenomena like *Faust II* or *Der Ring des Nibelungen*, it is worth, however briefly, seeing it in relation to the literatures across its borders.

Is the German Novelle, as Theodor Mundt suggested in 1834, a 'Deutsches Hausthier'?[2] No, it is not. Its name merely hides the family likeness to terms such as 'story' or 'tale' or 'sketch' or 'conte' or 'récit'. The German Novelle is part of the whole mass of short prose fiction produced in European and American literature during the nineteenth century, and it must ultimately stand or fall in comparison with that larger corpus. It would be an act of considerable hardihood to claim an absolute uniqueness for German story-writing in a century that produced works of the order of *The Murders in the Rue Morgue*, *Pique-Dame*, *Colomba* or *Benito Cereno*. And it is not without reason that, especially later in the century, German writers were looking over their shoulders at what Turgenev or Mérimée or Maupassant could show them. Paul Heyse's and Ludwig Laistner's *Novellenschatz des Auslandes* of 1884–7 testifies eloquently to this sense of belonging to a wider community of excellence. It can also be seen that those questions that preoccupied German writers and critics in the nineteenth century in respect of shorter prose fiction were shared by their foreign counterparts, with the exception that in France, England, America and Russia questions of practice took precedence over theory, and that, by and large, aesthetic theory was there a matter formulated more by writers as they went along than by professional critics.

But, it will be argued, none of the other literatures cited is so especially noted for short prose fiction as is German. Surely the century of Dickens, Thackeray and Henry James, Balzac and

Flaubert, Tolstoy and Dostoevsky, stands on its own merits without being reminded of its admittedly remarkable achievements in shorter stories. That cannot be denied. On the other hand, the sheer richness and weight of novels appealing to a special kind of middle-class consciousness in the nineteenth century can very easily make us overlook the merits of the shorter forms. The short story or 'conte' can even allow for an escape from considerations that are more especially, or even oppressively, social. Edgar Allen Poe, a master of brevity and imagination, drops this aside in a review of stories by Nathaniel Hawthorne in 1847:

Were I called upon, however, to designate that class of composition which . . . should best fulfil the demands of high genius—should offer it the most advantageous field of exertion—I should unhesitatingly speak of the prose tale as Mr. Hawthorne has here exemplified it. I allude to the short prose narrative, requiring from a half-hour to one or two hours in its perusal. The ordinary novel is objectionable, from its length, for reasons already stated in substance. As it cannot be read at one sitting, it deprives itself, of course, of the immense force derivable from *totality*. Worldly interests intervening during the pauses of perusal, modify, annul, or counteract, in a greater or less degree, the impressions of the book. But simple cessation in reading would, of itself, be sufficient to destroy the true unity. In the brief tale, however, the author is enabled to carry out the fulness of his intention, be it what it may. During the hour of perusal the soul of the reader is at the writer's control. There are no external or extrinsic influences—resulting from weariness or interruption.[3]

This review does not say what a short story absolutely must be and lays down no rules of composition. It lists certain advantages of the short prose work without prescribing the one or proscribing the other. But the relationship between novel and story in Flaubert or Turgenev might produce a similar pattern, in that the shorter work produces greater scope for, as the case may be, the exotic, the psychological sketch or the concentration briefly but in depth on the obsessions of one character.

The application of this wider analogy to German literature is, however, not without its difficulties. For there is the question, put so aptly and trenchantly by J. M. Ritchie,[4] as to whether German literature really conforms to the patterns of the other major literatures of the nineteenth century, whether indeed it had not cut itself off from the European mainstream. Had German literature, hemmed in by its peculiar political and social constraints, being part of a language and culture but not of a nation with an identifiable centre, not been forced to retreat from the kind of wide-scale comment and commitment which were possible in other countries? Had the Germans even failed to produce anything commensurate with European and American literature, so that a relatively minor form like the Novelle stands out all the more? Do we thus have in the Novelle a form *faute de mieux*?

There is no single answer to these questions or allegations. In some ways, German literature from about 1795 onwards does indeed seem to lag behind its counterparts in other countries. But we should not forget that, at certain times, notably up to about 1825, it seems remarkably ahead and is acknowledged by others to be so. Madame de Staël's *De l'Allemagne* of 1810 is one of the key works of the century in opening up to the French what German literature had to offer; August Wilhelm Schlegel could in 1836 state that his Vienna lectures on drama were a household word from 'Cadiz to Edinburgh, Stockholm and St Petersburg'.[5] There was a time when Germany seemed to be in the position of giving, with Poe and Nerval taking Hoffmann's stories, young Frenchmen imitating Schiller's tragedies, with Goethe's novels—but also Jean Paul's— being read and discussed by a wide circle of literati. The *Edinburgh Review* of October 1827[6] is even prepared to risk the comparison of modern German literature with that of the Elizabethans. That influence, and that fascination, never ceased during the century. Yet it did not lead to a literature along the same patterns as in other countries and to the same kind of intellectual and social groupings as in France or England or Russia.

We see this when we come to examine the German novel in the nineteenth century. The novel, due to its very dominance and sheer quality in the period under discussion, has come to be seen as the touchstone of literary quality. Where it fails, a whole literature is seen to fail; where the social conditions do not seem to exist for the novel to thrive, the society concerned is deemed to be inadequate. Few would wish to disagree with Roy Pascal's now famous dictum of 1956 that the German novel in the nineteenth century produced 'failure after failure'.[7] That is, in European terms. True, few scholars writing in English have taken up his challenge, issued at the same time,[8] to explore the further possibilities of the genre in Germany, and have been content with establishing a 'German tradition' in the 'Bildungsroman' while sedulously neglecting, say, the Romantic novel or Jean Paul or Immermann. By and large, however, Pascal's statement remains true. The usual argument adduced to explain this parlous state of the novel—and the conversely strong state of the Novelle—is the lack of social cohesion, the lack of a Paris or a London or a St Petersburg to provide the political and social focus for literature. The novel is the product of the city, the Novelle of the province. Again, the arguments seem incontrovertible. Admittedly, during the Napoleonic period, fragmentation seems not to have had a bad effect on German literature; but thereafter, the opposite seems to apply. And, in as much as so many of the novels of Balzac or Flaubert or Dickens or Thackeray or Tolstoy presuppose a society that is urban, sophisticated, polished, close to the centres of political power, knowing itself to be the arbiter and source of reference in matters of style and taste, the German novel—or Novelle for that matter—cannot compete. Freytag's novel *Soll und Haben* of 1855 teaches us how pernicious the *grand monde* is and how preferable it is to stay in one's station; Wilhelm Raabe's *Der Hungerpastor* of 1863-4 begins in 'ein Nest' in which the hero grows up and has him returning to another. We do not sense in these novels that same strain between urban values and those of the 'provinces' that underlies Balzac's title 'Scènes de la vie de province' or which is behind the tragedy of an Emma Bovary, who will never find in Rouen what there is in Paris. By contrast, we find the conscious desertion of urban values in Keller's *Der grüne Heinrich* or Stifter's *Der Nachsommer*, despite their being so different from each other in tone and emphasis. Gustav Freytag's words of 1853 seem to be those of resignation rather than of affirmation:

Wir haben kein Salonleben, wir haben keine Salonsprache, wir sind nicht in einer großen Stadt zusammenzubringen, und wenn wir einmal zusammengedrängt werden, präsentiren wir uns nicht vortheilhaft. Wer uns schildern will, muß uns aufsuchen in unserer Arbeitsstube, in unserem Comptoir, unserem Feld, nicht nur in unserer Familie. Der Deutsche ist am größten und schönsten, wenn er arbeitet. Die deutschen Romanschriftsteller sollen sich deshalb um die Arbeit der Deutschen kümmern. So lange sie das nicht thun, werden sie keine guten Romane schreiben.[9]

Here indeed is a writer, after 1848, saying that the Germans should not try to emulate others' sophistication; it is a tactical retreat from something that does not seem to be within German writers' scope.

He is saying, by implication, that where they have tried to be part of a *grand monde*, like the Young Germans (quite ambitious social novelists, incidentally), it has led, not to a capital of a united Germany, but to a political disaster.

But Freytag's words, which could also be a superscription over many of the best Novellen of the century, need not be an absolute criterion. The 'failure after failure' is not for lack of trying. Without wishing to plead for a 'deutsche Sonderlösung' which would remove the element of comparison with other literatures, or raise German novelists to a status they do not deserve, it is worth bearing in mind that German literature does nevertheless have its own peculiar emphasis; or rather that the spectrum of German culture from 1830 to 1880, of which literature is but one part, has different facets from other cultures. One could cite the intellectual and philosophical endeavour of its universities or the vividness of its historical writing, but the cases of music, and especially drama, are closer to our considerations. For one could say that no German work of prose fiction sums up the myths and urges of the nineteenth century as do *Faust II*, *Der Ring des Nibelungen*, or that substitute for tragedy, *Die Geburt der Tragödie aus dem Geiste der Musik*. In short, the *drama* is a major competitor for the literary esteem otherwise enjoyed by the novel. Nearly all the major writers before 1850 are successful dramatists (Schiller, Kleist, Grillparzer, Büchner, Hebbel); some of those after 1850 are failed or less distinguished dramatists (Freytag, Ludwig, Keller) who have retreated into prose. Even in the later decades of the century, when German drama was veritably in the doldrums, no other literary form could command such high esteem. Excluding the Realist school, every major movement of the century, up to and including Naturalism, found its outlet, and sometimes its quintessential expression, in the drama.

It is also essential to realize that prose fiction was not held in universally high esteem in Germany during the period under discussion.[10] This was not all the doing of conservative professional aestheticians and critics. Schiller thought little of it; Goethe had a bad conscience about it; Grillparzer and Hebbel disdained it despite occasional lapses of principle. The many comparisons made right through the century between drama and Novelle are between an accepted high form of poetry and one that has to struggle for recognition. Many of the best German Novellen are also by dramatists, a pattern begun by Schiller, which Gerhart Hauptmann suitably sustains in the last two decades of the nineteenth century. Indeed, the history of nineteenth-century literature is partly—but only partly—one of the struggle for prose fiction to find, and eventually to achieve, adequate status. The Romantics, the Young Germans and the Realists all had this in common that they saw prose as a medium *par excellence* for, as the case may be, poetic endeavour, social comment, or depiction of life. Yet Tieck and Arnim, Gutzkow and Laube, Freytag and Ludwig were paradoxically also all men of the drama or theatre. If in France Balzac and Stendhal saw the French Revolution and its aftermath in terms of the wide sweep of the novel, Grabbe and Büchner felt drawn towards the historical drama as alone suitable for the portrayal of such historical processes. Willibald Alexis did not succeed as a writer of historical novels merely because the Germans did not possess the rich tradition depicted by Scott ('Unsere deutsche Geschichte in fünf Bänden ist dagegen eine wahre Armut', was Goethe's comment to Eckermann),[11] but because the German writer still had to contend with the shadow and bulk of a work like Schiller's historical drama *Wallenstein*. There are more examples which one could, and perhaps should, cite. When in 1881 Theodor Storm made the much-quoted statement (which he significantly refused to publish himself) about the Novelle and the drama, he was saying something about the relatively late status which the Novelle, the prose work, had achieved, that it, too, had come of age: 'die heutige Novelle ist die Schwester des Dramas und die strengste Form der Prosadichtung'.[12]

By—perhaps fortuitous—contrast, it is interesting to note how Mérimée, writing to Turgenev in 1866, draws attention to the *distinct* properties *and* advantages enjoyed respectively by the dramatist and the prose writer.[13] For Turgenev and Mérimée the need to justify their art in terms of another genre simply does not arise. Storm, who, significantly, had never felt tempted or drawn by the drama, is constrained to say to Keller, who once was, that the Novelle can have and does have the 'classical' qualities associated with the other form. Keller and Raabe and Fontane may have been less worried by such issues and certainly did more than Storm to re-establish the *novel* in the later part of the nineteenth century. Yet Storm's credo comes at the end of a whole series of statements by others, the major ones of which we shall examine in detail. They betray a more than occasional looking over the shoulder at other genres and practitioners in other countries, even an assertiveness that is the product of uncertainty. This all belongs to a history of the German Novelle. It is, by the same token, unfair to visit all the alleged sins of the nineteenth century on the narrow shoulders of this genre. It is surely not correct to gauge intellectual culture solely by what is missing in one special area but abundant in fields more abstract and theoretical.

ii. The Novelle and twentieth-century theory

Anxiety about a supposedly 'ideal' form of the Novelle is a product of the twentieth century rather than of the nineteenth. The twentieth century sees the old worries about the status of prose dissipated. In their place come those about the strict form of the genre of the Novelle. It seems that, no sooner had prose-writing in Germany found its feet—in the traditional European sense—in Fontane, than reactions and strictures set in. This did not affect the actual writing of the genre; Robert Musil, one of the twentieth-century masters of the form, in a little essay of 1914, 'Die Novelle als Problem', was quite candid that it is possible to delimit the Novelle in very traditional terms, as was done in the Renaissance, but also in the nineteenth century, to 'eine Erschütterung [. . .] eine Fügung des Geschicks',[14] and was prepared to state the ideal case for it. But he goes on to say:

Man schreibt Dramen, Romane, Novellen und Gedichte, weil es diese Kunstformen nun einmal gibt, weil Nachfrage besteht und weil sie sich zu vielem eignen. [. . .] nur bis zu einem gewissen Grad ist das Ausdruck innerer Notwendigkeiten. In ästhetischen Fragen steckt oft mehr Praxis und gemeine Notwendigkeit als man denkt.[15]

Only then does he proceed to list certain 'traditional' qualities of the genre: brevity, silhouette, strong impressions of limited scope but incalculable depth. Musil is not being over-prescriptive. He is stating the manifest advantages of a certain short form of prose. He also knew what a novel could or could not do.

If however we examine the statements by other practitioners and theorists alike, in the period 1900 to c.1935,[16] we will see how criteria of a more absolute kind are being set up. They are not an account taken out of actual literary practice, as given by the modern writer like Musil, who acknowledges that theory and practice rarely marry; rather they are statements about how the Novelle ought to be and ought to have been, whether its history bears this out or not. They are attempts to re-order what has gone before and to prescribe for those who are to come. They are generally conservative voices, disturbed at the babel of Naturalism or Expressionism, the loss of values, the collapse of form. Paul Ernst, writing in 1901–2, starts this wave.[17] The George circle, seizing on the formal discipline and severity of Kleist, follows suit. Hofmannsthal's foreword to *Deutsche Erzähler* of 1912 sees his selection of stories as affirming old and lasting values and norms which are now under threat. There is much categorization and taxonomic distinction on the part of critics influenced by Heinrich Wölfflin's school, whereby pairs of opposites—Renaissance and Baroque, Classical and Romantic, open and closed form—are set up as aesthetic and formal criteria. There will be much talk, for instance, of 'Formenverfall',[18] of 'Abarten',[19] 'nordisch-moderner Novellenersatz'[20] on the one hand, of 'Essenz der "Novelle"',[21] or 'zeitlose Typen'[22] on the other. The Kleistian Novelle takes on a significance hitherto (wrongly) denied it, but with the consequence that forms that are lyrical or discursive or in other ways not formally severe, are rejected. By 1936, Johannes Klein can write an essay which represents a canonical position on what the 'genuine' Novelle may or may not be, with authors and works cited.[23]

Such criteria, which need not be discussed in detail here, amount essentially to a distillate of the theory and practice of the Novelle from the Renaissance to the present day. Like other such sets of statements, those by Hermann Pongs or Adolf von Grolmann, or Josef Kunz, they have the effect of superimposing theoretical distinctions on to the mass of historical material. They tacitly assume that historical practice and theoretical considerations go hand in hand, or at least that they should, or should have done. In terms of critical method, it is putting the cart before the horse. For any even approximately historical survey of the Novelle will show that writers generally did what they liked and cared very little for theory, or at most adhered to very wide and imprecise notions of what they were doing.

The position in critical discussion after 1945 has shifted somewhat towards attempts to examine the Novelle in its historical development, subject to the constraints which emerge from its times and from nowhere else. The clear and authoritative positions of 1900–35 are no longer accepted, but that has brought with it an attendant disunity and many more attempts at defining the genre. It is at least a disunity with an awareness of chronology and change. With this development—mapped out in K. K. Polheim's survey of 1964—has come a greater historical awareness of the development of the genre, and, as an attendant benefit, the widening of the 'canon' of reading, as questions of theory and practice become merged into one discussion.[24] For it is now almost axiomatic that studies on the Novelle must express some kind of historical sense, however tentative. This had already been Tieck's position in 1829, as he looked back to Cervantes and Goethe; or Heyse's in 1871, as he surveyed both the changes and the constants in the genre. There are no 'zeitlose Typen'. The survey which follows is written in that spirit and that indebtedness.

Chapter One

'OR AVENNE CHE...'
THE NOVELLE FROM THE RENAISSANCE TO 1790

i. Do we need a definition?

It may seem strange that no attempt has been made as yet in this survey to define what a Novelle is. Part of the difficulty in attempting to see the Novelle in its historical context is the awareness that definitions, or attempts at definitions, are themselves subject to the process of historical change. Inevitably the literary historian finds himself constrained to distil out of a variety of sometimes conflicting statements those factors which appear as constants, and on which nearly everybody seems to agree. But even this is not without its pitfalls. It does not automatically follow, for instance, that Goethe's attempt of 1827 to define the scope and purport of a Novelle coincides exactly with Paul Heyse's of 1871. Nor does it mean that statements which do not use the actual word 'Novelle' are invalid for our discussion, or that a work of literature which never refers to itself as 'Novelle' cannot be subsumed under that category.

Everybody, it would seem, agrees that a Novelle, as understood in German, is a short piece of fiction written in prose. Even if the eighteenth century could talk of 'Erzählungen' in verse, or Paul Heyse in the nineteenth could confuse the issue by publishing 'Novellen in Versen', the factor of prose does remain constant. The choice of the medium is crucial. We see this, for instance, in the way Goethe chose in 1798 to recast the prose anecdote of the Salzburg refugees in verse, as *Hermann und Dorothea*, but adapted certain French stories in their original medium for his *Unterhaltungen deutscher Ausgewanderten* of 1795. There seems to be agreement, too, that a Novelle is *short*. Emil Staiger's extempore statement in a seminar in 1946–7, that the Novelle is 'eine Erzählung mittlerer Länge'[1] is as useful a working definition as any in this respect; as is, say, Wolfram Krömer's from the area of Romance studies, 'kurze

Prosafiktion'.[2] Yet these definitions are not entirely without their problems, and it is not mere pedantry to draw attention to them. What, as K. K. Polheim argues, is 'short' or 'mid-length'?[3] Is Mérimée's *Colomba* (roughly 150 pages) short? Yet we generally call it in French a 'nouvelle', a term roughly related to its cognate in German. Does Kleist's *Das Bettelweib von Locarno* (three pages in the standard edition) belong to a different genre from *Michael Kohlhaas* (103 pages)? What is the essential difference between—an extreme example—Goethe's novel *Die Wahlverwandtschaften* (about 250 pages) and the work which Tieck airily termed a Novelle, *Der junge Tischlermeister* (350 pages)? What of Storm's *Der Schimmelreiter*, Meyer's *Jürg Jenatsch* or Fontane's *Schach von Wuthenow* or *Unterm Birnbaum*, all of which have the certain virtue of expansiveness?

Or should our criterion simply be that a Novelle is that which calls itself such by name? Or can we not employ 'Novelle' as a useful generic term for all sorts of works that call themselves 'Märchen', 'Erzählung', 'Fantasiestück', 'Sittengemälde', 'Skizze' and the like? It is not that attempts to delimit 'Novelle', 'Erzählung' and 'Märchen' have been lacking, in both the nineteenth and the twentieth centuries, in the same way that in French distinctions have been postulated between 'conte', 'conte fantastique' and 'nouvelle'.[4] The history of nineteenth-century literature and criticism shows that emphases are subject to considerable shifts, as tastes and criteria change. The actual use of the word 'Novelle' is not the final arbiter. Kleist never used it of his stories; and in 1821, Tieck, Kleist's first editor, never once refers to the other's stories as 'Novellen'. On the other hand, in 1909, a popular *Novellenbuch* in seven volumes can unquestioningly admit Kleist's *Anekdote aus dem letzten preussischen Kriege*[5] into the category, and shows how open the genre can be in terms of length.

The distinctions recorded throughout the decades are a useful guide, but never an absolute one. (Not every writer is as obliging as Diderot with his title, *Ceci n'est pas un conte!*) We can therefore accept Staiger's definition only under the express provision that it does not exclude works which historically deserve to be studied under the general head of 'Novelle', be they of medium length or not. But even then we may do so gratefully.

ii. The practice in the main Romance literatures of the Renaissance

In the Romance literatures of the Renaissance and succeeding centuries, in Italy, Spain and France, there were certain criteria for 'novella', 'novela' and 'nouvelle' which remained relatively constant. These are important for our considerations, for, with many provisos and qualifications, and whether acknowledged or not, they are ultimately the basis for most of the practice of the nineteenth century in Germany. This does not mean to say that there is, between different countries with an independent self-awareness, any great area of unanimity. And, as Walter Pabst has shown, both for our illumination and warning, the relationship between novellistic practice and theory in the Romance literature is one of irony:[6] *they very often act as if they are adhering to rules but in reality they are not*. Yet we find that, as the Germans join the ranks of those writing 'Novellen', and by the use of the term align themselves with other European literatures, certain criteria are implicitly assumed and explicitly stated, as valid for this mode of writing.

It may therefore do to examine briefly the main stages in the Romance literatures. One need only begin with the work normally regarded as the ancestor of the modern Novelle, Boccaccio's *Decameron* (1353). The Preface states:

> In these tales will be found a variety of love adventures, bitter as well as pleasing, and other exciting incidents, which took place in both ancient and modern times. In reading them, the aforesaid ladies will be able to derive, not only pleasure from the entertaining matters therein set forth, but also some useful advice. For they will learn to recognize what should be avoided and likewise what should be pursued, and these things can only lead, in my opinion, to the removal of their affliction.[7]

Here we can single out certain guiding factors, even a statement of intent. The hundred stories and anecdotes are 'adventures' and 'exciting incidents', events out of the ordinary, that 'took place'. This is not necessarily a stamp of authentication (for the sources are diverse, to say the least), but a general acceptance that the stories are based on events, are cases drawn not only out of the sphere of human experience, but out of its exceptional happenings. They give both 'pleasure' and 'useful advice'; that is, they conform to the classical principle of 'prodesse' and 'delectare' which is the spoken or unspoken assumption behind any literature adhering to that tradition. The 'moral behind the story', the recognition of what is right and what is wrong, is therefore a guarantee that telling stories of varying degrees of delicacy can be reconciled with matters of moral seriousness. The stories are told within a social framework, an identifiable society, one not esoteric or scholastic or pedagogical, but conforming and subservient to the accepted norms and *bienséances* of polite intercourse. The background to this society of story-tellers is real: they had escaped from the plague in Florence with its attendant horrors ('I am one of many people who saw it with their own eyes,' avers the author) and had sought diversion in this particular pastime. The narrators are named persons (noblemen and ladies), and the listeners, of both sexes, belong to the same group. The stories themselves bear out the author's general description in their wide range of plots and incidents; yet they are for the instruction of ladies, and their main underlying theme is the role of women, for good or ill, in human affairs.[8]

'Unusual' does not mean the same as 'original'; we have in Boccaccio a stock of stories, many themselves drawn from existing sources, which form a kind of model for later writers. Indeed, the seeming adherence to certain patterns of narration is one of the characteristics of Romance Novelle writing. It need therefore not surprise us later to find Goethe adapting a Boccaccio-type story (from the French *Cent Nouvelles nouvelles*), the tale of the 'Prokurator', for his *Unterhaltungen deutscher Ausgewanderten*. It has a central 'event': the Prokurator in Genoa makes a vow of asceticism. Into this is brought the account of the elderly merchant and his young wife, the merchant's departure and well-founded, stated fears for his wife's fidelity. The meeting of Prokurator and lady then ensues. The two agree to subject to the Prokurator's vow of abnegation and chastity their mutual attraction, with the result that both learn the moral and spiritual benefits of renunciation.

Goethe's choice of this quite decorous kind of story should of course not allow us to forget the duped and deceived husbands, the crafty and lascivious women, the friars behind the arras or under the bed, who are also part and parcel of the Boccaccian tradition. Indeed, deception is often one of the accompanying factors in events which are unusual, with the awareness that changes in fortune are attendant on our general state of human frailty. Yet in all the major Renaissance writers there is the awareness of an *ordo*, a structure of moral and religious values to which the extraordinary, and more than occasionally piquant, situations refer. The *Cent Nouvelles nouvelles* of 1486, which are the first major collection in French, admit their debt to Boccaccio and are also aware, as stated, that such narration belongs to the 'prouffitables passe-temps'.[9] By calling themselves 'Nouvelles' they are admitting that Boccaccio's anecdotes have, in the hands of his successors, become an accepted literary genre that is worth imitating.[10] The stories, however, purport also to come 'ès parties de France, d'Alemaigne, d'Angleterre, de Haynau, de Brabant et aultres lieux' and to be 'd'assez fresche memoire'.[11] This is by way of suggestion that they are not merely adaptations from the Italian (which many are) but 'authentic'. Marguerite de Navarre's *Heptaméron* of 1559 also has its obligatory reference to 'occupation plaisante et vertueuse'[12] and will similarly state: 'dira chascun quelque histoire qu'il aura veue ou bien oy dire à quelque homme digne de foy'.[13] But the narrators in these French stories are all men, and they stress with greater emphasis the weaknesses of womankind.[14] They retain an anecdotal quality, but their incidents are more uniformly racy and salacious than are Boccaccio's, closer in general to the conventions of comedy. And like most Italian and French collections, they come in batches or dozens, mixed in quality.

When we come to Spanish, and to Cervantes's collection of twelve *Novelas ejemplares* of 1613, we find that the indispensable adherence to *ordo* and *exemplum*, to 'prodesse et delectare', remains, whereas the subject-matter has been opened up to include all manner of things, such as the picaresque, the satirical, the implausibly adventurous, stories bordering on the fairy-tale in their improbability (but not mere fabulous impossibilities).[15] The framework of the plague in Boccaccio's Florence, or the floods and disasters in Marguerite de Navarre, which brings a society together for 'occupation plaisante et vertueuse', has been quietly dropped. There are fewer stories, and an according emphasis on literary quality. We are left to establish for ourselves how the stories cohere in their reference to that which is exemplary. The rules are there, but they are not always stated in the obtrusive fashion of the earlier tradition. These *novelas* all refer to Spain, and some have settings like Toledo or Estremadura, but this does not restrict them to 'real' event or plot.

In eighteenth-century France, the genre begins to flourish again. There, too, there is considerable contamination as 'conte', 'conte de fées' and 'nouvelle' lose their distinctions. Exotic, oriental, and English sentimental subject-matter now crowds into the collections, with titles like 'contes moraux' or 'contes philosophiques' remaining the only feature in common. And yet through all these changes in the different literatures and centuries, one can still detect certain constants which refer back to the origins of the tradition: the desire to address society in its expectations of entertainment and instruction (of whatever kind), the presupposition of some kind of 'moral' (however ironic), and the element of the unusual or exemplary (however improbable). Another continuing factor of a less formal nature is the element of adaptation and sheer pillage, from generation to generation, from century to century, as each succeeding set of 'ejemplos morales' or 'journées amusantes' draws without compunction or acknowledgement on the products of its predecessors. The result was that, by 1795, the claim of a given story to be unusual or extraordinary, original or authentic, often did not stand up to very close scrutiny. Eduard von Bülow, whose *Novellenbuch* of 1834 published one of the most comprehensive collections of such stories from many early European sources, admitted resignedly: 'geplündert [. . .] wurden die alten Novellisten in neuester Zeit mannichfalt und zwar auf eine sehr grobe Art'.[16]

It should be stressed that this, inevitably sketchy, survey has only taken account of the main representatives of a centuries-long tradition, and those which will play a significant role in the development of the genre in Germany. The real developments are never as neat as they seem, and writers adhere to 'rules' out of convenience rather than aesthetic sense.

iii. The Novelle in Germany up to 1790

What was the position in Germany?[17] Is the development in any way analogous? The answer is that there had been no dearth of short works in prose, but that they followed patterns different from those in Italy, France and Spain. True, there are late medieval romances and 'Schwänke' which draw on material substantially the same as that known to Boccaccio. There are even translations between 1462 and 1472 of Boccaccio and of another major representative of the Italian Renaissance, Enea Silvio Piccolomini. It is noticeable, however, that none of the adaptors approached Chaucer's rank. There were in both the sixteenth and seventeenth centuries stories

The Novelle from the Renaissance to 1790 17

which were racy and picaresque; some few also were collections of 'Gesprächsspiele' in the tried Renaissance mode. There were the 'Volksbücher', some like *Faust* of purely German origin, others like *Magelone* or *Melusine* of French provenance. Of all forms of short prose in Germany, they were the ones which survived longest, if in debased form, to await a literary revival in the second half of the eighteenth century. There was in the eighteenth century itself Schnabel's *Fata einiger Seefahrer* (1741–3), better known as *Die Insel Felsenburg*, using the framework of a Robinson Crusoe story to recount the various stories of its adventurers. By and large, however, it would be hard to disagree with the statement made in 1897 by Rudolf Fürst: that the modern German Novelle grew out of an existing body of eighteenth-century narrative.[18] That is, if the statement is taken to mean that, when in the last decade of the eighteenth century writers as different but as significant as Goethe and Tieck turned or returned to forms of short prose fiction, they were drawing on something that already existed in Germany. The significance, quality and implications of what they did are another matter.

To say that there existed around 1795 a corpus of short prose fiction in Germany is to give no indication of its quality. For we are dealing, with very few and significant exceptions, with works that are largely adaptations of the patterns of French and English stories; they bear many of the marks of uncertainty which betray an uneasy relationship to original sources. But adaptive receptivity is not a bad thing in itself, and the history of German literature in the eighteenth century bears this out. Without the willingness to open up to foreign impulses there could have been no indigenous creation of the drama or the novel as we have it. If the reception of Shakespeare in Germany is spectacular, we should not forget that of, say, Fielding. Indeed the pioneer of the modern German novel, Wieland, could not have achieved what he did without looking over his shoulder at what had been done in England, and to some extent France and Spain.

And it is to Wieland that we owe the first statement in German about the difference between novel and Novelle, in a footnote dating from 1772:

Novellen werden vorzüglich eine Art von Erzählungen genannt, welche sich von den großen Romanen durch die Simplicität des Plans und den kleinen Umfang der Fabel unterscheiden.[19]

Not only does Wieland in that same footnote refer specifically to Boccaccio and Cervantes; he also assumes that they are, with many others, known in Germany in the original and in translation. But the context, the novel *Don Sylvio von Rosalva*, also mentions 'die *Arabischen* und *Persischen* Erzählungen, die Novellen und die Feenmährchen';[20] it is itself, through a process of ironical adaptation and contamination, indebted to those very sources. Wieland is saying that his novel owes its pattern to the persistence of these prose forms, rather in the same way that *Don Quijote* cannot exist without a belief in the patterns of chivalric romance. Wieland's statement reminds us that the French[21] had, since the late seventeenth century and the beginning of the eighteenth, been addicted to the 'conte' (a term used much more frequently than 'nouvelle'): the 'conte oriental', the 'conte de fées', even the 'conte licencieux'; that the factor of entertainment seemed to have gained the upper hand over that of moral seriousness, the titillatingly erotic over the exemplary. True, there was much adherence to a notional moral, but little actual sign in the stories as narrated. Indeed, a form calling itself 'conte moral' had even evolved to restore the balance. In the hands of some, the 'conte moral' would draw on the sentimental and moralizing conventions of English fiction in the manner of Richardson. All this, however, would lead writers of the stamp of Voltaire and Diderot to undermine conventions which had already become trivial, in order by the use of satire to subvert the very moral expectations or entertainment value of modes they saw as debased. Diderot, in writing *Ceci n'est pas un conte* (1773), was delivering a programmatic declaration against the falsification of reality in the conte, in favour of a récit based rather on contemporary experience.

These patterns of French shorter fiction were seized upon in Germany, mainly by minor and popular writers. But they also embraced the character sketch of La Bruyère and Chesterfield, the tale of terror and the Gothic novel of English provenance, the chivalric romance that recounted medieval improbabilities, or the Newgate calendar of criminal stories. If today we do not read Wezel or Spiess, Lafontaine or Meissner, Eckartshausen or Langbein, and often only find their names mentioned by Wieland or Goethe or Tieck as models of vulgar debasement, we should not forget that these and others were forerunners who made it possible for works of greater quality to find an entry. By the same token, these works had also contributed to the process whereby German prose writing was generally opened up thematically, to take in more moral and social awareness, satire, and the realm of the fancy and romantic imagination.

It should, however, not be thought that these 'Erzählungen' were only restricted to popular taste and popular forms of dissemination. Wieland's highly influential journal *Der Teutsche Merkur* had not disdained them, and it was in this organ that Schiller published one of his lesser-known stories, *Spiel des Schicksals*. When Schiller, however, sought to launch himself in the 1780s as an independent writer and journalist, with the periodical *Thalia*, he also turned among other things precisely to short fiction—and wrote it himself. Briefly one can say that his three stories from *Thalia* show their provenance in existing patterns of fiction from the century; *Der Verbrecher aus verlorener Ehre* belongs to the 'Kriminalgeschichte', *Der Geisterseher* has the mystifications, seeming improbabilities—and explanations—of the English Gothic novel, and *Merkwürdiges Beispiel einer weiblichen Rache* is based on a manuscript of one of Diderot's 'récits'. Schiller's more ambitious journal, *Die Horen* (1795–7), in which he and Goethe laid so many of the foundations of Weimar Classicism, was also not to disdain this form.

Chapter Two

'UNTERHALTEND' AND 'BEFRIEDIGEND' GOETHE'S RENEWAL IN 1795[1]

It was at a suggestion of Schiller's, made on 28 October 1794, that Goethe revived the idea of adapting a story which was to become that of the 'Prokurator' in *Unterhaltungen deutscher Ausgewanderten*. That Schiller took the source to be the *Decameron*, whereas it is in fact from the *Cent Nouvelles nouvelles*, is of little consequence. The patterns are, as already seen, very similar. It was, for Goethe, a welcome relief from the 'Last', the burden, of writing a full-scale novel, *Wilhelm Meisters Lehrjahre*. And if neither Goethe nor Schiller could accord to the writing of prose fiction the dignity assigned to the epic or drama, they were nevertheless throwing their authority behind this form and helping it to gain recognition.

Out of this suggestion of Schiller's was to emerge Goethe's 'revival' of the old Boccaccian—or at least Renaissance—form, *Unterhaltungen deutscher Ausgewanderten* (1795). But, like all creative renewals, Goethe's work is more than just a readaptation, or even reissue of what was still there. The many collections of Italian, French and Spanish stories still current in the eighteenth century were keeping the older tales alive: Goethe's own copy of *Cent Nouvelles nouvelles* had been published as recently as 1786. And Goethe's collection only contained a *few* stories, not a hundred. By setting his *Unterhaltungen* in a framework of political and social disorder, during the French Revolutionary Wars in the Rhine provinces, Goethe was doing more than merely adhering to Boccaccio or Marguerite de Navarre. He was giving his collection a note of urgency which the older ones could no longer possess. That this sense of threat and undermining of cultural and social values was not limited to one kind of literary renewal is seen in the way it also determines the Homeric verse epic *Hermann und Dorothea* (1798) and the verse drama *Die natürliche Tochter* (1804). This does not mean to say that *Unterhaltungen deutscher Ausgewanderten* are 'classical'—that is left to *Hermann und Dorothea*. There is still a certain amount of the garrulity and ease of the older genre (compare his less successful collection *Die guten Weiber* of 1800).[2] There is quite a long way until we reach the artistic consciousness of *Novelle* (1828) or the stories in *Wilhelm Meisters Wanderjahre*. Traditional form nevertheless comes to the rescue of established and culturally indispensable patterns of life: it is not a mere exercise in itself. And so the *Unterhaltungen* have their own particular emphasis—in the framework of social narration. We do not learn here, as in *Hermann und Dorothea*, of the fate of 'Bürgertum' and 'Volk', or of the problems of statecraft, as in the drama of the natural daughter, Eugenie. The stories are narrated for the benefit of a group who are all 'ausgezeichnete Personen',[3] that is members of the aristocracy. That, too, is a reminder of the earlier associations of that class with the situation of framework and stories. They do not make the claim to speak, 'Nicht dem Deutschen geziemt es, die fürchterliche Bewegung/Fortzuleiten', which in the closing lines of *Hermann und Dorothea* is a popular appeal to *all* sections of the nation, regardless of class. They focus rather on a more special aspect.

The aristocratic society assembled shows, in its initial disagreements and surrenders to impatient impulse, that war, like all the 'überraschende Vorfälle'[4] of life, causes the breakdown of social intercourse and its most essential manifestation, 'Gespräch', gregariousness within the norms of decorous conviviality. For, as the Baroness avers, to be 'gesellig' also requires 'sich beherrschen müssen'.[5] It is not merely a question of an escape from unpleasant realities like the Florentine plague, but also of restoring and reintegrating within one selected group the values that are under threat outside. Hence the 'gesellige Schonung'[6] that story-telling revives is also related to events 'out there'. A story containing 'das Wunderbare' can be recounted and be made to refer to an equally remarkable and unheard-of event: a writing-desk in the house suddenly splits as its 'twin' in a nearby property falls a victim to the flames. The Abbé ('der Geistliche'), on whom the burden of narration falls, has the kind of 'unerschöpfliches Archiv von Menschen- und Weltkenntnis, von Begebenheiten und Verhältnissen'[7] that the society needs. But, if the stories are to serve the dual purpose of pleasure and instruction, to be 'unterhaltend' and 'befriedigend',[8] they must also adhere to certain formal criteria: they must have the advantage of brevity and recount one central event; they must have 'Reiz der Neuheit' and not be a mere *réchauffage* of the old collections; they must have a surprise turning, that 'geistreiche Wendung'[9] which will illumine and highlight the central event. They must therefore not be tedious, involved, or overpopulated with events and characters. These are the qualities required by society for its specific needs, in coming back to its senses, in restoring its self-respect and self-discipline.

The stories are not only taken 'aus alten Büchern und Traditionen',[10] but contaminate existing traditions as well. They refer back to these, but each time with a difference. The ghost story of the singer Antonelli is recounted as 'real' by the Abbé (for he was in Naples at that time—it is actually an anecdote about the French actress Clairon, whose lover was Marmontel, the writer of 'contes moraux'). The claim to be 'real' is, of course, part of the tradition. But the event is not explained; the equally strange episode with the desk *is*, and the two accounts are held in balance, the real truth lying somewhere between 'Unwahrscheinlichkeit' and 'Wahrscheinlichkeit'. So, too, the unnerving incident from the memoirs of Bassompierre is linked with an explicable one from the real family's own history. The story of the Procurator, which as number 100 of the *Cent Nouvelles nouvelles* is, in the original, kinder to female 'chaleur naturelle'[11] than most, becomes a 'moralische Erzählung';[12] not of the French sort, Marmontel's or Baculard's or their like, where the author superimposes a moral, but one where the moral conviction is developed from within the characters and is based on a psychological inner conviction. The improving story of Ferdinand, who seeks to make good an act of dishonesty, is also a gentle flea in the ear for Karl, one of the company who has earlier on spoken very much out of turn and still has much to learn about social deportment. This story comes, significantly, nearly at the end of the *Unterhaltungen*, as the 'real' family is beginning to feel that its private differences are being submerged in the desire for common betterment and reintegration. By now, however, the political moment has all but receded into the background. The very act of confraternity that is involved in story-telling, the awareness that listening is better than raising one's voice, that the humility of self-appraisal is preferable to the flight into self-defence, all this has, unspoken, produced the frame of mind which triumphs over outward adversity and dissension. The time is now ripe for the imagination to be given 'vollkommen freien Lauf'[13] in the concluding story, the artistically conscious *Das Märchen*. Here is opened up a world of serpents and will-o'-the-wisps, giants and golden kings, transmogrifications and transformations. It is not, despite its inherent charm and beauty, the usual 'cabinet de fées'. Its central symbols of disparity and disjection are resolved into harmony and interdependence: ' "Was ist erquicklicher als Licht?" fragte jener. "Das Gespräch", antwortete diese.'[14] 'Die Liebe herrscht nicht, aber sie bildet, und das ist mehr.'[15] These are central themes of the whole *Unterhaltungen* and raise it on to a level where the *whole* man and his needs, not just the signs and tribulations of the times, are the crowning concern.

With *Unterhaltungen deutscher Ausgewanderten* Goethe had rehearsed, either in the stories or in the framework, most of the forms of short fiction current in his century or enshrined in Renaissance tradition. He had also given some indication of how they might be adapted to the needs of a succeeding age. Nowhere does he use the word 'Novelle', yet the criteria he applies are those which are common to the 'novella' the 'novela' or the 'nouvelle'. He also makes it clear that there are some forms which ought to stay well and truly where they are—in the past. Wieland's *Hexameron von Rosenhain* of 1805,[16] which closely follows Goethe's *Unterhaltungen*, while less significant, is also a rehearsal of what there is in terms of short narrative material. Its reference is not to the troubled times but to a society where time does not obtrude, and the stories lack that dual adherence, to traditions and present disorder, to which Goethe's bear witness. Wieland, too, has his likes and dislikes: he abhors the gratuitously improbable, the sentimental 'Familiengemälde' or 'moralische Erzählung'. But his collection is also interesting for its heterogeneousness: it admits 'Märchen', 'Erzählungen' and 'Novellen'; stories which have the sequence of dream, where the impossible becomes natural, with their own special order and sense; those that are in the real world; those that are 'nicht alltäglich', but could happen. Neither Goethe nor Wieland is prepared to separate the various forms of short fiction so sharply that any one is excluded from the framework of social discourse. Both authors affirm a pattern that allows an interpretation of framework and narrated story, so that the doings of the narrator are thematically related to those of the people narrated. The element of the 'gesellig' remains firmly linked to this kind of fiction.

Goethe's continuing interest in 'kleine Geschichten und Märchen, die ich lang im Kopf herumgetragen',[17] which can only briefly be traced here, follows in the same patterns. Only one story, *Novelle* (see Chapter 8) stands completely on its own. The rest are either published as a collection, or incorporated into a larger context, that of the novels *Die Wahlverwandtschaften* and *Wilhelm Meisters Wanderjahre*, in which they bear a symbolic or thematic relationship to the main plot and themes. *Die wunderlichen Nachbarskinder* in *Die Wahlverwandtschaften* (1809), despite its clear points of reference to the novel in which it is narrated as a 'story within a story', still adheres, outwardly at least, to the lines established in *Unterhaltungen deutscher Ausgewanderten*; with the difference, however, that it now calls itself 'Novelle'. Similarly, five of the stories which are later incorporated into *Wilhelm Meisters Wanderjahre* go through a change of designation as Goethe moves from the use of words like 'Erzählung', 'Geschichte', or 'Märchen' (for one of them, *Die neue Melusine*, is really such) to the single term 'Novelle'. In fact, the original scheme of the second part of *Wilhelm Meister* was to be a garland of Novellen, a 'Novellenkranz' such as popular reading taste around 1815 was calling for (see Chapter 8). These stories, too, show the mark of the Renaissance tradition and their more recent predecessors in the *Unterhaltungen*. Indeed Goethe seems tacitly to have moved from a mixed set of German terms, such as Wieland had used, to accept the foreign word 'Novelle'. Seen another way, it also meant that, in the relatively short time since 1795, 'Novelle' had come to cover more or less the features which Goethe had defined in that year. That still gave it, as we saw, very wide terms of reference, inclusive rather than exclusive.

Chapter Three

'ETWAS MUSS GESCHEHEN' THE ROMANTICS

In encouraging Goethe in the enterprise which was to become *Unterhaltungen deutscher Ausgewanderten*, Schiller was supporting something that was both a publishing venture and a serious moral and social comment in agreeable guise. No such edifying thoughts had been in the mind of the young Berlin writer Ludwig Tieck in 1795–8, as he contributed to a collection of stories called *Straussfedern*, and in 1797 published his *Volksmärchen* containing both plays and stories. In Tieck's early writing we see that Renaissance models are an irrelevance and that other, more popular, modes predominate. Yet the prose works of Tieck from the 1790s also belong to the forcing-ground of what comes to be known as the 'Novelle'. It was not a term that Tieck used at the time. Why should he, when his intention was largely parody and entertainment? Working for the Berlin publisher Friedrich Nicolai, Tieck was not above producing stories for the older man's *Straussfedern*, a rag-bag of all kinds of fiction. Once, in the hands of Johann Karl August Musäus, famed for his *Volksmärchen der Deutschen* (1782–6), the collection had been a fairly true guide in translation to the trivialities of French contes ('moraux', 'licencieux', 'contes de fées'). Nicolai was continuing the enterprise for the sake of making money and was employing a slick young writer as translator or independent adaptor. Journalism makes for fast and adaptable writing, and there was no style of prose unknown to Tieck. The horror story, the oriental tale, the sentimental, the 'altfränkisch', he could do it without effort; and, what is more, he could parody them all, and did. For Tieck was using the *Straussfedern* mainly as a vehicle to demonstrate the fatuities of the mode in which he was writing. His *Volksmärchen* of 1797, with which is allied the closely related story *Peter Lebrecht*, 'Eine Geschichte ohne Abentheuerlichkeiten' (1795–6), are a further forum for parody, but also for advancing more serious forms, with some claim to originality.

If Goethe in 1795, as an established writer, could turn to tradition to enrich contemporary literature, Tieck saw first of all the need to laugh as much as possible out of court before advancing alternative forms. And so between his two major collections, with great wittiness and ease and elegance, he set about parodying: the far-fetched or contrived plots of the 'conte' tradition; the insistence on 'event', 'fate' or 'chance'; the avowal that the most implausible plot was 'true' because based on the memoirs of the Marquis de . . . ; the eternal moralizing; the cheap manipulation of sensation. By telling stories where nothing happens, by showing how the same story could be narrated in different modes, Tieck initiated a breakdown of accepted narrated patterns. That a clever young writer saw the need to act thus, is also an indication of how deeply entrenched the modes were. And no history of the Novelle should fail to mention somewhere that it is so often the tide of the trivial and pennydreadful that bears along the works of real quality; they do not spring from nowhere.

Into this framework, however, Tieck was able to insert a few stories that point away from popular taste. It was not that, both in parodying and presenting an alternative, Tieck was acting without predecessors, but his real achievement can stand without reference backwards.

There are two areas in which Tieck can be seen as innovatory. The first is the renewal of the old 'Volksbücher', or chapbooks: *Melusine*, *Magelone*, *Die Schildbürger*, even that quaint old eighteenth-century pack of lies, *Merkwürdige Lebensgeschichte Sr. Majestät Abraham Tonelli*. By re-creating the naïve, woodcut-like style of the chapbook, Tieck was introducing a 'medieval' 'alt-fränkisch' subject whose archaisms would seem more authentic than some robber-and-knight fantasy: for the re-creating of a Romantic Middle Ages belongs in the history of Romantic short fiction.

Possibly more important is what later generations have called the 'Kunstmärchen'. It, too, is not without precedents, but the publication in the *Volksmärchen* of *Der blonde Eckbert* is nevertheless something of an event. We have seen how both Goethe and Wieland were not so fastidious as to exclude 'Märchen' from their respective collections. Yet they were concerned either to leave 'das

Wunderbare' or other seeming improbabilities, without comment, as 'Begebenheiten' (the Antonelli and Bassompierre stories); or else it is to be the world of total fancy and utter surrender to the imagination that holds sway (*Das Märchen*, and the first three of Wieland's *Hexameron*). Tieck proceeds differently. In his first three so-called 'Kunstmärchen', *Der blonde Eckbert* (1797) *Der getreue Eckart* (1799) and *Der Runenberg* (1804), he makes the 'wondrous' world of the Middle Ages into something 'real'. There are touches of popular fiction, with farouche landscapes and dizzy heights and 'Gothick' castles, populated by 'real' people who are presented as living 'normal' lives. 'Pull up your chair to the fireside and I will tell you a story' says the heroine of *Der blonde Eckbert*: 'Nur haltet meine Erzählung für kein Mährchen, so sonderbar sie auch klingen mag.'[1] That is the old plea for authenticity, the suspension of belief that 'I am not making this all up', that all can be vouched for. It was part of the tradition of the Gothic novel. All the stories in the line from Walpole's *The Castle of Otranto* (1764) to Karl Grosse's shamelessly sensational *Der Genius* (1791–4) had made this same claim. All can be explained, and behind all there is some kind of purpose, guidance, providence even, often glimpsed but imperfectly by the characters themselves. *Der blonde Eckbert*, with its wondrous bird that sings 'Waldeinsamkeit', would be a 'Märchen' in anybody's terms. In a strange and sinister fashion, however, one of the listeners reveals himself to be someone who had, like the narrator, also once lived in that same, seemingly improbable, fairy-tale world. We no longer know where we stand; we cannot tell where our imaginings about the past end and present reality begins. The lost paradise of childhood (in the case of *Der blonde Eckbert*), where the natural order of things is suspended, suddenly becomes part of the present, part of a new sensation of guilt and powerlessness. For—another cliché of the Gothic novel— Eckbert and his wife discover that they are living in incest; the removal from the faery world of childhood is a progression into the terror of awareness and recognition—and madness. Who is responsible? Have we been deluded by supernatural forces bent on our destruction? Have we been lured into guilt for which we cannot bear ultimate responsibility? Can we ever be sure that life is secure against such incursions of psychological and psychical terror? The answer is: we cannot. When Tieck in 1812 published three further stories, *Liebeszauber*, *Die Elfen* and *Der Pokal*, he abandoned the medieval trappings and took a world more akin to that of his readers. In *Liebeszauber*, the hero's state of madness is 'real'. He can, by chance, look in at a window and see another world so authentic, so chillingly palpable, that we never know what is fevered imagination and what is actuality. This is the world in which occasionally Achim von Arnim, and especially E. T. A. Hoffmann, are to set so many of their stories. Edgar Allen Poe's 'mystery and imagination' will take over from there.

The Romantic 'Märchen' takes many forms: Novalis, for instance, is much closer to the pure world of Goethe's *Märchen*, where the writ of all normal laws of reality no longer runs. There is, however, no absolute division between Tieck's mode of story and what we call the 'Novelle'. It is part of the range of shorter prose fiction that is still with us when, in a less serious vein, later in the nineteenth century, Keller writes *Spiegel, das Kätzchen* and Storm *Bulemanns Haus*. And even if the Grimm brothers may have rejected any 'contamination' of their collection of *Kinder- und Hausmärchen* with popular prose fiction, they were really deluding themselves. For that intermingling of 'real' world, 'real' 'Begebenheit' and the fairy-tale did actually take place, and there is no certain line of demarcation between one and the other.

Neither the efforts of Goethe in *Unterhaltungen deutscher Ausgewanderten*, nor Tieck's 'Märchen', had escaped the attention of the most prominent Romantic critics, the brothers Friedrich and August Wilhelm Schlegel. A series of statements by the Schlegels between roughly 1798 and 1803 took the theoretical discussion a good stage further; indeed, one could say that, whereas Goethe discussed his criteria for the Novelle in a context of practice, the Schlegels actually initiated that discourse on the theory that was to run concurrently with the production of fiction. But here we must be circumspect; for only a few aphorisms in *Athenaeum* (1798–1800), and Friedrich's Boccaccio essay of 1801, were actually published at the time. Even such important pronouncements as August Wilhelm's Berlin lectures (1801–4) were initially restricted to an audience of hearers, not of readers. That is not to diminish the importance of what the brothers said. For both throw their authority behind *prose*, the novel and the Novelle. Friedrich's review of *Wilhelm Meister* (1798) is a crucial statement of the essentially poetic quality of the novel: the novel is not, as traditional aesthetics taught, excluded from the ultimate achievement of poetry, but is part of its veriest processes. When Schlegel seeks for a term which will sum up in one form the various seemingly conflicting forces of the poetic spirit, he chooses the word 'Roman', if in a sense wider and more embracing than our 'novel'. Joining Goethe as a main example of this is Cervantes. For the Romantics initiate the first major wave of Cervantian enthusiasm (as opposed to occasional influences) in Germany. Tieck produces the standard translation of *Don Quijote* (1799–1801) and he and August Wilhelm plan to do the same with Cervantes's whole œuvre. Soltau's translation of the *Novelas ejemplares* (1801) comes suitably to reinforce some of the theoretical statements. For Cervantes, like Dante, Shakespeare, Calderón and now Boccaccio, is one of the representatives *par excellence* of the 'Romantic', that universal, mythological, religious spirit or force which is one with the absolute. By and large, in the Romantic view, later times have lost touch with this spirit, and so it will be to the 'Romantic' age and its main representatives (in effect the Middle Ages and the Renaissance) that we shall have to turn for guidance. Only Goethe among modern poets provides an exception. All this does not mean that the Schlegels in their statements are ultimately concerned with historical accuracy: on the contrary, they seem to conflate the very different practice of Boccaccio and Cervantes.[2] But in doing so, they also establish that 'novella' and 'novela' are essentially the same as German 'Novelle'; also that the word, if rooted in Romance practice, is applicable to what Goethe has been doing and what the Germans should be continuing to do.

It should be noted at the outset that much of the Schlegels' theorizing relates clearly to what Renaissance writers themselves claimed to be doing and what Goethe had so recently reiterated: that the Novelle relates to real life,[3] is the product of polite and polished social intercourse ('feine Gesellschaft')[4] and its needs ('Unterhaltung'),[5] and is concerned with the new and extraordinary in real life ('das Unwahrscheinlichste [. . .] ist [. . .] oft gerade das Wahrste')[6] in moments where they are least expected ('frappant',[7] 'Wendepunkt').[8] The nice precision of a word like 'Wendepunkt'—as well as its subsequent persistent history—should not blind us to the fact that it is in effect the point about 'geistreiche Wendung'[9] made by Goethe. Both Schlegel brothers, if not for the same reasons, see the Novelle essentially as a collective form ('*Kränze* von Novellen',[10] 'Masse von Novellen'),[11] an observation clearly based on existing practice. And yet it would be ungenerous merely to suggest that the Schlegel brothers were indulging in clever reiteration, or that their respective statements did not have a particular emphasis. Common to both is the desire to relate the Novelle to other poetic genres or to distinguish it from them. Friedrich sees a link with the 'Märchen';[12] August Wilhelm draws the important parallel with the drama,[13] one which will run right through the century. He is, however, less concerned with accrediting the Novelle with the elevated status of the drama—for the Novelle, like the drama, is essentially also a poetic form, if in prose—but with stressing the unexpected, the need for incident ('In der Novelle muß etwas geschehen'),[14] and the proximity to tragedy. This last point, in its way, brings the Renaissance Novelle into the same ambit as the universal genius of Shakespeare. By contrasting Novelle and novel in terms of 'etwas muß geschehen' on the one hand, and 'graduelle Entwickelung'[15] on the other, A. W. Schlegel is demonstrating his adherence to Cervantes, Fielding or Goethe and his disdain for more popular traditions.

Friedrich seems more concerned with questions of tone and style, but also with the origins of the Novelle. It conforms to the highest poetic and stylistic criteria: 'Reinheit, Zartheit, Würde, Harmonie und Künstlichkeit des Stils und der Sprache'.[16] One can hardly accord greater praise; and the Novelle will thus be but one further step towards 'progressive Universalpoesie', that process by which the fragmented world of human experience and relations becomes involved with and merged into the universal, divine, supernal, the origin of poetry itself. Thus Friedrich takes care to stress that the Novelle was found in those past ages when the poetic spirit was closer to the real affairs of life, the ages of 'Ritterthum, Religion und Sitten';[17] but that, conversely, like the 'Romanze' and its 'Helden- und Kriegsgeschichten', or the 'Legende', with its 'Heiligengeschichten',[18] the poetic expressions of those times, it is yet another manifestation of the separation and splitting of the social classes and the attendant movement away from the true wellsprings of poetry. But Friedrich further perceives in the Novelle the workings of 'Witz',[19] that inexplicable and ultimately indefinable quality of the spirit which holds together the disparate and seemingly irreconcilable.

For the Novelle is a paradoxical form. It is all objectivity, truth, strictness of form, conformity to 'gemeinschaftlichen Gesichtspunct'.[20] But each story of Boccaccio is also 'subjective', with its own special emphasis and peculiarity. This also explains the difference in quality between one story of Cervantes and the next. And underlying it, too, is an irony: it is a 'Geschichte [. . .], die [. . .] nicht zur Geschichte gehört';[21] it is *true* in the sense that it is part of the collected possibilities of human experience, but it also has an inner truth of its own, its own 'Mittelpunct'[22] and centre of gravity.

August Wilhelm is marginally more interested in the subject-matter of the Novelle and its place in modern literature. He too makes the point that its task is 'zu erzählen, was in der eigentlichen Historie keinen Platz findet, und dennoch allgemein interessant ist'.[23] But, like all prose, its reference is to *reality*.[24] Indeed, given the fragmented state of our modern world, a 'Masse von Novellen [. . .], die in unsern Sitten gegründet und der Denkart des Zeitalters angemessen wären'[25] would be preferable to a mere reference back to the achievement of a Boccaccio, with his own peculiar, but yet essentially different, world. We see affinities with Friedrich's insight that a collection of several Novellen can make up a novel:[26] as a proof of this he cites the episodic structure of *Don Quijote*. This may hardly seem like encouragement for the traditional novel in the style of, say, Fielding. It is, nevertheless, an observation which, intentionally or not, fits so many German novels of the first part of the nineteenth century, from Tieck's *Franz Sternbalds Wanderungen* (1798) to Achim von Arnim's *Gräfin Dolores* (1810) to Eichendorff's *Ahnung und Gegenwart* (1815) to Goethe's *Wilhelm Meisters Wanderjahre*. They disintegrate formally into episode and sub-section, almost into a concatenation of partially self-contained stories, in Goethe's case with actual Novellen interspersed. That is one side of Schlegel's most acute observation. The other is that the Novelle is appropriate for all kinds of human experience. And there has scarcely ever been such a helpful, practical, unrestrictive, and generous encouragement to writing Novellen as August Wilhelm's concluding words:

Die Sache verhält sich so. Die Novelle ist eine Geschichte außer der Geschichte, sie erzählt folglich merkwürdige Begebenheiten, die gleichsam hinter dem Rücken der bürgerlichen Verfassungen und Anordnungen vorgefallen sind. Dazu gehören theils seltsame bald günstige bald ungünstige Abwechselungen des Glücks, theils schlaue Streiche, zur Befriedigung der Leidenschaften unternommen. Das erste giebt hauptsächlich die tragischen und ernsten, das letzte die komischen Novellen.[27]

It would be agreeable to be able to say that the Schlegels had 'said it all', had pre-empted any further need for definition. And indeed one could say that nobody during the whole of the nineteenth century was able substantially to 'improve' on their statements. Yet, as already observed, they were not addressing the wider public nor the closer-knit fraternity of traditional aesthetics. Their emphasis on prose is essential. Their stress on the encompassing capabilities and aesthetic dignity of a restricted form is crucial. They draw attention to both the *collective* and the *single* potential of the Novelle. Their indebtedness to Renaissance tradition is as manifest as Goethe's. But, like him in practice, they are in theory calling for a creative adaptation to the needs of their own times. It is part of their concern with national poetry, with the idea of people and 'Volk' and the relationship between the poet—the servant and mouthpiece of the universal—and the nation.

There is never such a neat coincidence of theory and practice as literary historians would wish. It can, however, be observed that the Schlegels' Romantic contemporaries did, for a time at least, turn to 'Kränze von Novellen' in significant fashion. Wieland's *Hexameron von Rosenhain* (1805) may seem too much a return to tradition and thus represent a step back from Goethe's *Unterhaltungen*. The same cannot be said for five major Romantic collections: Arnim's *Der Wintergarten* (1809), his so-called 'Novellensammlung von 1812', and his *Landhausleben* (1826); Tieck's *Phantasus* (1812–16); and Hoffmann's *Die Serapionsbrüder* (1819–21).

Goethe's *Unterhaltungen* had been both a revival of Boccaccio and an avowal of the pleasures, duties and conventions of social intercourse. The stories are an affirmation that 'Geselligkeit' is one of the things that hold a society together in times of disorder. It is a conservative credo, reinforced by the stories themselves. In Goethe's case it may seem rather as if he were holding on to the values of the *ancien régime*, but there is more to it than that. It is something the eighteenth and nineteenth centuries actually believe in and affirm—not only in Germany.[28] And the Novelle, with its indebtedness to gregariousness, is one of the many forms that mirrors it. 'Geselligkeit' is a way of life; for writers as different as Goethe, Arnim, Tieck, Mörike, Keller, Storm and Fontane, an essential: they cannot live without friendship, sociability, and the amiable discourse that this generates. Some have a 'conversational' style, some do not, but that is not the point. The so-called 'Rahmengespräch'—the framework of conversation around a story—is not merely a gratuitous literary device, although it can degenerate into one. It may give, as Sartre testily remarks of Maupassant's stories,[29] the impression that society has been 'caught' in the agreeable torpor of half-empty glasses and cigar-smoke, with all questions of social change and intellectual ferment as remote as the actual possibility of bandits or revolutionaries disturbing the proceedings. If Sartre only means the framework, and not the stories themselves, his statement is doubtless true, if unhistorical. The stories, however, in their insistence on 'Begebenheit', 'Vorfall', event or unusual relationships, open up insights that belie the sedentariness of the assembled company and may even challenge their very assumptions. Thus, for example, we will learn in the narrative substance of Storm's *Der Schimmelreiter* that the real point of the story is not the mystification with the supernatural that the framework encourages, but the true achievement of Hauke Haien, himself unsentimental to the point of harshness about popular superstition. Nor are nineteenth-century 'Rahmengespräche' a mere attempt to re-create Boccaccio; they are creative adaptation. Surely Paul Heyse was right in his insight: that the age that has produced a Schumann can no longer simply return to the objectivity of Haydn;[30] by the same token, the Novelle should not be restricted to themes once considered exclusively valid for it. And, if as K. K. Polheim observes, the Novelle of the nineteenth century is essentially different from Boccaccio,[31] one cannot escape the historical fact that the German writers who laid the foundations of the form—Goethe, Tieck, Hoffmann—looked back to the Renaissance for their initial situations. A little-quoted section from Tieck's *Phantasus* can perhaps make the question of adaptation clearer. The characters are talking of their proposal to tell each other stories:

Diese Einrichtung, wandte Manfred ein, ist vielleicht zu gefährlich, weil sie an den Boccaccio erinnern dürfte.
    Sie erinnert, sagte Ernst, fast an alle italiänischen Novellisten, die mit minder oder mehr Glück von dieser Erfindung Gebrauch gemacht haben.
    Doch werden Sie, sagte Emilie, uns in andrer Hinsicht nicht an diesen berühmten Autor erinnern wollen, denn gewiß verschonen Sie uns mit

dergleichen ärgerlichen und anstößigen Geschichtchen, deren er nur zu viele erzählt.

Wir können dergleichen wohl nicht so ganz unbedingt versprechen, antwortete Manfred, wenn wir uns nicht darüber erst etwas verständigt haben, was wir ärgerlich oder anstößig nennen wollen. Davor, daß wir keine Erzählungen, die ihm ähnlich oder nachgeahmt sind, vortragen werden, sind Sie hinlänglich gesichert, denn es erfordert das glänzende Talent seiner gediegenen, scharfen und bestimmten Darstellung, welche nie zu viel oder zu wenig sagt, die nichts verhüllt und doch immer von den Grazien gelenkt wird, um dergleichen allerliebste Seltsamkeiten vorzutragen:[32]

We see here the friend of August Wilhelm Schlegel: the artistic form of the Renaissance Novelle is unique and no longer attainable in its own form or own terms, but it may be applied in creative renewal to the present-day needs of a later generation.

Thus, when the theologian among the Romantics, Friedrich Schleiermacher, in 1799 published a *Versuch einer Theorie des geselligen Betragens*, he was reflecting a social need of his age. Arnim's *Wintergarten*, subtitled 'Novellen', is a collection in which the framework-society adheres to self-imposed rules of behaviour: they must not refer directly to the events of their times (the downfall of Prussia and the Napoleonic occupation). And yet their very sociability is in itself a symbol of the need for the nation to cohere, to show a united front against the loss of political and religious values. The stories, all set in past times, are what do the asserting. His other collections state this less directly: but as an ensemble they reflect the urges, weaknesses, recriminations and aspirations of a society seeking for liberation, or uncertain of its role under political restoration. Arnim proves another point of Schlegel's: his collections of Novellen are a more pertinent commentary on the age than his novels. Tieck's *Phantasus* is an affirmation of friendship and *causerie* (it is dedicated to the absent friend, August Wilhelm Schlegel). But it is also the vehicle for a wide-ranging discussion of the aesthetic and literary issues of the time. Tieck can now define what he meant all those years ago by writing 'Kunstmärchen' (putting 'Unschuld' and harmony, but also 'ungeheure Leere, das furchtbare Chaos',[33] the commonplace and 'das Wunderbare' on equal terms). Now, a story like *Liebeszauber* presents an even bleaker aspect:

die Kunstform beruhigt euer Gemüth nicht mit der Nothwendigkeit, ja ihr könnt oft in diesem Jammer nicht einmal ein Schicksal sehn, sondern nur das Blinde, Schreckliche, das was sagt: so ist es nun einmal! In dergleichen mährchenhaften Erfindungen aber kann ja dieses Elend der Welt nur wie von vielen muntern Farben gebrochen hineinspielen, und ich dächte, auch ein nicht starkes Auge müßte es auf diese Weise ertragen können.[34]

And so, for the society's benefit, he tells the little chap-book story *Magelone*, restoring the balance as the decrescendo from terror to 'Liebe und fromme Demuth'.[35] The very mobility of the conversation, seeking a balance between extremes, is what enables us to accept *Der blonde Eckbert* alongside 'Wunder' and 'Scherz'. So, too, Hoffmann's *Serapionsbrüder*, a direct follower of *Phantasus*, moves between 'Geselligkeit' and terror, the fairy-tale world (*Nussknacker und Mausekönig*) and the eerie and numinous (*Das Fräulein von Scuderi*), held together by 'das serapiontische Prinzip', the transference of the inner world of imagination into outer reality, the ratification of inner truth in the quotidian or conventional world.

The 'Rahmengespräche' of these Romantic collections have their special place at the beginning of the nineteenth century and are not necessarily a pattern for generations to come. The collection of stories or Novellen under a general title, signifying adherence to some kind of cohesive principle or underlying awareness, is however a constant during the century, not only in Germany. A bewildering variety of reasons may be offered for bringing together the disparate manifestations of life and experience. Washington Irving's *The Sketch Book* sets out to explore 'the charms of storied and poetical association' in Europe. Lermontov's *A Hero of our Time* wishes to assemble a portrait 'put together of the vices of our whole race in their most developed state'. Keller's *Die Leute von Seldwyla* casts an eye, alternately genial and malevolent, on the universal weaknesses which a small Swiss town may display. Melville's *Piazza Tales* take the vantage-point which gives them their name, in order to range out into the wide world of imagination. Each story can be read on its own. But the reverse is also true, that each collection cries out to be read as one. 'Novellenkränze' assembled from the *œuvre* of different authors, by Bülow or Heyse or Hofmannsthal, are surely also subject to this principle. Reading a single Novelle in context may also involve reading the others that accompany it: is for instance *Romeo und Julia auf dem Dorfe* different if read in the context which also embraces stories like

Kleider machen Leute and *Pankraz der Schmoller*?[36] (see Chapter 6). It is also possible to see the collective principle in operation in a single work, where the 'Rahmen' is not extended beyond the possibilities of one story, yet endows it with a multiplicity of perspectives. A good example, which also involves 'Geselligkeit', is Mörike's *Mozart auf der Reise nach Prag* (see Chapter 5).

Chapter Four
'MORALISCHE ERZÄHLUNGEN' HEINRICH VON KLEIST AND THE NOVELLE TRADITION

There has never been any lack of commentators who would see in Heinrich von Kleist the culmination of the German Novelle and the pattern for the rest of the nineteenth century. This was very much the view of some of the more doctrinaire writers on the Novelle (Pongs, Kunz, Silz) and one can see why. Kleist's stories seem to exhibit in exemplary fashion all the qualities of strictness, narrative economy, tragic concentration and eventfulness which an 'ideal' Novelle might be expected to demonstrate. Indeed one might go so far as to say that the espousal of Kleistian criteria on the part of critics has led to many nineteenth-century Novellen being interpreted in a Kleistian way. It has even led to a preference for stories by certain authors which have affinities with Kleist: Achim von Arnim, for instance, was for decades known almost exclusively through a very untypical story, *Der tolle Invalide auf dem Fort Ratonneau*, which has superficial affinities with Kleist.

It is, nevertheless, difficult to escape the conclusion that Kleist is indeed different from most of his contemporary Novelle writers, both in technique and quality. One of the presuppositions on which so much of the writing on the German Novelle is based is that far too few writers have followed in Kleist's pattern. But it is equally difficult to avoid the observation that the nineteenth century itself did not wish to adhere to Kleistian patterns and may have had very specific reasons for finding them unsuitable or inadequate. That is not to deny the recognition that Kleist's stories had enjoyed from quite early on: Brentano tells Arnim that they are being 'verschlungen' by the reading public;[1] they are praised by Tieck[2] and Eduard von Bülow[3] as being 'classics' of their genre. But the nineteenth century also wanted certain other things in which Kleist was notably deficient, and we fail to understand the century if we do not appreciate the reasons which led it to write in a mode quite at variance with Kleist's. For, at different times and in the hands of different authors, the nineteenth century calls for reflection, or it calls for plausible explanation, for more humour or more sentiment, more mystery and imagination, more of the 'Normalfall', or more integration of psychology and event.[4] It clearly recoils from much of Kleist's baldness and starkness; or it wishes Kleist's stringency to be tempered with other qualities:

> Es ist schwer diesem Dichter gerecht zu werden, von welchem man sich ebenso gewaltig angezogen als abgestoßen fühlen muß.[5]

This is the verdict in the preface to Heyse's and Kurz's highly influential *Deutscher Novellenschatz* of 1871. We have only to think of the different ways in which the nineteenth century treats a murder story (Brentano, Hoffmann, Droste, Sealsfield, Ludwig, Fontane) to see how, say, *Der Zweikampf* or *Der Findling* are not a pattern. Or the many examples of crossed love, from Goethe to Keller. The twenty-four volumes of the *Novellenschatz* contain but one story by Kleist, *Die Verlobung in St. Domingo*, a reflection of what the market will 'stand'. If the nineteenth century therefore is not Kleistian, then it is so of its own volition.

But what *is* the 'Kleistian Novelle' and what are its characteristics? Is it the ghost story, *Das Bettelweib von Locarno*, with its absolute reduction of plot and psychological insight, or is it the rather rambling *Michael Kohlhaas*? Is it *Das Erdbeben in Chili*, with its muted tribute to human dignity at the end, or *Der Findling*, with its ferocious rejection? *Die Marquise von O . . .* , where one individual reaches out to the other over an abyss of uncertainty and improbability, and finds a hand to seize, and eventually claim; or *Die heilige Cäcilie*, where 'higher forces' lift man out of sanity into unreason? Is it that story that calls itself 'Nach einer wahren Begebenheit' (*Marquise*), 'Aus einer alten Chronik' (*Kohlhaas*) or 'Legende' (*Heilige Cäcilie*)? One could go on; for in Kleist's stories one is confronted by variety, disparateness and shifts of emphasis. The sources for the stories are various; the subjects seem arbitrary, until one sees that they have, in their settings at least, been chosen for maximum effect: medieval, or at least historical (*Kohlhaas, Zweikampf, Heilige Cäcilie*), with their 'altteutsch' associations; Italy (*Bettelweib, Findling, Marquise*) and the evocation of southern passion; the Americas, with Spanish fanaticism or racial hatred. Kleist seems to have looked around for those genres and subjects which would best suit his consuming ambition. His tendency toward extremes ('wer beschreibt das Entsetzen'),[6] his love of the exotic, his anticlericalism, his use of seemingly extravagant devices like faints or blushes or pallor, all these show Kleist wishing to wring as much as possible out of *established* patterns of narration.

Indeed Kleist, in his only recorded statement about his collected stories, suggested for them a title that reminds us of the whole Novelle tradition lying behind him: 'Moralische Erzählungen'.[7] And he did, in 1810–11, publish his stories as a cohesive collection, if without the title. But, as already stated, it is cohesion in disjection. At most, only a few stories seem to belong together, and then as pairs (e.g. *Erdbeben* and *Verlobung*, *Marquise* and *Zweikampf*). Also, the proposed general title was never used. We are concerned, therefore, too, with the problem of whether the *collection* should determine our reading of the *individual* stories, or vice versa. But could Kleist really have been serious with 'moralische Erzählungen'? Surely this title would suggest everything that Kleist does not stand for, associated as it is with mainly French, and minor German, writers? Yet the 'contes moraux', whatever else they may have been, were also usually collections drawn from the disparate events of human life, held together only by an underlying belief in providence or human goodness. In that respect, too, Kleist's projected title, and collected stories, would remind his readers of the most famous set of Novellen written outside of the Boccaccian mode: Cervantes's *Novelas ejemplares*.

And yet the only real point of comparison between Cervantes and Kleist could surely lie solely in the element of collective disparity.[8] For Cervantes assures us in a preface that, despite the heterogeneity of his stories, they all have an exemplary moral quality in common, be they satire, or picaresque, or character type-study, or love adventure. They are certainly not to be associated with the scabrous Italian tradition[9] and embrace a wider range of subject-matter than this. There are twelve stories, which, following Christian number symbolism, suggests some kind of order and pattern. And common to all the stories, applying as the case may be to heroes or victims alike, is the principle of 'desengaño', that awareness of the fragility and unsoundness of the foundations on which natural man stands, and the conviction of an undergirding security in divine providence.[10] That is the framework, if one will, which replaces the explicit reference to a moral and social order set out in the collections extending from the *Decameron* to *Unterhaltungen deutscher Ausgewanderten*, *Der Wintergarten* and *Phantasus*.

The range of human experience and narrative style in Kleist's stories is considerably reduced as against Cervantes (no picaresque, no satire). Kleist concentrates more uniformly on *event*, 'Begebenheit', catastrophe even, and in a way that is more exaggerated, or unrelieved, than Cervantes's novelas or most of the collections already referred to. Whereas Cervantes presents us with some kind of theological or moral *ordo*, we are hard put to it to find such a frame of reference in Kleist's stories. Some of his most horrendous accounts do, it is true, like Shakespeare's tragedies, return us to some kind of order after the chaos. There is the child at the end of *Das Erdbeben in Chili*, which, even if its parents have been massacred, and another baby killed in its stead by mistake, is better than nothing at all ('so war es ihm fast, als müßt er sich freuen'). Readers, may, if they wish, remark the monument erected in memory of Toni and Gustav from *Die Verlobung in St. Domingo* and reflect on their love and how it might have been. But it is small comfort. After some stories, characters take active steps to see that these things do not happen again, or submit to the authority against which they have rebelled: the rules of trial by duel are changed at the end of *Der Zweikampf* (but will it help?); the mother of the four sons reduced to imbeciles by some higher agency in *Die heilige Cäcilie* returns to the bosom of the Catholic church (but will that explain what happened?); Michael Kohlhaas dies knowing that his children will be provided for (but will that bring back his wife?). Even the relatively serene end of *Die Marquise von O* . . . represents an ascent from the depths of a despair unto madness ('Engel', 'Teufel'). Two stories even run headlong into catastrophe and total loss (*Das Bettelweib* and *Der Findling*). It is quite manifest that events do not speak for our having an anchor or security in any kind of pre-established moral or social order; moreover, we cannot relate the *events* of the stories to any kind of system of explanation or instance of higher justice. We are left to read the signs, to test reactions, tentatively to establish relations, to sift evidence—and *then*, and only then, to trust other persons. Those who do not, perish.

And so, we find ourselves, in examining Kleist's stories, inevitably beginning, not with an 'ordo' but with the *events* themselves, the 'Begebenheit'. 'Etwas muß geschehen' had been August Wilhelm Schlegel's way of describing the central event of a Novelle, or at least its general tenor. And, in stating that, Schlegel was summing up the tradition that began with Boccaccio and was being renewed in his own times through Goethe. The Boccaccian 'or avenne che', the 'advint ung jour' of *Cent Nouvelles nouvelles*, runs right through to Kleist's 'es traf sich', or 'gerade zu der Zeit', or 'dergestalt . . . daß', announcing so many of the events in his stories and suggesting a state of affairs that is now about to be interrupted.[11] In many of Boccaccio's more serious or even tragic novellas, we find that the 'or avenne che' is actually about to lead us out of the world of the norm into that of the exception. An agent, be it Fortune or Providence or some force inaccessible to human reason, paralyses temporarily the accepted way and constellation of things, to make way for the unnatural or even catastrophic. It comes unexpectedly (otherwise it would lose its force). When it does happen, human reason has no ultimate answer. The story of the unfortunate lovers in *Decameron* IV, 7, who both die from the effects of putting leaves from a sage bush to their mouths, has everybody dumbfounded and groping for a satisfactory explanation. Only when the judge orders the destruction of the bush and a huge toad is found underneath it, is the *immediate* cause of the deaths revealed: but man is not let into the ultimate secret of why the lovers must die. Man cannot know certain things and he cannot repair the attendant damage. Similarly, in the famous story of the falcon (*Decameron* V, 9), the lady's son is ill and believes that possession of Federigo's falcon will make him well again. When the lady goes to Federigo, who is in dire penury, to make her request, he believes it is his duty as a gentleman to set some meal before her: the beloved falcon. The son dies. Would he have died anyway, or was it a direct cause of the unfortunate series of events, Federigo's misunderstanding of the lady's visit and her ignorance of his devotion to her? The son's death does make her heir to the family fortune, and she can marry Federigo and make him a richer and wiser man.

But, unlike the couple Jeronimo and Josephe in Kleist's *Erdbeben in Chili*, they have greater respect for the unseen workings of providence. They submit, they do not speculate. For them, it is not the naïve 'raison suffisante' 'wie viel Elend über die Welt kommen mußte, damit sie glücklich würden',[12] the answer of supposedly emancipated and enlightened modern man which, however, comes so perilously close to the optimism so fiercely harried by Voltaire in *Candide*. Boccaccio's characters do not proceed beyond the obvious solutions of cause and effect. Goethe's, too, in *Unterhaltungen deutscher Ausgewanderten*, do not pursue the question too far, and the assembled society is left in ambiguity. The phrase used more than once by Kleist, that 'Wahrscheir' ʰkeit nicht immer auf Seiten der Wahrheit ist',[13] shows that his characters have begun to speculate, are seeking explanations, are not content to regard the chance events as a bolt from the blue, where it is at variance with their inner sense of innocence or justice (*Marquise, Zweikampf, Kohlhaas*). Or they are pitched into a set of events for which an explanation, of a harshly matter-of-fact kind, is present: the maltreatment of the beggar woman at the beginning of *Das Bettelweib* leads to the blanching bones of the Marchese in the ruins of the castle at the end; St Cecilia really *did* intervene to save the church from the iconoclasts. *Suum cuique*. But even then we cannot be sure. For in the short *Bettelweib* story, Kleist rushes us through the events with such breathless speed that we have no option but to believe the outcome. In *Die heilige Cäcilie* we are presented with a state of affairs (four men reduced to imbecility), with 'events' which are patched together from several accounts, yet which call nothing into doubt (until we remember that the story begins and ends with the word 'Legende').

Yet for all that Kleist exploits events and arranges situations of peril and extremity, his relationship to the old 'etwas muß geschehen' is by no means straightforward. The rapport between narrator and reader in the German Novelle, from the 1790s on, is no longer that direct and unchallenged one which we know from Boccaccio or Cervantes. We have already noted that Kleist refuses to assist his readers with a general preface or a framework discussion. But these devices, too, were no longer what they had been in the Renaissance: they had become to a large extent an aesthetic forum, a means of characterizing the events about to be narrated, a guide to formal interpretation. The breakdown of the traditional relationship between narrator and reader in the novel, which can be seen in the second half of the eighteenth century, with attendant ironization and various other strains, also has its parallel, while not entirely analogous, in the Novelle. In the novel, sustained narration of the expected, whether third-person or first-person, or epistolary, is the first feature to suffer. The Novelle can hardly abandon that, for it still calls for the old-fashioned virtues of story-telling.

In France, by about 1760, however, the 'nouvelle' and its various modes of narration had reached a state of super-saturation. It was scarcely possible to become more exotic, exciting, moral, or 'licencieux'; mass-production meant triviality.[14] One notable reaction to this was Voltaire's *Candide* (1759). For Voltaire was willing to take the conventions of the 'nouvelle', but to such extremes that a satirical intention was obvious and a purpose more serious than mere entertainment showed through. A story whose first few pages alone present us with all the horrors of the Seven Years War, the earthquake in Lisbon, and the Inquisition, with enough attendant improbabilities and seeming absurdities, is no longer a mere exotic adventure story. We could otherwise not bear the implications of the narrated horrors with which we are regaled as if they were the most natural things in the world. The events would be too profoundly disturbing if the author were not also making something else clear through them. That is one possibility for dealing with 'etwas muß geschehen'.

Another is straight parody. Coming nearer home, we saw how the young Ludwig Tieck, a reader of Sterne and Diderot, but also of the Gothic novel, set out to write stories in which nothing happened, deliberately foiling the readers' expectations. 'Begebenheit' ceases to have any meaning when the author addresses us: 'Dear reader, I could begin my story, "Der losgelassene Sturmwind zog mit aller seiner Macht durch den Wald",[15] but I choose not to.' A writer who is able to proceed in this fashion has clearly seen through the techniques involved in direct narration of events. Hence in *Der blonde Eckbert*, when he turns to a serious vein, the uncertainties about what really happened, what was real and what in the imagination. This is not the same as the traditional mystifications of the Gothic novel, which are concerned with unnerving, and then explaining. Tieck refuses to 'explain' something which—'kein Märchen'—is partly memory, imagination and fevered delusion. But which is which?

On a less extreme level, it was noted that Goethe in *Unterhaltungen deutscher Ausgewanderten*, while concerned with renewing a tradition, also makes it clear that he is not merely adapting existing patterns: the events in the stories become associated with new considerations. Stories from known sources are narrated in such a way that we are left to work out for ourselves the problems of truth and appearance, the supernatural, the effects of chance on the moral character. Even Wieland is adamant that certain narrative traditions, with attendant improbabilities of event (the 'conte moral' of Baculard, for instance) have had their day.

Kleist's stories seem to reflect some or all of this reaction. Yet there is still some of the older tradition of the 'novelas ejemplares' and the 'conte moral', with their insistence on the *human implications* of unlikely events, where certain human constants assert themselves amid tribulations and trials (virtue, human goodness, natural justice, providence). Indeed, the very way Kleist writes his stories makes it clear that he is impelling us towards a portrayal or discussion of such basic human concerns or is forcing us to read the story in a certain way. Clearly he is not, like Cervantes, telling us, as at the end of *La Española inglesa*, 'how much virtue and beauty can achieve' and 'how heaven may turn even our worst misfortune into our greatest fortune'. Nor even, like Goethe, at the beginning of *Werther*, telling his readers that they must not identify with the hero. He is, however, making it clear that the 'Begebenheit', the spectacular or unnerving event, is not the only, or even real, point of the story.

Here Kleist the dramatist and storyteller meet. For we can see in his tragedies a progression: from the eventful 'fate' tragedy, *Die Familie Schroffenstein*, with its insistence on what we cannot know, on how we cannot reach out to the other person without being thwarted; to plays, with truly Shakespearean stage action, where the events are less important than the inward consciousness of the characters who act in them. Thus a Käthchen, a Penthesilea, a Prinz Friedrich von Homburg, act, or bring about actions; these are, however, of more purely *personal* importance than their immediate implications for others or their social effects. The main characters are not the ones who comment on the extraordinariness of their own behaviour; it is so much part of them that they cannot do otherwise. And so the 'event' of *Das Käthchen von Heilbronn* is the dream-like devotion to her cherubic vision, not all the attendant trappings of the 'großes historisches Ritterschauspiel'. The 'event' of *Prinz Friedrich von Homburg* is not so much the battle of Fehrbellin, as the Prince's inner interpretation of outer reality and the merging of the truth in one's heart with the pragmatic facts 'out there'.

Commentators have noted the similarities between Kleist's dramas and his stories and have observed the congruence of motifs and symbols, even of stylistic features. But a story in the Novelle tradition will require perhaps a greater insistence on that central event, that 'Begebenheit', that extraordinary case, than is normal in the drama. Yet in many of the stories, Kleist seems to get the main event 'over and done with', to lead us on to consider the effects and implications of what has happened. The three best examples are *Die Marquise von O . . .* , *Das Erdbeben in Chili*, and *Die Verlobung in St. Domingo*. Here we see how Kleist, less radically than Voltaire, manipulates extraordinary events so that we are forced to ponder not them but what they entail. The amazing, monstrous, first sentence of *Die Marquise von O . . .* does not have its effect solely because of the seeming 'event' of the story: 'ohne ihr Wissen, in andre Umstände gekommen'. The dishonouring of a sleeping or fainting woman is in itself an old motif and can be traced in the European novella tradition back to at least the fifteenth century;[16] its most notable representation is in Cervantes's story, *La Fuerza de la sangre* in the *Novelas ejemplares*. Where Kleist found the motif is irrelevant (there are even variants involving necrophilia!);[17] that is not, in itself, the so very extraordinary event in the story (even if we do find it hard to believe that the Marquise has absolutely no notion of what has happened to her). True, the subtitle, 'Nach einer wahren Begebenheit', the device of keeping the readers in a certain state of suspense, may show Kleist adhering to traditional narrative patterns. But he makes us immediately aware that the story is not to proceed on traditional lines, by telling us in the first sentence of the newspaper announcement. For this is the story of someone who, having undergone what other writers would have considered an event sufficiently remarkable or even outrageous in itself, wishes to gain inner moral and spiritual certitude, and has recourse to a device more extraordinary than the happening that first caused it.

Similarly, the point of *Die Verlobung in St. Domingo* is not merely 'als die Schwarzen die Weißen ermordeten'. That first sentence is chilling enough. But Kleist cajoles his readers into believing that they know all that already ('Nun weiß jedermann, daß im Jahr 1803 . . . ').[18] He keeps us waiting for nearly two pages before the hero, Gustav, is introduced. He tells us less of the horrors of the insurrection than, by implication, that all the enlightened and libertarian talk of the National Convention, the humanitarianism of an Abbé Raynal or a Count Schimmelmann, could not triumph over man's basic instinct to avenge injustice. The quick run-through of events in the first two pages prepares us for the inevitable: blacks will kill whites at all costs, and Gustav is doomed the moment he knocks at the door of Congo Hoango's dwelling. Even then, Kleist impels us on to the real point of the story, that white will help white. Toni invokes her half-European origin; her very first action, the lifting of the lamp to show her white skin, leads over to the eventual mutual attraction. It is part of the basis of trust and tragedy; she will not betray her own kind, especially one who has himself suffered through the Revolution before coming to Haiti.

Again, there is nothing so particularly remarkable itself in an earthquake in Chile (Santiago had had several; this happened to be the one in 1647); it is almost what one expects. What surprises the reader is that phrase 'wollte sich erhenken'. For this is a story about those who seek to draw their own conclusions from events. A chance (the word 'Zufall' or 'zufällig' occurs at least four times in the first six paragraphs of the story) is immediately interpreted by those to whom it occurs as being unfortunate or auspicious as it affects them. The hero, Jeronimo, has read all the signs given him by fortuitous occurrences in such a way that the same 'Zufall' can offer, in succession, the joys of love, the chance to end his life, and the grace to save it again. Amid all the cataclysmic chaos and ruin, the characters find time (or are given it by the author) to assign the events to cause and effect. Jeronimo, in the fluctuations of his fortune, ascribes them successively to chance, then to God, then to some malevolent agent ruling the world, then to heaven again and its angels. This culminates in that 'wie viel Elend über die Welt kommen mußte, damit sie glücklich würden!' Others, however, notably the church authorities, are equally certain in their own minds how the event is to be seen: on an apocalyptic scale, or at least as a visitation on the sinful. Unlike the optimists in Voltaire's *Candide*, who have their speculations cut short by: 'Quand Sa Hautesse envoie un vaisseau en Egypte, s'embarrasse-t-elle si les souris qui sont dans le vaisseau sont à leur aise ou non?'[19] and the curt advice not to concern themselves with the ways of providence and theodicy, Kleist's characters relentlessly pursue their delusions. When the same citizens of Santiago who were, shortly before, hoping to burn Josephe at the stake, are now stripped of all their possessions and have returned to a kind of paradisal equality, Jeronimo and Josephe believe in a kind of Rousseauistic reversion of human society to its original, 'free' state. Without possessions, and equal, man is 'good'—and seems to demonstrate it.[20] The story goes on, however, to prove, not that *man* is good, but that only some few *men* can be capable of the highest virtue and selflessness. The rest of mankind seems only bent on proving not Rousseau but Hobbes: that man is by nature a predator. To reach the ending, with Don Fernando, 'der göttliche Held', and the child of love that has survived the cataclysm, we have been speeded through a series of events which prevent us from concentrating so much on the 'Begebenheit' as on its implications. It seems as if Kleist has deliberately projected us towards the two reflective sections of the story: the idyll, with its false paradise, and the final paragraph, with its subdued acceptance of 'diese Begebenheit' and the re-establishment of a family amid loss and bereavement.

Whether Kleist tells his 'Begebenheit' in the first sentence or not, we also notice his technique of interrupting all superfluous reflection or digression or explanation ('wie bekannt', 'Nun weiß jedermann', 'die zu entwickeln zu weitläufig wäre', 'aus mancherlei Gründen', 'lassen wir dahin gestellt sein').[21] This is in part the old technique of pretending to initiate the reader into some secret, in order the more to mystify him. But it has special import in Kleist's longer stories, notably *Michael Kohlhaas*. The first sentence proclaims the main character paradoxically to be compounded of both the 'entsetzlich' and the 'rechtschaffen' and makes a causal link between 'right' and 'wrong'. It is also an invitation to run helter-skelter through the 'entsetzlich', Kohlhaas's deeds of revenge, with their half-truths, inadequate explanations, dubious appearances, in order to present us with the second, and more discursive, part of the story, with the moral rehabilitation of the hero and his concern to atone for the effects of his deeds. Hence Kohlhaas rises in stature against the Elector of Saxony, who deludes himself as to the nature of appearances, whereas Kohlhaas is gradually freeing himself from trust in a dubious 'Wahrscheinlichkeit'.

This is, however, not an absolute pattern for the stories. For Kleist, like Cervantes, varies his approach to narrative. *Der Findling* and *Die heilige Cäcilie* concentrate as much on the effects of a human *decision* as on a central *event*. Piachi could, after all, leave

Nicolo the foundling behind; but his kindness leads him to decide otherwise. He is, therefore, to some extent 'responsible' for the viper he has nurtured in his own breast; in adopting a strange child to replace their own and re-establish their domestic order, Piachi and his wife are giving themselves up to the uncertainties of chance. And so the story moves from an account of virtue and human pity to one of desperate and frenzied hatred. The decision to desecrate the church in *Die heilige Cäcilie* similarly involves the brothers in events and consequences which they cannot foresee: 'die *Gewalt* der Musik'. An irrational and fanatical resolution seems to make them susceptible to the total force of an irrational art form. They are not overwhelmed by violent events like the attack on the Kommandant's house in *Die Marquise von O . . .*, or the earthquake, or the massacre on Haiti. Indeed, such events are glossed over or not allowed to take place, as Piachi's loss in the plague is made up for or the feast of St Cecilia runs its course without disturbance. We can see this pattern right down to the sentence-structure of Kleist's stories. Much has been made of the famous opening sentences, with their compression of several statements and events, their contortions of normal periodic and syntactical sequence, their uneasy marriage of the incongruous, their refusal to permit the reader a moment's relaxation. But this is Kleist's own reaction to a device which itself is part of the tradition in which he was writing. A comparison with a text contemporary with Kleist, but by a much older author, may bring this out:

Die Familie Moscoso von Altariva, eine der ältesten und angesehensten in Galicien, war auf den gewöhnlichen Wegen, worauf große Häuser mit der Zeit in Verfall zu geraten pflegen, nach und nach so weit herabgekommen, daß die reichen aber abgenützen Gerätschaften einer alten, den Einsturz drohenden Burg, nebst der Herrlichkeit über ein paar kleine Weiler, und ein sechs Ellen langer Stammbaum, beinahe alles waren, was Don Lope Moscoso, Graf von Altariva, der letzte Sprößling des ältern Zweiges der Familie, vom Glanz seiner Vorfahren übrig behalten hatte. Fern vom Hofe, und sogar in der Hauptstadt seiner Provinz selten gesehen, lebte er mit seiner Gemahlin Donna Pelaja in einer beinahe einsiedlerischen Abgeschiedenheit von der Welt, einzig mit der Erziehung eines Sohns und einer Tochter beschäftigt, welche, in der nämlichen Stunde geboren, eine so große Ähnlichkeit der Gestalt und Gesichtsbildung mit auf die Welt brachten, daß es, in der Folge, den Eltern selbst nur durch die verschiedene Kleidung des Geschlechts möglich war, sie von einander zu unterscheiden.

Durch einen Glücksfall, der, wiewohl nicht ohne Beispiel, doch in Romanen und Komödien häufiger als in der wirklichen Welt vorzukommen pflegt, kehrte Don Jago, der einzige Vatersbruder des Don Lope, nach einer vieljährigen Abwesenheit, mit einem in West-Indien erworbenen unermeßlichen Vermögen aus Mexico zurück, mit dem Vorsatz, dasselbe, da er ohne Leibeserben war, zu Wiederherstellung des alten Glanzes seines Hauses anzuwenden.[22]

It is the opening of Wieland's story, *Die Novelle ohne Titel*, from *Das Hexameron von Rosenhain*. Beside it one can set the opening of Kleist's *Der Zweikampf*:

Herzog Wilhelm von Breysach, der, seit seiner heimlichen Verbindung mit einer Gräfin, namens Katharina von Heersbruck, aus dem Hause Alt-Hüningen, die unter seinem Range zu sein schien, mit seinem Halbbruder, dem Grafen Jakob dem Rotbart, in Feindschaft lebte, kam gegen das Ende des vierzehnten Jahrhunderts, da die Nacht des heiligen Remigius zu dämmern begann, von einer in Worms mit dem deutschen Kaiser abgehaltenen Zusammenkunft zurück, worin er sich von diesem Herrn, in Ermangelung ehelicher Kinder, die ihm gestorben waren, die Legitimation eines, mit seiner Gemahlin vor der Ehe erzeugten, natürlichen Sohnes, des Grafen Philipp von Hüningen, ausgewirkt hatte. Freudiger, als während des ganzen Laufs seiner Regierung in die Zukunft blickend, hatte er schon den Park, der hinter seinem Schlosse lag, erreicht: als plötzlich ein Pfeilschuß aus dem Dunkel der Gebüsche hervorbrach, und ihm, dicht unter dem Brustknochen, den Leib durchbohrte.[23]

There is, naturally, one very obvious difference: Wieland's tone is one of gently nudging irony, while Kleist's is serious, as befits his almost total concentration on the tragic—his main contribution to the genre. The technical structure, however, reveals similarities. Wieland's two main clauses may be reduced to 'Die Familie . . . war . . . herabgekommen' and 'lebte er'; Kleist's to 'Herzog Wilhelm . . . kam . . . zurück' and 'hatte er . . . erreicht'. All the additional information is in the form of subordinate clauses which begin almost to take on an existence of their own, to introduce us to dynastic complexities unknown to the main clause, to bring in characters left out of the main statement. Both mention in these subordinate structures characters who are to play an important part in the story (Galora, one of the identical twins, and the Holy Roman Emperor, who is later to convene the duel). Both bring a surprising or perplexing turn into the story after the space of little more than a paragraph.

The fact that Wieland is using this display of rhetorical artifice at the outset of a work significantly entitled *Novelle ohne Titel*, suggests that he is both identifying himself with the conventions of this mode of narration—and parodying it. That 'Durch einen Glücksfall, der [. . .] in Romanen und Komödien häufiger als in der wirklichen Welt vorzukommen pflegt', is an indication that the story is rather more of an exercise in 'etwas muß geschehen' than a work of absolutely serious motivation. For the 'Glücksfall' follows on from the already remarkable statement that there were boy and girl twins so absolutely identical as to be somewhat of a phenomenon. The first paragraph and its continuation have introduced the unusual, then the even more unusual, and have commented on it ('auf den gewöhnlichen Wegen, worauf große Häuser mit der Zeit in Verfall zu geraten pflegen'). Even a short examination of Boccaccio and Cervantes reveals that Wieland's opening sentences are part and parcel of the tradition. Boccaccio's falcon story, for instance, less convoluted in its rhetoric, has us within about as many lines at almost the same place in Wieland's story: 'In the manner of most young men of gentle breeding, Federigo lost his heart to a noble lady', 'Federigo lost his entire fortune (as can easily happen)', 'one falcon', 'resigned himself to a life of poverty', 'Now one day . . .'.[24] Similarly, Cervantes's *La Fuerza de la sangre* has, within its first paragraph, the family, the place, the first event (an evening walk), with a short characterization of persons and the unusual event about to be adumbrated: the well-policed town of Toledo, its peace-loving citizenry, the honourable family, then the observation that misfortune usually arrives when one is least expecting it, the second paragraph ('For there lived in that town a young nobleman') leading into Leocadia's abduction and rape. We know more or less what we are to expect, and why, for there are certain constants—or inconstants—of human behaviour ('as can easily happen', 'when we are least expecting it'). Because they are based on observation of general human circumstances, but are also narrating an exceptional case, a 'caso portentoso y jamás visto', Boccaccio's and Cervantes's will be exemplary: as demonstrating what may happen (fortune, *desengaño*) and what is the best way of reacting (recognition of a noble deed, in Boccaccio; admission of guilt and the willingness to make amends through love, in Cervantes).[25] Occasionally, Cervantes will even produce an opening sentence which will pack all this information together very tightly and will, through the very periodic structure itself, have us well into the story within a few lines. Soltau's translation of the beginning of *La Española inglesa*, of 1801, runs thus:

Unter der Beute, welche die Engländer aus *Cadiz* wegführten, befand sich ein kleines siebenjähriges Mädchen, welches *Donald*, ein englischer Cavalier mit sich nach *London* nahm, ohne Mitwissen, und wider den ausdrücklichen Befehl des Grafen *von Essex*, welcher befohlen hatte, das Kind mit allem Fleiße aufzusuchen, um es den Aeltern wieder zu geben, die sich bey ihm über den Verlust desselben beklagt hatten.[26]

Leaving aside other considerations (the quality of the translation, the question of whether Kleist knew it), we see how Cervantes refuses to allow us to become involved with statements that might in themselves be interesting (the sack of Cadiz, the role of the Earl of Essex), in order to concentrate on the illegal abduction of Ysabela by Clotaldo. Soltau, no stylist like Kleist, has to put a full stop to regain his breath, for Cervantes's sentence does not end where the translation indicates: Cervantes finishes the opening period by telling us that Ysabela was the most beautiful girl in the whole city and the light of her parents' eyes, the first suggestion, from an urbane observer of human behaviour, that a long and involved story is perhaps going to turn out happily in the end.

Where does this leave the first sentence of *Der Zweikampf*? We could say that, despite everything, Kleist is following an established rhetorical tradition. But there is an important difference: the first paragraph lacks that element of common human wisdom, of laconic reflection, of relation to some kind of norm of human behaviour or human experience. Kleist does not wish us, at the outset, to begin ratiocinations about whys and wherefores. The narration of the story moves on inexorably through phrases like 'unverhofft', 'plötzliche Wendung', 'Nun muß man wissen', 'Dieser plötzliche Sturz', 'wer beschreibt das Erstaunen', 'Inzwischen war', 'eine besondere Fügung des Himmels', 'ein heilloser Fehltritt', 'eine sonderbare Schickung des Himmels', 'Es traf sich', 'unerwartete Wendung der Dinge', 'die ganze Wendung'. It is worth knowing that, for at least twenty-five pages of this set of fateful events, the heroine Littegarde, is left with 'nichts, als die Unsträflichkeit ihres Lebenswandels'[27] as a surety. Indeed, of all Kleist's characters, one might say that Littegarde, even more than the Marquise, is tried and tested by events, 'Begebenheiten', to an almost inhuman degree.

Unlike Jeronimo and Josephe, who are prepared to interpret events in their own favour, Littegarde must see every incident (the murder, the investigation, the accusation, the trial by duel, the outcome) as speaking *against* that sense of inner integrity and innocence which is all she can pit against them. Until 'das geheiligte Urteil Gottes'[28] is made to coincide with her own conviction of blamelessness, it seems that man's dignity and decency has no hope against coincidence, appearance and the adventitious. Kleist clearly does not believe in the efficacy of stating commonplaces of human experience at the opening of a story, because chance, or fate, or 'Fügung', 'Schickung' or 'Wendung', will call them into question and upset them. When by contrast Cervantes is about to accompany us on a set of adventures which would test the constancy of any lovers, in *El Amante liberal*, he tells us at the beginning that blows of fate may cause us to abandon our reason and give way to despair; but the 'exemplary' nature of the story assures us from the outset that reason and generosity will prevail. Kleist's world is too fragile for such a commitment at so early a stage.

We see this particularly in *Die Marquise von O . . .* , not only in that story, but in the way it notably differs from others which use the same motif: Cervantes's *La Fuerza de la sangre* and Hoffmann's *Das Gelübde* (1816).[29] Cervantes's story runs as follows: Leocadia, the daughter of an impoverished noble family, is abducted by Rodolfo, of wealthy and influential parentage, while out walking. She is blindfolded, faints, is raped, and abandoned. Rodolfo goes off to Italy, while Leocadia lives with her family and the child that has resulted from the incident. A chance accident to this child reveals its true identity to Rodolfo's parents. He is summoned back from Italy and a scene of reconciliation takes place.

In Hoffmann, we have: the flighty Polish Countess Hermenegilda is originally in love with Count Stanislaus, whom she however spurns. She is, instead, strangely attracted to Count Xaver, his cousin, who bears a remarkable similarity to Stanislaus. One day, with Xaver, in a kind of trance, she imagines her wedding to Stanislaus, a battle raging in the background, the subsequent consummation of the marriage, and Stanislaus's death. She has, however, lain in Xaver's arms; Stanislaus having, at that moment, in fact died a soldier's death far away. Hermenegilda, regarding herself as Stanislaus's widow, is discovered to be pregnant. The family refuses a marriage with Xaver, arranges for the mother to have the child in secret before she enters a monastery. Xaver comes and abducts the child, which dies. Hermenegilda takes the veil as Sister Cölestine, and dies shortly after. Xaver also enters a monastery.

There are similarities of motif and detail between Cervantes and Kleist's and Hoffmann's stories. But it is not a question of who had read whom or borrowed what from whom. The motif, as we have already stated, is not original. It is evidence of how much all the great story-writers are indebted to tradition in their respective collections. Common to all three stories is the unpremeditated or impulsive nature of the act, which is caused by weakness in the face of occasion, opportunity or chance. In all three stories, the seducer goes away, returning dramatically to face the consequences of his deed. Cervantes can stress both the 'event' and the moral consequences it bodes, by claiming to be writing a true story (the real names have been changed). Kleist's, too, is 'Nach einer wahren Begebenheit, deren Schauplatz von Norden nach dem Süden verlegt worden'; but it is doubtful if that means much more than Goethe's changing the site of his 'Antonelli' story from Paris to Naples. It is by now the indispensable claim to authenticity, into the spirit of which readers are prepared to enter for both amusement and instruction. Or at most it has something to do with the statement elsewhere by Kleist that only the 'Geschichtschreiber', recording true fact, is warranted to recount events that strain normal credulity.[30] When, however, we examine the narrative structures of the older story and the two more modern Novellen, we see how the Renaissance *exemplum* has given way to other considerations.

Cervantes's story takes the form of a straight narrative, told from one event to the next, with very little digression, and a concentration on a necessarily small number of characters. This enables him to trace a clear pattern: misfortune comes when we are least expecting it and even in places where civic order is assured; Rodolfo and his companions are likened to wolves among sheep as they prepare for the abduction, the whole action of which only takes a few minutes. Leocadia is left with little hope that the dishonour done to her can be righted; she is indeed fortunate that her father does not invoke the honour code and kill her. In a moment of the story reminiscent of that where Kleist's Marquise acknowledges 'die Weltordnung', the family comes to the conclusion that, in the world, human evil inevitably will triumph over reason, and that honour is best preserved by silence. But both before and after this moment of spiritual resignation, we have the mention of a crucifix which Leocadia removes from the scene of her misfortune; this becomes the symbol of an *ordo*, an earnest of future justice and recognition, a surety that a misdeed will some day be converted into, as does indeed happen, marital bliss and a happy line of descendants. The crucifix becomes part of that 'power of blood', the natural drawing together of those joined by consanguinity, into a family which accepts its responsibilities and shows magnanimity and forgiveness. After the introduction of the crucifix, the outcome is to some extent assured; we are, at least, reminded that behind human suffering there is divine pity and compassion. Our expectations are not built up towards tragedy.

Cervantes's characters try in adversity to read signs that point to some kind of higher order and providence. Kleist's are not far behind in trying to do the same. Yet the structure of *Die Marquise von O* . . . has one or two crucially different features. The first sentence deliberately does not tell us the actual circumstances of those 'andre Umstände', and the first twenty pages have something of a comedy of errors in which the Kommandant's family *mis*reads every hint which Graf F . . . drops, while the reader is initiated more and more into the secret that eludes the main characters. That element of mystification is foreign to Cervantes's story. And whereas Cervantes states a general *maxim* about human experience in his opening paragraph, Kleist tells us a *fact*—the startling newspaper announcement—which immediately puts the mere 'andre Umstände' in the shade. Yet it refers us paradoxically to a search for the kind of order that for Cervantes is an assured factor governing our existence. Like Cervantes, Kleist pitches us into events with some speed: 'sonderbarer [. . .] Schritt', 'Drang unabänderlicher Umstände': *'plötzlich'* [my italics]. No time is wasted: Cervantes's wolves become Kleist's hounds. The order which countermands chaos and rapine is soon also to hand; Graf F . . . is 'ein Engel des Himmels'; the honourable surrender, the politenesses and conventions duly observed, mark the restoration of order. Similarly, when later the false news of Graf F . . .'s death comes as an 'unglücklicher und rührender Vorfall',[31] this is followed by 'Alles kehrte nun in die alte Ordnung der Dinge zurück.'[32] It is this order, this sense of things belonging in a certain way, that

Heinrich von Kleist and the Novelle tradition 55

makes it impossible for the family to understand what Graf F . . . is referring to when he makes his impetuous suit. The Marquise's 'berief sich auf das Gefühl der anderen'[33] at the same time is a further indication that things are as they should be, that there are congruities in human behaviour. Yet gradually the signs of disorder and disparity appear; the doctor ('hielt sich für verrückt, wenn sie an den letzten dachte'),[34] and the midwife ('dergleichen Fälle wären ihr schon vorgekommen')[35] point to the imminent situation where not the secure supporting unanimity of the family but 'dein innerliches Gefühl' is to be pitted against an 'Umwälzung der Weltordnung',[36] against 'wie denn die Natur auf ihren Wegen walte'.[37] As the outer order of the family falls away, the Marquise is 'mit sich selbst bekannt', reduced to reconciling herself and her inner conviction of blamelessness, to the 'große, heilige und unerklärliche Einrichtung der Welt', and 'Schicksal'.[38] The family's sense of moral appeal ends where nature has its limits and will not make the step into a world where appearance and reality are at odds. The midwife only gives support to this, with the irony that her explanation *empirically* is true, but for the Marquise not *absolutely* true. The 'große, heilige und unerklärliche Einrichtung' is a formula suggesting the possible coincidence of family and Marquise, as each abandons his absolute position and seeks for a plausible explanation. That the Marquise's very purity and integrity, but also the incontrovertible evidence of her own condition, actually prevent her from approaching the truth, is seen in the way she rejects Graf F . . . as he visits her in her seclusion, still representing in her eyes as he does the 'Engel des Himmels'. Only as the Marquise's mother is willing to admit 'ein unerhörtes Spiel des Schicksals'[39] in preference to the mere appearance of truth, can the way be opened for the recognition of the order which rules the world, that 'gebrechliche Einrichtung der Welt'.[40] For if there is a system of reference in the world, it is not one of 'Engel' or 'Teufel', not one of appearance on the one hand and conviction on the other, or irreconcilable opposites, a situation which would leave Graf F . . . as the only character knowing the truth and assuming that others will be equally percipient—and pragmatic.

In Cervantes's story, there is no disbelief; Leocadia's family trusts her account without demur, as does later Rodolfo's. The whole point of the story would be lost if the links of trust were once broken. What could we then refer to? Where would we be? Could a crucifix be a useless symbol? In Kleist, all such questions have to be asked anew and each time a new answer provided. *Die Marquise von O* . . . happens to be one of the few stories in which characters are permitted to formulate their relationship to a newly established order; for the story, beginning by outdoing the usual 'caso portentoso', proceeds then to explain how an adherence to order and system and congruity led to that 'caso' (the newspaper announcement), and how 'Gebrechlichkeit der Welt' becomes, not a formula for *explaining* human behaviour, but one for permitting the business of living with other persons as they are. Graf F . . .'s deed is only explained in terms of his inner desire to atone, to make amends, to wash white again the besmirched swan; Rodolfo's brutal misdeed, on the other hand, is actually put down to inexperience, parental insouciance and the easily explained desire of youth, a system of passions which appeals to established categories of Renaissance thinking. It is thus interesting to note that both Cervantes and Kleist are able to reach the traditional happy ending by such different means. Given the terms of *La Fuerza de la sangre*, it is possible for forgiveness and rehabilitation to appear as norms which annul the unspeakable and adventitious. The Marquise, on the other hand, has to reconstruct, through a tremendous moral effort, a modus vivendi in which pardon and love are possible.

Hoffmann's story does not have a happy ending. Nor does it proceed in the relatively direct fashion of Cervantes and Kleist. It begins with total mystification: the arrival of the prioress with a veiled lady, and attendant enigmas; the discovery of the lady's condition; that she wears a mask to cover her true identity; the abduction of the baby. Only then do we learn the whole story of Hermenegilda, Stanislaus and Xaver and place them into the web of intrigue in which the opening has captured us. Hoffmann is here much more indebted to the narrative traditions of popular fiction and the Gothic novel. A mystery is there and must be solved; the most intriguing aspects are presented first, with veils and masks as the symbols of a truth yet to be revealed. And here the Gothic fascination with the Catholic rite and monastic mummeries comes out to good advantage.

Yet, as with Kleist, the 'Begebenheit' is not merely that Hermenegilda has been seduced in a faint or trance, but that she absolutely believes that Stanislaus embraced her. In her somnambulistic state she also sees him carried to his death. She is his bride and widow—a delusion—on the one hand; but her vision also coincides in real fact with the actual moment of Stanislaus's death. A marriage between Xaver and Hermenegilda, which might avert the shame of their encounter, is rejected by her family after such a mixture of, for them, the dastardly and the preposterous; and Hermenegilda persists in her own peculiar vision that excludes any union with another. For she adamantly believes she is pregnant by an embrace from the non-corporeal sphere. Her love for Stanislaus admits of a psychic consummation, the achievement of total spiritual union. When she learns of Xaver's agency, she punishes herself rather than rectifying the pure and innocent side of her love for Stanislaus. She becomes Cölestine, veiled and masked, taking 'das Gelübde' of the title. The ending—not without its sensationalism and implausibilities—is terrible; the story is allocated by Hoffmann to the 'Nachtstücke'. The intervention of so base a reality prevents any kind of order from being established or any kind of harmony achieved. There is a plausible explanation for her pregnancy, but not for her clairvoyant identification with Stanislaus in the moment of death.[41] The family also makes no real effort to enter into the 'spiritual' aspect of this vision. In the face of inexplicable higher powers there is nothing to do but place a veil or mask over a reality which refuses to be subsumed under the usual sets of cause and effect. Where death, consummation, and inner vision coincide, there can be no appeal to an *exemplum*, or even to 'Gebrechlichkeit der Welt'. That which is inside, which has validity for the inner eye, becomes the authority for the interpretation of the outside world. Until Xaver's explanation, whatever the world may say, Hermenegilda is Stanislaus's widow and her vows are sacred. The Marquise had been both innocent *and* the victim of Graf F . . . ; the 'Gebrechlichkeit' involves reconciling these two, her forgiving him and his proving worthy of that forgiveness. Hermenegilda's total and inexplicable vision removes any grounds for reconciliation. She may have the element of the unexplained, the strange coincidence, the rare conjunction of events, on her side, which makes the world's viewpoint appear rigid and inadequate. But she cannot, like the Marquise, find a formula of accommodation or compromise. That is why Hoffmann's story ends tragically. Cervantes's could not; Kleist's agrees not to.

Chapter Five

'SCHILDERT ALLES'
THE BIEDERMEIER NOVELLE

When in 1871 Paul Heyse in his survey of the German Novelle which takes up a large part of his preface to *Deutscher Novellenschatz*, took stock of the development of this genre, he was at pains to point out that it was not a mere by-product of Renaissance practice, but something indigenous and an essential part of the national literature. One could, for instance, look back to Goethe, to Kleist, and to Tieck.[1] Not everything that had happened in the last three generations finds Heyse's favour, but the Novelle's place in the establishment of German poetic literature is assured. This is by no means all that Heyse had to say, but it can provide a useful starting point for an examination of what took place between roughly 1815 and 1870 and beyond.

How did the Novelle develop to the extent that Heyse could describe it as a form treating 'die tiefsten und wichtigsten sittlichen Fragen'?[2] For Heyse, despite the special emphasis which his own poetic self-awareness entailed, was saying with certain qualifications something that others, from earlier generations of the same century had also said, but even more emphatically: that the Novelle is 'die berufenste Kunstform, das Höchste darzustellen'[3] (Theodor Mundt in 1834), is the 'Mittelpunct ... für unsere jetzige Literatur'[4] (Karl Rosenkranz in 1838), 'schildert Alles'[5] (Heinrich Laube in 1833). This was certainly higher praise than Heyse was prepared to accord, but it suggests that the Novelle had, in the years since the death of Kleist (1811) or the appearance of Tieck's *Phantasus* (1812–16), come of age.

We have to come to terms first of all with the fact that, in the period of the German Restoration (1815–48), the age of 'Biedermeier' as it is now generally known, the Novelle was the most popular form of prose writing and probably the most popular literary form in Germany. Like all manifestations of popular taste, it brought with it accreditation, approval and wide dissemination, but also reaction, dismay and reappraisal.[6] It is all part of the history of the genre, in Germany and elsewhere. Boccaccio, who after all started with a *hundred* stories, was followed by dozens of writers producing their hundreds in turn (*CENT Nouvelles nouvelles*). In France, in the 1740s, 1750s and 1760s, there had also been something close to mass production of what the more disdainful called a 'litanie d'historiettes usées'.[7] The genre has by nature always had, rightly or wrongly, something of the appeal of mass entertainment, follows easily established patterns, and can be reproduced more or less *ad libitum*.[8] What earlier generations did not possess was the phenomenon current in Germany in the first half of the nineteenth century: the literary almanach. These small collections, produced by assiduous and enterprising publishers, become somewhat of a fad or a craze. The format is small (duodecimo—hence 'Taschenbuch'), the contents multifarious and of varying quality, the production attractive, often with gilt edges and engravings. The titles, *Iris*, *Urania*, *Taschenbuch zum geselligen Vergnügen*, *Frauentaschenbuch auf das Jahr* . . ., *Novellenkranz*, and so on, betray the collective rather than the individual, popular taste rather than the esoteric. All the great publishers (Cotta, Reimer, Brockhaus) know their selling power, as do many smaller. None of the major writers of the period is too proud to be associated with them: neither the survivors of the Romantic movement (Arnim, Eichendorff, Hoffmann, Tieck), nor the up-and-coming (Alexis, Hauff, Laube, Gutzkow), nor the masters of the new generation (Stifter, Droste, Mörike, Gotthelf, even Grillparzer).

If we are in the English-speaking world less acquainted with good writers like Alexis or Hauff or the later Tieck or Sealsfield (pseudonym for Karl Postl), we do know, say, Droste's *Judenbuche*, Stifter's *Bunte Steine*, Mörike's *Mozart auf der Reise nach Prag*, or Gotthelf's *Die schwarze Spinne*. We are, with these titles, acquainted with some few of the very best of a mode that reached almost epidemic proportions in its time. We will, understandably, not wish to read the thousands of others that have sunk without trace. Or, to put it differently, we are reading stories which, while masterpieces of their genre, still show many traces of their provenance in a mass movement, while standing out because of some special mastery or transcending quality. These origins may not be readily apparent. Yet we might ask ourselves: why does

Droste so stress the social and moral order in the midst of a detective story? Why does Stifter, such a conscious artist, choose such modest titles for his collections as *Studien* or *Bunte Steine*? Why does Mörike choose a merely convivial and everyday incident from Mozart's life? Why does Gotthelf set his demonic story amid a country christening celebration? Why does Stifter again, with all his powers, so programmatically opt for stories of such limited ambit, some only a hair's breadth away from conventional sentimentality or idyllic harmlessness? Why does Grillparzer, a dramatist of classical ambition and achievement, write a Novelle at all? The answers to all these questions have something to do with the traditions and modes in which they were working and the extent to which they were indebted to them.

The Schlegel brothers at the turn of the century had advocated the Novelle by stressing both its inherent poetic, 'Romantic' qualities, and its relevance for the literature of its day, all this through reference to Boccaccio and Cervantes. Commentators from 1825 on were now able to refer to models inside Germany, notably Goethe and Tieck. Goethe is understandable, given his general authority and his continuing interest in 'kleine Erzählungen'. But Tieck, of whose later Novellen, if any, perhaps at most *Des Lebens Überfluss* (1839) is still known, may surprise. 'Der herrliche Tieck bei dem ganz Teutschland in die Schule gehen sollte', writes Wilhelm Hauff.[9] Yet Tieck was the senior Romantic, a writer with a fine sense of shift and change in literary taste, but also with a newly won awareness of the writer's need to blend 'Poesie, Mährchen und Schertz' with the actualities of real life. He had stated as much in the 'Rahmengespräch' of *Phantasus*; but it was quite another matter when in the 1820s he threw his authority behind the less esoteric mode of the 'Taschenbuchnovelle'. Although Tieck does not shake off Romantic narrative habits overnight (or ever, for that matter), it can be noted that many of his subjects are real people, in an identifiable society, with their qualities, but their weaknesses and eccentricities, which somehow must be resolved. For Tieck is concerned with resolution, harmony and reintegration, of the disparate and conflicting—through the means of conversation and polite intercourse. It is the old Boccaccian cliché perhaps, but much more the 'gesellige Schonung' of which Goethe had spoken.

If only one can converse, can observe the decent conventions of civilized society, Tieck is saying, one can turn away wrath, malevolence, intemperate zeal or even revolutionary fury. Conversation means putting different points of view, and it means generally a slowing down of the pace and a greater degree of digression. One can appreciate from Tieck's position of authority why the Kleistian pattern, or even Hoffmann's, did not have the appeal which one might otherwise expect. One example may suffice. Kleist had written a story about 'die Gewalt der Musik', in which an irrational and impalpable art form had become merged with religious fanaticism and had lifted the characters of *Die heilige Cäcilie* from one state of fury and exaltation into another—madness. Hoffmann had, in *Rat Krespel* or *Ritter Gluck*, shown how music and the daemonic, music and the obsessional *idée fixe*, may make a person no longer fit for the congruities of everyday life and force the inner vision out, to dominate the reality enjoyed by the 'normal' world. Perhaps it is small wonder that Hoffmann's creative influence was greater in France, on Nerval and even Baudelaire, or on Edgar Allen Poe, in this period than on his German contemporaries. But Mörike, an admirer of Tieck's, when coming to his late masterpiece *Mozart auf der Reise nach Prag* (1856), had chosen a completely different method to depict the problems of artistry and genius: conversation.

Mörike is constantly aware in the story of the darting, febrile, consuming and darkly ominous aspect of genius—but it is also *creative* genius. The seizing of the orange on an impulse is also the seizing of the moment of artistic intimation, the delving into a past reality that makes present and past and future mastery all merge in the creative process. But the shadow of death, as well as the refulgence of immortality, is over Mozart:

> Sie werden schrittweis gehn
> Mit deiner Leiche;
> Vielleicht, vielleicht noch eh
> An ihren Hufen
> Das Eisen los wird,
> Das ich blitzen sehe!

Mörike does not gild with the afternoon sun of comfort or happiness, he does not transfigure. But the *technique* is in keeping with the moment-to-moment fulfilment of genius: loose, almost improvised, now in the present, now returning through some 'Histörchen' to the haphazard and hectic rush of artistic improvisation, or to the but brief moment of rest and wit and conviviality that genius may enjoy. It is 'gesellig'. Mozart is held, true, at a moment of creativity, on the eve of the culmination of rococo grace and the terrible retribution that is *Don Giovanni*; but society comes, polished and elegant, to his aid and envelops him in its *bienséances*, its 'Schonung', its ease and unhurried pace. As no such social occasion should be oppressive, one-sided, without flow of conversation and accommodation of all present, so the tone of the story involves all parts of the society present, bringing them out in gaiety and laughter and music. The narrative perspective changes constantly, anecdotes flow backwards and forwards, past lapses and future hopes, frustrations and moments of glory, are lightly mingled. Mozart can be the life and soul of the occasion because the society enters into the spirit, not because he forces genius upon them. A 'Begebenheit', if one so will, is allowed to be swallowed up in the lighter and less obstructive conventions of conversation.

Mörike's *Mozart* is a Novelle of rare and consummate artistry for reasons that do not apply readily to the very different techniques of Kleist or Hoffmann. It is by the same token undoubtedly greater than anything that Tieck essayed in a similar mode. But Tieck's contemporaries had seen in his Novellen a number of other features which are significant for the practice of his generation. For if one looked around the mass of Novellen that were being produced in the 1820s, one could see that anything went, that strictness seemed to have gone to the four winds, that improvisation and confusion held sway; that one could try one's hand at the fantastic, the idyllic, the sentimental, the reflective, the fairy-tale, the detective story, or whatever—and it would sell. Nobody seemed to know what a Novelle was and nobody seemed to care. Even the prescriptiveness of length seemed to have been lost sight of. Statements by critics and writers of Novellen alike concentrate less on what a Novelle *is* than on its scope, what it is able to do, how much its terms of reference have been expanded, what we can yet expect from it. This helps to explain why Goethe and Tieck sought to reintroduce a little order into what they considered a Novelle to be (see Chapter 7). The sketch, the 'Studie' (to use the title that Stifter chose for his revised stories in the 1840s and 1850s) seemed more common than artistic consummation. Wilhelm Hauff could speak for many (although few achieved his standard), in finding the Novelle not strict, but 'bequem'.[10] Others, however, did concentrate rather on what the Novelle could achieve as *poetry*, as conscious artistry; it could be, as Georg Reinbeck said in 1817, a 'poetische Erzählung'.[11] For Willibald Alexis, it need not be a mere 'Jagd von Begebenheiten',[12] but have 'höheres Interesse'.[13] And few would agree with Grillparzer's rather disdainful finding that it meant a 'Herabneigen der Poesie zur Prosa'.[14]

We notice that the Boccaccian anecdote, the account stripped of unnecessary detail, is less favoured than the Cervantian *novela*. Tieck, in his famous preface of 1829 (Chapter 7) explicitly referred to Cervantes as he made his own statement of intent. Two important considerations seem to emerge. Georg Reinbeck again is our witness. The Novelle is:

poetische Erzählung einer Thatsache, welche als dem wirklichen Culturleben eines bestimmten Zeitraumes angehörig erscheinen soll[15]

It should, he says, reflect all 'Lebensverhältnisse';[16] 'alle Stände, alle Verhältnisse der neuen Zeit'[17] were Tieck's words in 1829; 'schildert Alles' were Laube's. Indeed, Laube the Young German, programmatically interested in prose as a medium of critical dissemination and progressiveness, speaks of a 'Demokratismus' brought about by the Novelle, the opening up of spheres of life and of circles of readers both for 'literarische Auffassung'[18] and for poetic representation. It would seem that the Novelle in the pre-1848 years had usurped much of the function enjoyed by the novel in other literatures. For the only major distinction drawn between the two genres in the period is that of length and scope, of 'einzelne Situation'[19] (Reinbeck), not the totality of life, 'Makrokosmus' and 'Mikrokosmus' (Mundt).[20] There is no denying that these are not good years for the German novel,[21] despite what was achieved by Goethe or Tieck or Alexis or Immermann or Gutzkow. Notable writers plan (Grillparzer) or even start novels that they either cannot finish (Droste) or cannot find the creative energy to revise (Mörike's *Maler Nolten*). Alexis and Tieck find that the historical novel in the mode of Scott is not a mode that is readily adaptable to German conditions; after the failure of his unfinished *Der Aufruhr in den Cevennen* (close to *Old Mortality*), Tieck only manages to achieve mastery in the late historical novel, in the far too little known *Vittoria Accorombona* (1840, closer to Manzoni's *Promessi Sposi*). Stifter, significantly, comes to *Der Nachsommer* in the 1850s, when the novel begins to come into its own again. But the

Novelle, in drawing attention to the potential of prose writing for 'Poesie' and 'alle Lebensverhältnisse', would have prepared much of the ground for the later recovery of the novel.[22]

'Alle Lebensverhältnisse' needs to be read with some qualifications (it is not a 'comédie humaine' in Balzac's sense); but it does mean that the Novelle will actually record the views that society did hold in Metternich's day[23]—and they are generally conservative. For if we do not appreciate that most of the major writers of this period were convinced of an underlying religious order and harmony, stood in horror of the elemental and of exaggerated passion, upheld the values of family life and saw over all a providence upholding all, then we may misread many of the signs in their works. We may, by the same token, fail to understand why the Young Germans, reacting against the moral and political order, put such stress on human reason, the emancipation of the flesh, or the opiate influences of religion, in the writings which led to their ban in 1835.

Take Droste's *Die Judenbuche*. True, this story is based on an eighteenth-century source, but its attitudes are those of its aristocratic nineteenth-century authoress. The circumstantiality with which she narrates how Friedrich Mergel, finding himself on the slippery slope, slides eventually to murder and suicide, is not one of chance, but design. The symbolism of hearth and home on the one hand, and on the other of elemental nature (the forest, not just the one beech tree), the demonic uncle, the crass whiff of corruption on the last page—all this is part of an intention. She is too good a writer for us merely to read an edifying pattern into events which are full of sinister mystery; all the same, her account has Friedrich, fatherless, without the guiding hand of parental care, falling into unregeneracy and depravity (in the theological sense), as his identity is merged with the dark sphere of the Brederholz. There is an inexorability with which he moves, not just by the tree and its Hebrew inscription, but by inner conviction, towards the retribution of an unshriven death by his own hand. Significantly, he is drawn, on his return, towards the sphere of authority, the country house, where the Schlossherrin, at Christmas, the time of greatest family cohesion and religious inwardness, recognizes who he really is. If the Schlossherr is too obtuse to see the real state of affairs and is merely interested in clearing up a mystery, there is no doubt *we* are to read the ending as a culmination of misdeed and neglect, denial of the means of grace—and spiritual damnation. That is why we smell that corpse.

Droste does not withhold pity and compassion from her hero. Jeremias Gotthelf on the other hand is usually less accommodating. He does not indulge in mystification, but in exemplary reward and punishment. His characters are usually good or bad, with no area in between. One has the ordered, happy, resolved world of *Hans Joggeli der Erbvetter* or the fearful godlessness of *Harzer Hans*, to quote two of his very good, and regrettably little known, stories. A writer who can call a story *Wie fünf Mädchen im Branntwein jämmerlich umkommen* is not going to beat about the bush, especially if he is a pastor. His justly famous story, *Die schwarze Spinne*,[24] is accordingly carefully set in a framework of natural harmony (sunrise and sunset, reflecting God's providing and regular care), with a baptism (the extension of grace to the weakest and most helpless), the family, master and servants. All is order, polish, tidiness, everybody knowing their place. It is patriarchal Swiss peasant society, and Gotthelf, not without the occasional twinkle in his eye, likes it that way. There is no question that it will ever change or could change. But that is the point of the black spider story. It once *did* change; man in his dire distress did not turn to God, but to the Devil. Old Testament notions of sin and retribution and judgement are interspersed throughout the story to bring us to our senses lest we should be too fascinated with the sheer horror of the narrative. The rhetorical phrases, the allegorical view of nature, the links between earthly nature and the heavenly order that created it, all indicate that this is a preacher with a message: 'daß es sich mit dem Teufel nicht spaßen lasse'.[25] And so the story is polarized, with sin and grace, rise and fall, black and white. The inhabitants of the valley are not presented as evil in themselves, but easily led. By whom? By Christine, a foreigner (from Lindau) or later by a farmhand of whom it is said 'man wußte nicht, woher er kam'.[26] It is these two from outside who unleash the power of the devil in the terrible form of the spider; and it is Christine who receives for the devil's kiss the punishment in her own body. Significantly, Gotthelf makes little of the popular folklore elements in the story. The message is rather that the spider is still there in the beam of wood. That which in the story witnesses to the power of good (the innocent child, the priest) is also still with us. A people that takes the story to heart can be assured: 'Denn wo solcher Sinn wohnet, darf sich die Spinne nicht regen, weder bei Tage noch bei Nacht'.[27] With this, the sun and moon images become merged into a providential order, the 'Rahmen' and the 'Begebenheit', reflection and action, linked. And that order will be asserted as society resists the temptation of change, of foreign influence, revolution, 'socialism', the 'Zeitgeist'—all the things that the deeply conservative Gotthelf hates. For divine providence is also part of the order of the here and now; there is a continuity between the legend and its hearers and all others 'who have ears to hear'.

This is an extreme example. But even a much subtler narrator like the Stifter of *Bunte Steine* is stressing very similar things, although he does not make everything quite so simple for his readers. Yet all of these stories will stress order, home and family, fear of disorderly passion and elemental forces, resignation rather than self-assertion, providence rather than fate, 'Gemüt' and sentiment rather than extreme emotions, country simplicity as opposed to urban sophistication. There is no place here for the Kleistian 'Zufall'; there is a framework of reference to which we can appeal. There, too, people will know their places. Society is not mobile, but a stable hierarchy. There can be a 'sanftes Gesetz' if only we will grasp it and ratify it. Nature is not there for its own sake, but is part of a teleological order or is a force of which we stand in sacred awe, bringing home man's weakness and helplessness outside of a shelter or cover or habitation. It is worth reflecting that even a very different writer like the Büchner of *Lenz* will not use nature as a force independent of the human situation he is depicting; it is the rhetorical accompaniment to Lenz's deteriorating mental state; the question of man and the, for Büchner, missing universal order, man's piteous state and the (empty) heaven is always in the forefront.

The other constant which emerges from critical comment on the Novelle in the period is the desire for reflection,[28] that 'Schilderung und Reflexion',[29] that Alexis so approvingly notes of Tieck's practice. It is all part of the commodious attitude to the genre. We are not merely to read the 'Sonderfall', the stark central event of Boccaccian or, more recently, of Kleistian provenance. There will be room for detail, for comment, for moralizing even. We note the way in which Gotthelf can adopt two starkly contrasting modes: the 'Behaglichkeit' and expansiveness of the 'Rahmen', with its edification and humour, before moving over to the tighter and crasser central story. Or how Droste introduces her narrative with a poem as superscription, in case we forget her serious intention—'Laß ruhn den Stein—er trifft dein eignes Haupt!'[30]—and then spends many pages on the historical and social background, not just on the motivation of Friedrich's character. The warning example cannot be divorced from documented reality, any more than Droste's religious poems are incompatible with very close observation of animate and inanimate nature. And so a 'Sittengemälde aus dem gebirgichten Westfalen',[31] a story about retribution with a marked moral and religious intention, will have its effect even more if its message can be linked to accredited and documented reality. 'Dies hat sich nach allen Hauptumständen wirklich so begeben';[32] the appeal to social and historical detail thus stands at the close of the story just before the German translation of the Hebrew text, the 'message'.

This appeal to the 'true story' is somewhat of a cliché of the nineteenth-century Novelle, now as later.[33] A claim to authenticity had, of course, always been part of the tradition, by way of asserting that the unheard-of could also be true or that the 'exemplum' was not merely far-fetched. As the nineteenth century progressed, however, as the Novelle became open to the principle 'schildert Alles', this claim was taken more seriously. When Wilhelm Hauff, in his satirical 'Vertrauliches Schreiben an Herrn W. A. Spöttlich' of 1828 could advise his addressee to read his stories as 'getreue Wahrheit'[34] rather than mere 'Dichtungen', that was surely jest. But the preface to his 'romantische Sage' *Lichtenstein* talks more seriously of 'historische Wahrheit'.[35] For a historiographical century that enjoys its Walter Scott will not wish to abandon the search for historical credibility to the professional historians, but will see no contradiction between historiography and the poetic representation of history. This explains in part Droste's insistence, although *Die Judenbuche* is not strictly a 'historical' Novelle like some by Alexis or Hauff or Tieck. But the historical dramatist Büchner will base his story *Lenz* on documented *fact*. Real historical personages—Raphael, Rembrandt, Jud Süss—come increasingly to populate the pages of the Novelle. Thus, as we saw, Mörike's *Mozart* records a precise moment in the composer's life 'auf der Reise nach Prag', with Mozart caught between intrigue and patronage in Vienna, hopes of preferment in Berlin, and the dream of success in Prague. It is the eve of the real *Don Giovanni*, first performed in Prague in 1787, as the first sentence announces. The increased interest in topographical detail—often written off as mere 'regionalism'—is also part of this same process. Again, as Cervantes demonstrates, this had never been absent from the mode. Yet we suspect that for him the 'caso' is more important than any precise account of its surroundings. The man in *El Licienciado vidriera* who believes he is made of glass commands more attention than the fact that the story is set in Salamanca. Even Hoffmann's 'Märchen aus der neuen Zeit', *Der goldne Topf*, with its precise mention of the topography of Dresden, evokes a 'toller Zwiespalt'[36] between 'real' and 'unreal' spheres. Yet one senses that Grillparzer in *Der arme Spielmann*, for all his 'Plutarch', his 'anthropologischer Heißhunger', and 'psychologische Neugierde',[37] is also concerned to place this story in the city every corner of which he knows and whose populace he so acutely observes. The psychological 'Sonderfall' is enhanced by the carefully chosen details of his surroundings; the everyday world, in its turn, becomes capable of being host to someone—who is not of glass (Cervantes), who does not see salamanders (Hoffmann)—but whose singular relationship both to musical notation and to quotidian necessities has something of the 'divine'.

The appeal to veracity also favours one of the century's favourite devices: the 'Rahmen'. This convention becomes more and more entrenched as the century proceeds. It may develop out of the old Boccaccian technique, but it now takes on rather more existence of its own as a constitutive part of the individual story than as the setting for a collection. It is part of the reduction of the 'Sonderfall' to the 'Normalfall', or it is a way of integrating the extraordinary into 'das wirkliche Culturleben eines bestimmten Zeitraums' (Georg Reinbeck).[38] Authors, as in Stifter's *Die Mappe meines Urgrossvaters*, take rather more seriously the old cliché of 'Aus den Memoiren des . . . ' or 'Aus den Papieren des . . . '. Stifter's story *Der arme Wohltäter* (1848), better known in its revised form as *Kalkstein*, has in this respect an opening that is typical of so many:

Wir erzählen in den nachfolgenden Zeilen eine Tatsache, welche uns von einem Freunde mitgeteilt worden ist, der den Mann, von welchem die Tatsache ausgegangen ist, noch recht gut gekannt hat. So unglaublich es auch klingen mag, was dieser Mann sich vorgesetzt und seiner Meinung nach ausgeführt hat, so hat uns doch der eben angeführte Freund so viele einzelne Züge von ihm erzählt, daß wir begriffen, daß der Mann nicht nur diese Handlung unternehmen konnte, sondern daß er sie unternehmen mußte. Wir verzichten auf den Ruhm künstlerischer Gegenständlichkeit, die wir am Ende doch nicht erreichen würden und erzählen durch das Auge unseres Freundes von dem Manne, wie er ihm erschienen ist, wobei wir uns nur zwei Dinge erlauben, die uns unerläßlich erscheinen: nämlich daß wir das, was uns der Freund in weit auseinanderliegenden Zwischenräumen und ohne Ordnung erzählte, in eine Gattung Reihenfolge bringen, in der es sich zugetragen haben konnte, wann eines aus dem andern hervorgegangen ist—und daß wir in den die Wesenheit der Sache nicht berührenden Nebenumständen und Nebenhandlungen so viel veränderten, daß die noch etwa lebenden Verwandten des schon längst gestorbenen Mannes sich nicht unangenehm betroffen fühlen, wenn etwas zu größerer Verbreitung kommt, was sie nur einem kleineren Kreise bekannt glaubten.[39]

While noting that Stifter adheres to the conventions of 'Tatsache' and 'unglaublich' and restricts his own role to ordering what has been narrated by another source, we should observe that the 'Begebenheit' of the story is not Droste's murder, not Gotthelf's demonic plague, not even Grillparzer's obsession, but the exemplary asceticism and selflessness of a country pastor. The *Kalkstein* version even avers: 'Ich erzähle hier eine Geschichte, die uns einmal ein Freund erzählt hat, in der nichts Ungewöhnliches vorkömmt, ...'[40] Stifter can in certain stories dwell in painterly detail and perspective on the natural surroundings of his narrative, so that we have the relation of man to surroundings, order and human endeavour, inner acceptance and outer immensity, in the proper setting. But by stressing that 'nichts Ungewöhnliches', he is slipping into another mode much favoured by the century: the idyllic.[41]

In the idyll, we have a *state*, that which does not change, the constants of human behaviour, not their upsets and climacterics, patterns that can be repeated, community rather than individual. This is not to say that nothing *happens* in *Der arme Wohltäter* (there is, after all, a terrible thunderstorm) but that which on the surface is insignificant and unprepossessing takes on some kind of universal significance. *Detail*, not the hurrying on to the next incident, becomes important: the frugality of the meal described is a good example, or the sparse fittings of the pastor's dwelling.

The idyllic can merge easily with other modes, or it can stand on its own as something valid and in no need of expansion. Gotthelf can be content to tell of *Der Sonntag des Grossvaters*, which catches the rhythm and order of one existence at one particular moment.

He can, however, integrate another idyll—the 'Rahmen' of *Die schwarze Spinne*—into a more drastic message. In *Mozart auf der Reise nach Prag*, the 'naïve' mixture of conversation and conviviality, the deliberate concentration on that which is homely, domestic or humorous, the rest amid the otherwise frenetic haste, is merely the foil, the foreground for an insight into the tragic potential of self-consuming and threatened artistry. Droste can, near the end of *Die Judenbuche*, pause for a page or two to dwell on that most sentimentally idyllic occasion, Christmas, before she turns with a will to guilt, death and corruption. Stifter's *Bergkristall*, by contrast, begins in the idyllic, timeless sphere and leads us through a moment of potential and actual peril, to return to the significance of family reconciliation on Christmas Eve.[42] Man and nature, the lights and associations of the festive tide, stand in marked and irreconcilable contrast to the awesomeness of nature and the fragility of human existence. The sentimental cliché takes on new significance as it is subjected to the discordant and the dissonant.

The 'Biedermeier' Novelle does not suddenly undergo a change in mid-century to become the Novelle of Realism or 'poetic realism'. One could even say that it reaches its highest artistic expression in the 1840s and 1850s, in Grillparzer's *Der arme Spielmann*, Droste's *Die Judenbuche*, and the many Novellen of Gotthelf and Stifter—Stifter, who is, already in the 1840s, recasting his Novellen in a more reflective artistic mode, with the sense of programmatic commitment that the preface to *Bunte Steine* sets out. Heyse's and Kurz's *Deutscher Novellenschatz* of 1871 is a monument to the pertinacity of many of the old narrative modes, not merely in its set task of rediscovery of, and reacquaintance with, the works of older writers, but also in its demonstration that the modes current in 1871 still included the sensational, the irrational, the sentimental, or the mere 'Begebenheit'. Yet it is interesting to find Heyse referring to *Der arme Spielmann*, surely not open to any of these charges, as an unjustly forgotten work,[43] or the critic L. Friedländer speaking in 1868 in similar terms of *Die Judenbuche*,[44] an indication that the past twenty or thirty years had indeed brought about considerable changes.

For, if we do examine representative Novellen by the Biedermeier generation, and by the writers who succeeded them, taking a span of about forty years, we can see considerable differences. Take Droste's *Die Judenbuche* of 1841 and Theodor Storm's masterpiece, *Der Schimmelreiter* (1888). One could immediately say that Storm's work is no longer really typical of the scope and subject-matter of the Realist Novelle, even that some features seem to anticipate aspects of Naturalism. It can, however, serve as an example of its own movement. A passage from *Die Judenbuche* describes the development of the hero, Friedrich Mergel:

> In seinem achtzehnten Jahre hatte Friedrich sich bereits einen bedeutenden Ruf in der jungen Dorfwelt gesichert durch den Ausgang einer Wette, infolge deren er einen erlegten Eber über zwei Meilen weit auf seinem Rücken trug, ohne abzusetzen. Indessen war der Mitgenuß des Ruhmes auch so ziemlich der einzige Vorteil, den Margret aus diesen günstigen Umständen zog, da Friedrich immer mehr auf sein Äußeres verwandte und allmählich anfing, es schwer zu verdauen, wenn Geldmangel ihn zwang, irgend jemand im Dorf darin nachzustehen. Zudem waren alle seine Kräfte auf den auswärtigen Erwerb gerichtet; zu Hause schien ihm, ganz im Widerspiel mit seinem sonstigen Rufe, jede anhaltende Beschäftigung lästig, und er unterzog sich lieber einer harten, aber kurzen Anstrengung, die ihm bald erlaubte, seinem früheren Hirtenamte wieder nachzugehen, was bereits begann, seinem Alter unpassend zu werden und ihm gelegentlichen Spott zuzog, vor dem er sich aber durch ein paar derbe Zurechtweisungen mit der Faust Ruhe verschaffte. So gewöhnte man sich daran, ihn bald geputzt und fröhlich als anerkannten Dorfelegant an der Spitze des jungen Volks zu sehen, bald wieder als zerlumpten Hirtenbuben einsam und träumerisch hinter den Kühen herschleichend, oder in einer Waldlichtung liegend, scheinbar gedankenlos und das Moos von den Bäumen rupfend.[45]

That from *Der Schimmelreiter* records a significant moment from the boyhood of the hero, Hauke Haien. He has gone to investigate the apparitions on the seashore that popular imagination has made into ghosts:

> Er lief nach Hause; aber an einem der nächsten Abende war er wiederum da draußen. Auf jenen Stellen war jetzt das Eis gespalten; wie Rauchwolken stieg es aus den Rissen, und über das ganze Watt spann sich ein Netz von Dampf und Nebel, das sich seltsam mit der Dämmerung des Abends mischte. Hauke sah mit starren Augen darauf hin; denn in dem Nebel schritten dunkle Gestalten auf und ab, sie schienen ihm so groß wie Menschen. Würdevoll, aber mit seltsamen, erschreckenden Geberden; mit langen Nasen und Hälsen sah er sie fern an den rauchenden Spalten auf und ab spazieren; plötzlich begannen sie wie Narren unheimlich auf und ab zu

springen, die großen über die kleinen und die kleinen gegen die großen; dann breiteten sie sich aus und verloren alle Form. 'Was wollen die? Sind es die Geister der Ertrunkenen?' dachte Hauke. 'Hoiho!' schrie er laut in die Nacht hinaus; aber die draußen kehrten sich nicht an seinen Schrei, sondern trieben ihr wunderliches Wesen fort.

Da kamen ihm die furchtbaren norwegischen Seegespenster in den Sinn, von denen ein alter Kapitän ihm einst erzählt hatte, die statt des Angesichts einen stumpfen Pull von Seegras auf dem Nacken tragen; aber er lief nicht fort, sondern bohrte die Hacken seiner Stiefel fest in den Klei des Deiches und sah starr dem possenhaften Unwesen zu, das in der einfallenden Dämmerung vor seinen Augen fortspielte. 'Seid ihr auch hier bei uns?' sprach er mit harter Stimme; 'ihr sollt mich nicht vertreiben!'

Erst als die Finsternis alles bedeckte, schritt er steifen, langsamen Schrittes heimwärts. Aber hinter ihm drein kam es wie Flügelrauschen und hallendes Geschrei. Er sah nicht um; aber er ging auch nicht schneller und kam erst spät nach Hause; doch niemals soll er seinem Vater oder einem anderen davon erzählt haben. Erst viele Jahre später hat er sein blödes Mädchen, womit später der Herrgott ihn belastete, um dieselbe Tages- und Jahreszeit mit sich auf den Deich hinausgenommen, und dasselbe Wesen soll sich derzeit draußen auf den Watten gezeigt haben; aber er hat ihr gesagt, sie solle sich nicht fürchten, das seien nur die Fischreiher und die Krähen, die im Nebel so groß und fürchterlich erschienen; die holten sich die Fische aus den offenen Spalten.

'Weiß Gott, Herr!' unterbrach sich der Schulmeister; 'es gibt auf Erden allerlei Dinge, die ein ehrlich Christenherz verwirren können; aber der Hauke war weder ein Narr noch ein Dummkopf.'[46]

The passages have no special similarity except the particular function of telling the reader what he needs to know about the hero's character for the rest of the story. Friedrich Mergel is caught up in the popular superstition which even turns his own dead father into a ghost; Droste does not dispel this, for it is part of the web of mystification into which the murder is to be woven. The uncanny, the atmosphere of the forest, is for Droste harnessed into the service of the moral order, without becoming sensational or gratuitously far-fetched. Hauke Haien, as the other passage demonstrates, the boy who wants to find things out for himself, is actively seeking to penetrate behind the assumptions of folk tradition and—quite literally—stand on the foundation of empirical reality. Friedrich Mergel's development, on the other hand, is one of alternate unproductive self-assertion and idleness.

Both Droste and Storm are making it clear that their descriptions are a key to the later development of their respective heroes. Friedrich Mergel has fallen into vanity and indolence, a concern for 'sein Äußeres', because he has neglected 'sein Inneres'. The lack of parental care, of concern for all aspects of his welfare, is beginning to form and determine his character. Hauke Haien, no less deprived of parental affection, turns his natural curiosity to useful purpose, begins to explore, to question, to establish cause and effect. His feet are on the ground. His authority is immanent, not transcendent; he looks to this earth for an order of things, a world where it is possible for the individual, the 'Bürger', to find his way and make his mark without recourse to some superterrestrial force. The Christian moral hierarchy is no longer superimposed on characters who will find a healthy, sound and satisfactory ethic for life with not so much a conscious rejection of Christian belief, as an indifference to matters beyond normal human ken and competence. The character will demonstrate, by the work of his own hands and the operation of his own will, how the community of man operates and coheres. Occasionally, as does Hauke Haien, he will find himself pitting his forces against both man and nature: but he will also be doing this in the interests of the wider community, not for mere self-aggrandizement. Like so many of Keller's characters, like Apollonius the steeplejack in Otto Ludwig's *Zwischen Himmel und Erde*, the hero will both stand out against the crowd and also strive for a way of reintegrating himself into the community. Hauke Haien becomes the Deichgraf by dint of sheer ability and seeks to work for the benefit of his fellow-men. His status, and the whole expectations of the community have changed in the course of the story.

As the quotations indicate, both Droste's and Storm's stories are overprinted with signs and indications, one heavily, the other less so. Yet Droste is narrating directly, Storm through an intermediary. Droste can state categorically: it was so; Storm will retreat behind an introduced character and leave us to work out the trustworthiness of the account so given. There will be in Storm a greater attempt to present the *character*, not so much as an example or prodigy, but as someone who has come up through his own society—and by application of real, active resources of intelligence and initiative, not through some 'Vorfall' or 'Begebenheit'. This permits us a full perspective of how hero and society hold together and how the values of one affect the other. For Droste, they are the same values which hold for all members of society—and that society is hierarchical. It is not her concern to show how a character may rise in status (even if he could), but to show his place in the fore-ordained estates. Where providence has placed him, at the lowest end of society, Friedrich Mergel has failed to achieve what potential he could, through his and others' fault, and becomes a warning *example*. Society does not change, only the character within it. That, too, is the message of stories by Stifter like *Granit* or *Kalkstein* or *Katzensilber*. Gotthelf's peasant world is equally rigid, but within that particular ambit there is room for a considerable range of social and moral comment. For Gotthelf is not just interested in the development of, say, a young farmhand through series of tests and trials; he can also be trenchant and merciless on the subject of tight-fisted masters and their stony-hearted wives, young people left without the means of self-improvement, or faithless pastors. It is a world where evil is sternly judged, punishment inexorably meted out, sins visited upon the deserving; and the situations are extreme—either for good or ill. It is as intolerant of the irreligious *Zeitgeist* as—its converse—Büchner's *Lenz* is intolerant of a Christian God who permits suffering. The years in which Gotthelf is writing are polarized between those who—radically—are for the old order, and those who are—radically—against. Hence Gotthelf's insistence on the continuation of the existing order: the end of *Die schwarze Spinne* deliberately returns us to the patriarchal, clearly marked structure of a society which will only prosper, Gotthelf insists, if it remains true to the faith of its forefathers.

At the end of *Der Schimmelreiter*, by contrast, the 'Ich' to whom the story is narrated actually rides out on to the Hauke-Haien-Deich. The schoolmaster says:

Hauke Haien mit Weib und Kind ging unter in dieser Flut; nicht einmal ihre Grabstätte hab ich droben auf dem Kirchhof finden können; die toten Körper werden von dem abströmenden Wasser durch den Bruch ins Meer hinausgetrieben und auf dessen Grunde allmählich in ihre Urbestandteile aufgelöst sein—so haben sie Ruhe vor den Menschen gehabt. Aber der Hauke-Haien-Deich steht noch jetzt nach hundert Jahren, und wenn Sie morgen nach der Stadt reiten und die halbe Stunde Umweg nicht scheuen wollen, so werden Sie ihn unter den Hufen Ihres Pferdes haben.[47]

Heaven does not intervene; there is no grave or memorial save that which man himself has created. Man returns in death whence he came, but leaves a lasting monument for the benefit of his fellows. Gotthelf's heaven is that of an anthropomorphic God who reaches down and holds men in his hand; Storm's is empty and there is nothing to be gained from transcendental speculation.

Chapter Six

'FREUDE AN DER WELT'
THE REALIST NOVELLE

It may be argued that a comparison between Droste and Storm is an extreme one, suggesting an abruptness in social and literary development where indeed there was none. Yet, when we are looking at Novellen by Storm, or Raabe, or Keller, or Ludwig, later by Fontane or Saar, we are dealing with specimens of a literature which was written in years spanning the abrupt and catastrophic years of 1848–9 (when the young Storm was in trouble) and the developments from 1864 and 1866 to the 'Reichsgründung' of 1871, also years during which a once unruly and schismatic Switzerland became politically stabilized. Gotthelf's canton of Berne—the 'Berner Geist' which his conservative instincts hold against the 'Zeitgeist' in the polemical novel *Zeitgeist und Berner Geist* of 1852—is not Keller's Seldwyla, the quirkily peaceful Gotham of a 'sonniger und wonniger Ort [. . .]irgendwo in der Schweiz', or his Zurich, the place whose 'Bürgerstolz' is lovingly celebrated in *Das Fähnlein der sieben Aufrechten*. Gotthelf's reaction is to become rampageous, shrill, the voice of lamentations as bitter as the prophet's whose name Pastor Bitzius had assumed in his pseudonym. Stifter's is to avow, with greater artistry, but no less tenaciously, 'das sanfte Gesetz' which, in his novel *Der Nachsommer*, reaches its apogee as an affirmation of all the order, political, social and moral, which seems under threat. Even Hebbel writes of his historical drama *Agnes Bernauer* (1852) that it is a reflection 'des alten, ehrwürdigen Reiches, [. . .] das jetzt begraben zu werden scheint'.[1]

This is not the reaction of the younger generation, especially of those who have embraced, like Keller and Storm, an agnosticism which was not concerned with the indivisibility of God or 'Weltgeist' and 'Reich'. By the same token, writers who deliberately turn to 'modern' themes are not necessarily abandoning the old order.[2]

The Realist Novelle

When the Austrian writer Ferdinand von Saar writes a love story set against the background of industrial and technical progress (*Die Steinklopfer*—the building of the Semmering railway) or political change (*Schloss Kostenitz*, and the breakdown of Metternich's rule) or the problems of emancipated Jewry (*Seligmann Hirsch*) he is not abandoning the conventional idyll or love story. But Saar is recording the eternal human conflicts as they take place against a background of change and restructuring. That is not the same as Gotthelf's rearguard action after 1848, or even the fierce polemics before 1848 of a Büchner, a Heine or a Marx. And writers of Saar's generation—Keller, Raabe, Storm—will find a place not for an acidulous and destructive wit, but for the kindlier and milder device of humour.[3]

Already in 1849, the young Gottfried Keller had expressed his doubts about Gotthelf in a review containing reactions which others would set out more programmatically and which he himself would seek to remedy poetically. Keller's review acknowledges the need for gradual and sensible change, for 'Bildung', for 'steten Fortschritt',[4] but not for the old Jehovah, not for 'Opposition gegen die Zeit', not for 'Tendenzen', 'verbittertes, versauertes Wesen' which has lost 'das schöne Ebenmaß'.[5] Rather, he maintains:

Es wäre die Aufgabe des Dichters gewesen allfällige eingeschlichene Roheiten und Misbräuche im poetischen Spiegelbild abzuschaffen und dem Volk eine gereinigte und veredelte Freude wiederzugeben, da es sich einmal darum handelt in der gemeinen Wirklichkeit eine schönere Welt wiederherzustellen durch die Schrift.[6]

And the quintessential Keller is contained in the words which end his 'Prolog zur Schillerfeier in Bern 1859':

> Was unerreichbar ist, das rührt uns nicht,
> Doch was erreichbar, sei uns goldne Pflicht![7]

Much of this was to be stated with greater programmatic earnest by writers and critics of the stamp of Julian Schmidt, Gustav Freytag, Hermann Hettner, Friedrich Theodor Vischer, and others during the years 1850 to 1870. It is not for nothing that they are often referred to as 'programmatische Realisten', for indeed they meant business.[8] A few quotations may suffice to demonstrate that Keller was not alone in his view of 'Wirklichkeit' and 'schönere Welt'.

Der Realismus der Poesie wird dann zu erfreulichen Kunstwerken führen, wenn er in der Wirklichkeit zugleich die positive Seite aufsucht, wenn er mit Freude am Leben verknüpft ist,[9] [. . .] (Julian Schmidt)

Der gesunde Realismus ist die Freude an der Welt, an der wirklichen Welt, wo sich immer aus der Erkenntniß auch die Schönheit und Gesetzmäßigkeit offenbart.[10] (Berthold Auerbach)

Das hohe Streben unserer Zeit ist dies, [. . .] die himmelweit gerissene Kluft zwischen dem Geist und der Materie auszufüllen durch das Glück, die Freiheit und die Einheit des Menschengeschlechts.[11] (Theodor Mundt)

Wer menschliches Thun und Leiden in Roman oder Novelle künstlerisch behandeln will, muß dasselbe zweckvoll so zurichten, daß der Leser eine einheitliche, abgeschlossene, vollständig verständliche Geschichte empfängt, die ihn erfreut und erhebt, weil ihr innerer Zusammenhang dem vernünftigen Urtheil und den Bedürfnissen des Gemüthes völlig Genüge thut.[12] (Gustav Freytag)

The consequences of such a view of art may be summarized briefly as follows. That the typical is more important than the extreme or particular; that the ethically sound and positive is more to be affirmed than the pathological or aberrant; 'Volk' in its various spheres of activity is to be preferred to the extreme or recherché or exotic; poetry is to be not exclusive, but inclusive and commodious, taking in 'Alltag', reality, the times in which we live. The figure in the story is to stand on his own merits, in the terms in which he is depicted, rather than being the 'Sonderfall'. We are to have depiction, direct narration, rather than what Julian Schmidt called 'die ewige Reflexion'.[13] The general *and* the particular, idea *and* matter, the ideal *and* the real, the subjective *and* the objective, are both to be subsumed under the one and indivisible sway of art. The name 'poetic Realism' has been given to this aesthetic, and, rightly so. For Otto Ludwig, writing about the drama, had headed a study 'Der poetische Realismus' and given a convenient short formulation which could encompass so much of what other critics had been adumbrating:

Der Zauber schwindet nicht vor dem Wirklichen, umgekehrt; in der That ist es das Gesetz des Wirklichen, welches über dessen bloß zufällige Erscheinung siegt.—Die Kunst soll nicht verarmte Wirklichkeit sein, vielmehr bereicherte; nicht weniger Reize soll sie bewahren, sie soll neue hinzuerhalten durch das Medium des phantasieentquollenen Gedankens, alle die, welche aus dem gedankenhaft bezüglichen Neben- und Ineinander der beiden Welten des Ernsten und des Komischen hervorgehen. Sie soll nicht eine halbe, sondern eine ganze Welt sein.[14]

Although these statements are not necessarily made in the context of the Novelle, and, in the case of Otto Ludwig, are more directed towards the drama, they go much further towards explaining the position of authority enjoyed by this short prose form in the second half of the nineteenth century than many of the actual theoretical statements precisely relative to the genre. For, even if important theorists like Ludwig and Freytag did devote much of their energy to the actual *technique* of the drama, these were not years in which the German drama (as opposed to the theatre) had much to offer. The careers of Otto Ludwig himself, or even Ferdinand von Saar, which begin under the shadow of Schiller and Shakespeare, end in the resigned awareness that times have changed. But the benefits of dramatic construction—characterization, psychological concentration, the struggle or sufferings of a central character, the relation of hero or heroine to subsidiary characters—could be applied to the medium of condensed prose narrative. And here we can see the fulfilment of much of what August Wilhelm Schlegel had formulated in theory at the turn of the century.

When Fritz Martini pronounces the Novelle to be the main achievement of the 'bürgerlicher Realismus' of the second half of the century, this can only be seen to mean that this excellence was achieved at the expense of the novel proper.[15] Which does not mean that novelists like Freytag or Spielhagen or Raabe, to mention only three, had proved incompetent. But the 'fragmentary' quality of the Novelle, its deliberate shutting out of universal depiction in favour of concentration, its renunciation of omniscience, the 'Strahl' as opposed to the 'Lichtmasse' (F. Th. Vischer),[16] meant that it could achieve greater discipline and artistry than most of the novels written during the period. Indeed, one might go so far as to say that when the German novel, in the hands of Fontane and Thomas Mann, did achieve true greatness, it was partly because it could at last manipulate the sheer mass of the Dickensian, Flaubertian and Tolstoyan novel, by leaving much unsaid, and bringing out through symbol or recurrent motif what the older tradition had felt the need explicitly to state.

The age's interest in *technique* (Spielhagen, Freytag, Ludwig, Heyse) could not but assist the Novelle as an art form. Yet, apart from Vischer's comparison already quoted, or Riehl's analogy between sonata and Novelle, symphony and novel,[17] we find that the very suitability of the Novelle to the depiction of the age's concerns is paramount. Heyse's much-quoted falcon theory (see Chapter 8) follows on from his more significant observation that the Novelle is the art form most suited to the presentation of 'moderner Individualismus' and 'Sittlichkeit' and life 'auf dem Boden des Thatsächlichen',[18] that it therefore shares the major concerns of art in general. Its powers of observation, its strictness of form, its concentration on situation, its symbolical potential, its intimacy, all lend themselves to writers.[19] And, a factor as important as its commercial exploitation earlier in the century, there were suitable journalistic media like *Westermanns Monatshefte*, the *Deutsche Rundschau* or *Die Gartenlaube*, to continue its popularity among the different tastes of the reading public at large. Heyse's preface to his *Novellenschatz* refers specifically to this particular sociological factor.[20]

Wilhelm Riehl did, however, repeat the time-honoured truth that the Novelle must get on with telling the story;[21] it should not get lost in too much situation or atmosphere. This emphasis may explain why, in Germany in the second half of the nineteenth century, the work of Mérimée, Maupassant and Turgenev enjoyed such popularity and esteem, a point further underlined by Heyse in his *Jugenderinnerungen* of 1900.[22] The words of Maupassant on the novel could apply equally to the Novelle: it is not cumulative or comprehensive, but a product of artistic selection:

Voilà pourquoi l'artiste, ayant choisi son thème, ne prendra dans cette vie encombrée de hasards et de futilités que les détails caractéristiques utiles à son sujet, et il rejettera tout le reste, tout l'à-côté.[23]

But Turgenev?—the 'vollendeter Künstler [. . .] in der Darstellung kurzathmiger Stimmungen',[24] as Julian Schmidt calls him. Turgenev, who with Mérimée leads off Heyse's *Novellenschatz des Auslandes* and to whom Heyse dedicates one of his collections,[25] appeals for several reasons. His brevity, his eventfulness, his 'objectivity', his limited sphere of action, cannot always be separated from resignation, pessimism, melancholy even, or idyllic 'Stimmung'.[26] The appeal of this side of Turgenev can help us to understand why Biedermeier sentiment or 'Kleinmalerei' do not cease with Stifter but carry on over to Storm, Keller or Raabe; why Oskar Walzel can see in the German Novelle tradition a love of the 'Verweilen in Nebendingen' which he establishes as an artistic principle in Keller.[27] For Turgenev knows both the 'muß erzählen' and the 'Verweilen'. Turgenev it may be, too, who confirms the German writers in their love of the 'Rahmenerzählung'. The Russian narrative device, 'skaz', retreats behind the interposed story-teller, who then takes over and, as it were, relieves the real narrator of the responsibility for omniscience, or comment, or for the veracity of what has been told, so that he can then withdraw into reminiscence and reflection. But Turgenev, an acute observer of German literature and a considerable connoisseur of its traditions, also laid his finger on some of its weaknesses when he wrote of 'das leidliche Motivieren' and 'die ganz vermaledeite Idealisation der Wahrheit',[28] and these remarks, meant for none other than Theodor Storm (see Chapter 8), could also be laid fairly and squarely at the door of Otto Ludwig and Keller.

Chapter Seven

'DIE SCHWESTER DES DRAMAS'
SHAKESPEAREAN THEMES IN THE NOVELLE

The twentieth-century theory of the German Novelle, which, as we have been attempting to demonstrate, has more to do with what a Novelle ideally *should be* than with what it actually *was*, has made much of the dramatic qualities of the genre. The dramatic concentration and the tragic peripeteia are factors which have been noted—rightly—in studies of the Kleistian model.

It could be argued quite generally that any story-teller worth his salt is bound to have dramatic elements in his narration, and it would require no ingenuity to demonstrate this obvious point. It would further seem reasonably manifest that a form like the Novelle which 'soll erzählen', which is given to 'Begebenheiten', 'Wendepunkte', or whatever one may call them, would allow for analogies with the drama. But that again would apply to the prose narrative in general. It is significant that, as the German novel began to find its feet in the eighteenth century, as seen in Friedrich von Blanckenburg's *Versuch über den Roman* (1774), the analogies—and differences—between novel and drama were made apparent.[1] And the Gothic novel, whose insistence on incident and *coups de théâtre* is both one of its qualities and besetting sins, is, in all its theatricality and occasional meretricious sensationalism, also one of the ancestors of modern fiction. How lovingly Goethe leads the hero in *Wilhelm Meisters Lehrjahre* from a mere reflective discussion of drama and novel over to the mysteriously terrifying appearance of the ghost of Hamlet's father! How consciously the young Tieck prefaces his blood-curdling pot-boiler *Abdallah* (1795) with a Shakespearean quotation! How appropriate that Hoffmann's decidedly Gothic *Die Elixiere des Teufels* (1815–16) should have an important section headed 'Der Wendepunkt'! And we could say of most of the good stories of the nineteenth century,

Novellen or not, that the sections of 'dramatic' narrative, where the author pulls out all the stops and has us on the edge of our chairs for sheer excitement, are often the most memorable. The Germans knew this as well as anybody else. Kleist the narrator was as much aware of it as Kleist the dramatist. It tells us something of the century when Otto Ludwig complains about dramatists' inability 'die Spannung zu sänftigen';[2] this, as we saw, is just what Kleist does not wish to do. But any reader of Gotthelf, or the lesser-known Charles Sealsfield, will know that these more 'mixed' writers, too, are quite capable of almost shameless dramatization when they so choose.[3] It is therefore appropriate to repeat the point that many of the best narrators of the nineteenth century are also dramatists, not just in Germany, as the examples of Mérimée and Pushkin demonstrate. It should come as no surprise that the analogy drawn between Novelle and drama by August Wilhelm Schlegel is one which runs right through the century. The point made by Theodor Storm about the 'Schwester des Dramas' is one which can be traced back for three generations before him. It is perhaps also worth reiterating that this tells us quite a lot about the status of the drama, even in years when production was at a fairly low ebb.[4]

Yet we do have examples in the nineteenth century of writers whose instinct for the drama was not sustained in practice and who accordingly sought to fulfil this in prose. The best-known of these is Otto Ludwig. His story *Zwischen Himmel und Erde* (1856) is a prime example of how a theorist of the drama may fail as a writer of 'Kunstnovellen' simply because he attempts to satisfy in a more restricted genre the expectations of a dramatic subject. For *Zwischen Himmel und Erde* tries to do everything:[5] it has 'das Volk bei der Arbeit', it has the idyll, it is replete with symbol or recurrent motif; it has the archetypal Cain and Abel enmity between brothers (the title even suggests David and Absalom). It has the dramatically sudden peripeteia of classical tragedy, but not without its melodramatic moments. It tries to draw everything together in the central symbol of the church tower on which the steeplejack hero, Apollonius, works: a kind of 'Erkenntnis', resigned awareness, somewhere between the transcendent and the earthly. But it simply does not hold together as a story. We see how, compared with Keller or Storm or Saar at their best, Ludwig is unable to succeed in that essential concentration and restriction of motif and character that the genre so often calls for and generally achieves.

Analogies with the drama do not always mean 'peripeteia'[6] (the point made by Hermann Hettner) or bear out Friedrich Spielhagen's dictum of 1882 that 'beinahe jede Novelle in ein Drama umgedichtet werden [kann]'.[7] It should not be forgotten that Tieck made his significant 'condescension' to the popular Novelle also as a transition from *comedy*,[8] and that the conversational tone of his, and many others', Novellen is a product less of the severity and stringency of tragic necessity than of the easier rhythms and situational hilarities of social comedy. All the same, it cannot be reinforced too much that this affinity with the drama represents one aspect only of nineteenth-century practice. If we wish to preserve a sense of historical accuracy, we should not attempt to force the Novellen of that period into a dramatic mould or take as sole criteria terms analogous to the drama, like 'Begebenheit' or 'Wendepunkt'.

But what does happen when prose writers borrow their subjects from the drama? It had been often enough remarked that Shakespeare had drawn on the Italian *novella*, a point made first with some insistence in German by the Schlegels. Can the opposite process work? It might be enough to point to Balzac's *Le Père Goriot* and *Lear*, or *Eugénie Grandet* and *L'Avare*, or Zola's *La Terre* and *Lear*. Here we see that continuity of great dramatic subjects, be they from classical antiquity or of more modern provenance, from one generation to another. The modern writer will simply choose the mode and the setting which is most appropriate to his own situation and adapt, add, combine, leave out, as it suits him. The modern work of art will need more than the 'classical' archetype to make it something of memorable quality.

It is no different in Germany. Sometimes, as in Wilhelm Hauff's story *Othello* (1828), a mere reminiscence from the original is retained, although the title invites the reader to see analogies with Shakespeare. For in this story we are in fact at several removes from the original, the *Othello* referred to being in fact Rossini's opera. And the opera, a less subtle medium than the tragedy proper, will bring out with greater pathos and sensation the high moments, rather than their motivation. So it is that, in the story, Desdemona's willow song (a bravura aria) and murder are almost all that is left of Shakespeare. The connection between this stage event and the 'real' plot—the death of an innocent heroine through jealous passion and misunderstanding—is, to say the least, tenuous. Hauff is, in fact, much more interested in the old questions of 'Zufall', 'Schickung' and 'Verschuldung', which make up most of the plot, than in a Shakespearean analogy. Passion is, it is true, a destructive force, but so is fate and chance. For his Novelle has more analogies with a more modern, and rather suspect, form of drama than with Elizabethan tragedy: the fate drama. Eight days after every performance of *Othello* in this residence town, a member of the ruling family dies (with attendant ghost)! We are left to ponder the workings of 'Zufall' versus 'Schickung' (the old 'or avenne che'), but enjoined also to reflect on the complexities and responsibilities of a passionate intrigue between persons prevented by their status from ever fulfilling their inclinations. It is this that redeems the story from being just another, if very competently written, Biedermeier 'Taschenbuchnovelle'. Yet it is interesting to recall that the rather Hoffmannesque pattern of this story, with the attendant incidence of the supernatural, can still be seen much later in the century in one of the Russian masterpieces, Leskov's *Lady Macbeth of the Mtsensk District*. But in Leskov, we do have a heroine who, even in her limited ambit and vulgar surroundings, is actually worthy of comparison with her archetype.

But are these modern-day Lady Macbeths or Desdemonas not really little more than prose versions of the old 'bürgerliches Trauerspiel', where the young Schiller could warn the readers of the preface to *Die Räuber* not to be offended at finding a Richard III or a Iago in modern guise? Yet when Gottfried Keller wrote his *Romeo und Julia auf dem Dorfe* in 1856, there was more in his mind than just the question of character; there was the very real question of 'auf dem Dorfe' and what that entailed. For a story which is part of the collection *Die Leute von Seldwyla* is clearly different from a tragedy where social questions can only be tackled through character and dramatic situation, not description or reflection.

Romeo und Julia auf dem Dorfe is part of a cycle, and if commentators have, surely rightly, seen it as the masterpiece of its collection, it also has its place first and foremost there and nowhere else, subsumed as it is under the general preface and account of Seldwyla and its denizens.[9] Indeed Keller seems to have underlined this fact by placing it in 1874 as the second story, after *Pankraz der Schmoller*. The whole collection will set out to show how different characters manage to find—or not find—the other person necessary for their integration into society and their fulfilment in happiness. Pankraz learns this through learning to be adaptable and useful—and through renunciation. Some need the assistance of well-meant deception to enable them to seize the modest prize which fortune extends them (*Kleider machen Leute*); others need unkinder means to awaken them from gross self-delusion (*Die drei gerechten Kammacher*). Sali and Vrenchen in *Romeo und Julia auf dem Dorfe* find a form of inner fulfilment but only at the expense of social and personal tragedy. The cycle extends from the good-humouredly harmless to the stark and sombre. In all the stories, too, the worthy citizens of Seldwyla have their own commentary on what happens and their suitable portion of 'Schadenfreude'.

'Auf dem Dorfe' also means that Keller is taking a form of popular fiction, the 'Dorfgeschichte', and giving it some universal significance by the opening reference: 'zum Beweise, wie tief im Menschenleben jede jener Fabeln wurzelt, auf welche die großen alten Werke gebaut sind'.[10] But the 'Dorfgeschichte' never really is given the chance of full unfolding: the point of the story is *not* that those, like the 'Schwarzer Geiger' who lack the means of legitimizing their claim to property, are excluded from their citizen's rights by the landowning classes. It would not even be crucial for the story if we did not know at all who owned the parcel of land which causes the insoluble dispute between the two families. Nor is Keller's real concern the proletarization of the dispossessed or the fate of those whom society fails to accommodate in its structure of respectability.[11] But the village, the land, the pauperization, are that 'gemein-empirische Wirklichkeit' which Otto Ludwig sees ideally as merged with 'Ideen' to produce 'realistische Motivierung'.[12] Indeed, Berthold Auerbach, the best-known writer of 'Dorfgeschichten', when reviewing Keller's story, would have preferred a less literary title, as an indication that the story 'vom Leben ausgeht',[13] which he takes *Romeo und Julia* to do.

Otto Ludwig's theory was not always so easily realized in practice, as we have seen. What about Keller? It is interesting to note how the nineteenth century saw the story of Romeo and Juliet, which by way of analogy—and that alone—can tell us something about Keller's approach. Ludwig Tieck, in 1826, had wished to counteract romantic and sentimental interpretation of the play by stressing Romeo's inadequacies as a lover, the 'Grab, Tod, Verzweiflung mit allen Schrecken der Verwesung'.[14] This was not

Georg Gottfried Gervinus's view in 1849, which saw the play as 'lyrisch', 'idyllisch', with 'rührende Treue und Beständigkeit über die Grenze des Todes hinaus'.[15] Even Otto Ludwig was to speak of 'der harmonische, schöne Eindruck dieser Tragödie', the 'rührende Situation' of the tragedy produced not by outer forces of fate but 'nur von innen selbst'.[16] One could say—again by analogy alone—that Keller has some of this desire for reconciliation, for harmony, for tragic satisfaction free of force and terror and sublimity. Indeed, he seems to see no contradiction between the 'idyllisch' and the 'veredelnde' and 'verderbliche Kraft'[17] of love (Gervinus). To achieve such a reconciliation in a work of art was a task to which Keller only just proved adequate. Surely a fine sense of narrative economy enabled him to allow the family feud to lapse into the background and not recur, as in Shakespeare, as a reconciliation at the graveside. And few stories in any language in the nineteenth century can match the sheer Homeric grandeur of the opening, or the sinister monumentality of the bark of death, like in a Böcklin painting, which slides down the cold waters of Lethe and brings the lovers to their union in consummation and despair. But what of the story in between? It is true that every strand of the story is held together by clusters of symbols, and these are there for the inquisitive reader to find.[18] But do they satisfy? Is there not the feeling that Keller has let the reins slip, has untethered those monumental ploughmen and horses and started to gild, to sentimentalize, to play with the grotesque—to try too many of the accepted modes of his century? Later in the century, Theodor Fontane, whose critical view of Keller indicates an impatience with this kind of modal polyphony, was unkind enough to speak of a dualism between realism and sentimentality in the story, between the art of the Netherlandish genre-painter Ostade and the Pre-Raphaelism of the Düsseldorf school.[19] Otto Ludwig, some years earlier, also had used a—more flattering—analogy from painting: the story evoked 'das glühende Giorgionische Kolorit' but also 'schmerzwonnebehagliche Auskostung'.[20] And indeed the simple grandeur of Vrenchen setting off as a bride to her union in death might have something of a Giorgione Madonna or Palma Vecchio's Rachel. For Fontane it was a fatal eclecticism, an unequal marriage of modes where a unified style might have been called for. But for us it is not possible to wrest *Romeo und Julia auf dem Dorfe* away from 1856 into the 1880s and 1890s, where Fontane's instinct led him to a more uniform 'middle style' or Conrad Ferdinand Meyer espoused a similarly consistent, but utterly different, grand and heroic manner.

Our third Shakespeare example leads us to a writer who, while never achieving Keller's fame, was able to adapt a Shakespearean story and preserve one tone and level of style: Ferdinand von Saar in *Seligmann Hirsch* (1889). One suspects that the beneficent influence of Turgenev, whom Saar admired to the point of adulation, may have come to his aid. For Turgenev was no stranger to the Shakespearean adaptation: there are for instance *The Hamlet of Shchigrov District* in the *Huntsman's Sketchbook* and *King Lear of the Steppes*. As in both of Turgenev's stories, the narrator is involved, is there, and records his impressions of the characters taking shape around him. Like Turgenev, Saar takes us well into the account before he introduces the Shakespearean theme: King Lear. We are first to gain an impression of the narrator, why he is where he is, what he is doing, the company he keeps, his expectations, before the crux of the story is recounted. In Turgenev's Hamlet story, we are given over ten pages of description and conversation— a tedious dinner on a provincial estate—before we meet the character whose sheer lack of the remarkable, of decision-making or incisiveness, makes him into an 'original', a role which he stylizes into that of Hamlet. The narrator himself does not give him that predicate: the character makes the comparison himself and lives out that symbiosis of personal nothingness and symbolic identification. Similarly, the monstrous Lear of the steppes has first to be seen in the estates which he precipitately and foolishly chooses to leave to his ungrateful daughters and son-in-law. Only then does his grotesque figure become tragic and terrible.

Saar's story is dense, reduced to an absolute minimum, contenting itself with a few strokes of characterization and a little conversation. There is no attempt to tackle the 'ungeheuer gedrängt' 'Reichtum des Stoffes', the compact 'Massen' which Otto Ludwig saw as the chief characteristic of *Lear* the play.[21] Saar has removed Maupassant's 'l'à-côté'. We are given a few deft touches instead: the Galician Jew whose loudness, grossness, Gargantuan appetite, and flashiness awake in the narrator the native Viennese's anti-Semitism. Our worst expectations of grotesque and pitiless satire are awakened—until Saar lets Hirsch speak for himself, until we learn the real tragedy of his life, his consuming and irrational love of his family and his fatal passion for gambling. The story is then taken out of old Hirsch's hands by the introduction of the polished and successful son, the apple of his father's eye, the man who stands between Hirsch and his idolized grandchildren. The uneasy transition from the ghetto to the Viennese salons and *grand monde* is brought home to us tragically as the father is thrust aside as an embarrassment, an encumbrance in the way of social preferment. Not Jews, but the whole society which worships status and Mammon, are the villains of the tragedy. And Saar places the blame by introducing a Viennese Jewish salon *habitué* as the real critic, the acute observer of his own people, but also the one who sees through the underlying fraudulence of a social structure in the process of decay. The unprepossessing material of Hirsch senior is raised in a few pages to tragic greatness as the society around him—Gentiles and Jews alike—dances round the golden calf. The Lear analogy is mentioned but once—Saar does not wish to force comparisons—but it is all the more appropriate for summing up a man's isolation in a real, identifiable society, where, in his aching loneliness, a stumbling and half articulate reminiscence of Shakespeare is enough to remind us that 'Idee' and 'Stoff' can be merged into a work of art.

Chapter Eight

'UNERHÖRTE BEGEBENHEIT', 'WENDEPUNKT', 'FALKE' DEFINITIONS IN THEIR CONTEXT

The 'major statements' selected here for special discussion are those by Goethe, Tieck and Heyse; 'major' because they have always been associated with attempts to define the Novelle and very often have provided the criteria for the survey of its historical development. The 'major statements' proceed out of practice but seem to embody theoretical considerations as well. Our examination of statements on the Novelle during the nineteenth century makes it clear that most writers simply adapt Renaissance practice for their own use and are not interested in questions of theory. Not a word from a Kleist too urgently concerned with making his mark as a writer; next to nothing from the Romantics like Arnim or Brentano or Hoffmann; nothing from Droste or Stifter or Gotthelf or Mörike; Storm says very little, and that in a preface which he decided not to publish anyway; Keller refuses point-blank to become caught up in the theoretical discussions of 'Novellerei' and the like.[1] Were it not for the fact that writers once successful in their day, of the stamp of Laube or Riehl or Paul Ernst, were prepared to go on record with some kind of prefatory or definitive statement, we might even go as far as to say that on the one hand the theorists (beginning with the Schlegel brothers), or the literary historians, said what they had to say; and that on the other the practitioners, the creative writers, induced by different urges, got on with the task of telling the stories without recourse to theory. This would be a convenient schematic arrangement were it not also for the fact that Goethe, Tieck and Heyse actually wrote down attempts to say what they were doing and why. We are arrested by their statements both because *in their time* they could command respect and because today their phrases, 'unerhörte Begebenheit', 'Wendepunkt', and 'Falke', are terms that can help us clarify what we may wish to see as the essential characteristics of a Novelle. Their statements, it cannot be repeated enough and with too great emphasis, were never canonical, prescriptive or definitive. At most, they helped to clear the air and, like other statements quoted in earlier chapters, like that of Poe, for instance, Goethe's, Tieck's and Heyse's statements are concerned with effect, context, personal taste and stated intention.

When Goethe in 1795 introduced his adaptation of the Boccaccian mode into German, he was, as we saw (Chapter 2), concerned to relate his practice to what had gone before. The discussion sections of *Unterhaltungen deutscher Ausgewanderten* take up the questions of 'Neuheit', 'Tausendundeine Nacht', 'moralische Erzählung', and 'Märchen', none of these alien to the practice of the Italian, Spanish and French writers on whom Goethe roughly based his own stories. The emphasis and the critical tendency were of course, Goethe's own. There was no attempt to define absolutely what a Novelle might or might not be (the word 'Erzählung' is used throughout.) Rather Goethe is generally concerned to explore the possibilities this mode might entail. That was in 1795. When in January 1827, however, Johann Peter Eckermann recorded a conversation with Goethe that has become so familiar, his partner was by now the author of *Die Wahlverwandtschaften*, the first part of *Wilhelm Meisters Wanderjahre* and was teasing out the last details of a story to be called simply *Novelle*. If we examine Goethe's career as a prose writer, we notice that *Unterhaltungen deutscher Ausgewanderten*, far from representing a finished stage of Goethe's development, marks the beginning of an intensive preoccupation with stories which he calls successively 'kleine Erzählungen', or 'romantische Erzählungen', 'Geschichtchen' and finally, almost incidentally, 'Novellen'.[2] *Die Wahlverwandtschaften* emerged out of this period of creative reading and study of 'kleine Erzählungen', indeed one of Wieland's stories from *Das Hexameron von Rosenhain* first brought him to the idea of a plot involving the exchange of partners in love.[3] By including within his novel a 'story within a story', the Novelle *Die wunderlichen Nachbarskinder*, Goethe was extending the pattern of the *Unterhaltungen*, but also preparing the way for his more loosely textured late novel, *Wilhelm Meisters Wanderjahre*. This novel was in fact first conceived as 'Ein Novellenkranz',[4] a collection of stories whose exemplary character (in the Cervantian sense) was to set off, illuminate and illustrate the main themes of the novel or point to alternative models of behaviour, or even to warn and gently admonish. These stories have their independent genesis over some years before they gradually form part of the texture of the larger work; Goethe did not disdain to publish them as 'Taschenbuchnovellen' in Cotta's *Damenkalender* between 1809 and 1818,[5] and he had between 1800 and 1801 begun a less successful series of Boccaccian anecdotes called *Die guten Weiber*. The whole process of receiving and adapting 'kleine Geschichten und Märchen, die ich lang im Kopf herumgetragen',[6] from the late 1790s on, involves stories very different from the one to be called *Novelle*: there is in *Wilhelm Meisters Wanderjahre* the 'Zwergengeschichte', 'Das Märchen mit dem Weibchen im Kasten',[7] called *Die neue Melusine*, and another from the 'Novellenkranz', *Die pilgernde Törin*, which are, by Goethe's own admission, adaptations from French sources.[8] *Die neue Melusine* is merely another version of the old fairy-tale which Tieck had rewritten for inclusion in his *Volksmärchen* of 1797. We see Goethe, therefore, adapting and assimilating, re-creating and creating afresh from sources that are there to be drawn on by all. It is the same as Achim von Arnim's *Der Wintergarten* of 1809 had done with this common fund of anecdotal and narrative material from older periods of literature.

Goethe's statement to Eckermann in 1827 seems to contain fairly strict notions of what a Novelle should and should not be. Yet when in 1826 he mentioned to Wilhelm von Humboldt that he was reviving his old plan where 'Bei einer modernen Jagd kamen Tiger und Löwe mit in's Spiel', a subject which Humboldt had years before discouraged him from pursuing, Goethe sounded almost apologetic:

und enthalte mich nicht, ihn prosaisch auszuführen, da es denn für eine Novelle gelten mag, eine Rubrik unter welcher gar vieles wunderliche Zeug kursiert.[9]

He is, of course, referring to the story published as *Novelle*. But how are we to understand 'gar vieles wunderliche Zeug'? Had the Romance *novella* as we have traced it ever been anything other than this? Had not Cervantes even likened his stories to a market-place with its booths and sideshows? Or was Goethe looking with disfavour at the flood of almanach Novellen since he had embraced this popular and convenient form, being turned out in seemingly endless series by the Claurens, the van der Veldes and the Pustkuchens of this world? Had perhaps the time come to call a halt, to state one's position, to prevent association with a mode that might bring its author into discredit? There might even still be some of the touchiness of the same Goethe who had seen the first part of his *Wanderjahre* parodied in 1821.

The conversation with Eckermann of 25 (29) January 1827 contains less concession to the heterogeneousness of tradition or existing practice than the letter a few months before to Humboldt:

'Nun', fuhr Goethe fort, 'wie steht es mit der Novelle?' Ich habe sie mitgebracht, sagte ich. Nachdem ich sie nochmals gelesen, finde ich, daß Eure Exzellenz die intendierte Änderung nicht machen dürfen. Es tut gar gute Wirkung, wenn die Leute beim getöteten Tiger zuerst als durchaus fremde neue Wesen mit ihren abweichenden wunderlichen Kleidungen und Manieren hervortreten und sich als Besitzer der Tiere ankündigen. Brächten Sie sie aber schon früher in der Exposition, so würde diese Wirkung gänzlich geschwächt, ja vernichtet werden.

'Sie haben recht', sagte Goethe, 'ich muß es lassen, wie es ist. Ohne Frage, Sie haben ganz recht. Es muß auch beim ersten Entwurf in mir gelegen haben, die Leute nicht früher zu bringen, eben weil ich sie ausgelassen. Diese intendierte Änderung war eine Forderung des Verstandes, und ich wäre dadurch bald zu einem Fehler verleitet worden. Es ist aber dieses ein merkwürdiger ästhetischer Fall, daß man von einer Regel abweichen muß, um keinen Fehler zu begehen.'

Es kam sodann zur Sprache, welchen Titel man der Novelle geben solle; wir taten manche Vorschläge, einige waren gut für den Anfang, andere gut für das Ende, doch fand sich keiner, der für das Ganze passend und also der rechte gewesen wäre. 'Wissen Sie was', sagte Goethe, 'wir wollen es die Novelle nennen; denn was ist eine Novelle anders als eine sich ereignete unerhörte Begebenheit. Dies ist der eigentliche Begriff, und so vieles, was in Deutschland unter dem Titel Novelle geht, ist gar keine Novelle, sondern bloß Erzählung oder was Sie sonst wollen. In jenem ursprünglichen Sinne einer unerhörten Begebenheit kommt auch die Novelle in den Wahlverwandtschaften vor.'[10]

In a way not recorded for any of the Novellen from the *Wanderjahre*, Goethe is concerned with the technical details of his story and their effect on the reader. He is preoccupied with questions of motivation (what is the best time to introduce characters into the story?) with the successful rounding-off of the narration, the satisfaction of seeing a story brought to a proper conclusion. He is grateful, even if Eckermann's account is not exactly self-effacing, for the reaction of an attentive reader and the confirmation of what was already in his own mind. But these are details concerning the story itself. What of Goethe's attempt to define the Novelle, to produce 'der eigentliche Begriff'? We have to ask ourselves two questions. The first posed by so many commentators on this passage: what does Goethe mean by 'sich ereignete unerhörte Begebenheit'? The second, asked less often: what is the relation of this to Goethe's other statements and his several Novellen outside the confines of *Novelle* and *Die wunderlichen Nachbarskinder*? Was Goethe in fact trying to say something significantly new, applying only to a narrow, and therefore, special, canon of his works? The lack of a comma between 'ereignete' and 'unerhörte' suggests that the first two words can be taken to qualify the second two: we are dealing therefore with nothing more nor less than the old 'cas étrange' or 'caso estraño' of Renaissance practice. In the usage of the early nineteenth century, as Adelung's dictionary records it, 'unerhört' simply means 'außergewöhnlich', 'ungewöhnlich',[11] without any of the negative connotations which it today possesses. And so 'unerhörte Begebenheit' is one that is chosen out of the fullness of the fortuitous and the adventitious. Again, the 'sich ereignet' is nothing more than the old 'véritable histoire' and its variants, that are a cliché of the tradition and which writers treat with increasing and ironical disregard. It is the insight that we do not wish to be assailed all the time with the merely far-fetched, the meretriciously sensational, or the gratuitously preposterous. We wish to accept that, even if the story is fiction, it could have happened.

But did Goethe need to restate all this? Much had already been said in the *Unterhaltungen deutscher Ausgewanderten*. In *Die guten Weiber* he had dropped the phrase: 'Eine wahre Geschichte ist ohne Exaggeration selten erzählenswert'.[12] And in arguably his finest story from the *Wanderjahre* Novellen, *Der Mann von funfzig Jahren*, he had added to the ironical balance of the whole story by interspersing phrases like: 'Nur wurden sie denn doch zuletzt auch wieder die Welt um sich her gewahr, und diese steht selten mit solchen Empfindungen im Einklang';[13] 'Nun war aber durch ein unerwartetes Ereignis der ganze Zustand verruckt'; 'es war schwer vorauszusehen, was die Sache für eine Wendung nehmen [. . .] würde'.[14] These are phrases that are recognizably familiar, from Boccaccio to Kleist. Goethe uses them here not so much to speed us on to new events, but to bring us to the dilemma of the central hero and his acceptance of an order and *bienséance* based on self-restriction and renunciation. Yet, in another of the *Wanderjahre* stories, Goethe can make comment on his own use of narrative celerity like the following:

Wir haben, wie an dieser Stelle auffallend zu bemerken ist, die Rechte des epischen Dichters uns anmaßend, einen geneigten Leser nur allzu schnell in die Mitte leidenschaftlicher Darstellung gerissen.[15]

Of course he has, of course we appreciate that he has, and naturally we enjoy being gently nudged by the author. For the Novelle form has throughout the centuries always enjoyed that direct, and sometimes chatty, relationship with the 'esteemed reader'.

The fact of the matter is that Goethe's stories, from 1795 to 1829, do not diverge from the standard Renaissance patterns. At most they preserve a certain distance in both subject-matter and quality from the mass of stories, half fairy-tale, half anecdote, half memoir, half ghost-story, that were to flood the German market. Only one story stands out as markedly different: *Novelle*. The aim, as stated in an earlier conversation with Eckermann, was on the face of it not appreciably different from some of the *Wanderjahre* stories, *Der Mann von funfzig Jahren* or *Nicht zu weit*:

Zu zeigen, wie das Unbändige, Unüberwindliche oft besser durch Liebe und Frömmigkeit als durch Gewalt bezwungen werde, war die Aufgabe dieser Novelle.[16]

That could also be read as a variation on insights from *Unterhaltungen deutscher Ausgewanderten*. But whereas Goethe's stories in the *Wanderjahre* involve a range from 'Märchen', to 'Schwank', to romantic mystification, to misreading of appearances, almost to the brink of tragic passion—and contain the French, and also a fair spectrum of the Renaissance, tradition— *Novelle* is different. This story is not so much concerned with the *events* that make up 'das Unbändige, Unüberwindliche' as with *states of mind*. That does not mean to say that nothing happens—a lion and a tiger escape from a circus during a fire—but that the implications of these events are resolved on a symbolical and contemplative level. This is a Novelle which allows a considerable space to observation of the links and connections between the natural order of plants or geological formations, and the harmony and order which man must achieve if he is to fulfil his true potential. These reflections are controlled, strictly narrated and free of any gratuitous garrulity. But as such they are different both from 'etwas muß geschehen', and from mere interspersed maxims. The story, in its reflective structure, is a kind of microcosm of human activity and industry, reflecting a hierarchy of existing states, but also a movement upwards in growth, and true, responsible self-awareness. It is as if the many reflective sections of *Wilhelm Meisters Wanderjahre* had been concentrated into a space short enough to permit the interrelating presentation of maxim, symbol, outer and inner processes, song, and dramatic event. Because of this dense structure, the old 'etwas muß geschehen' becomes only one factor in the story. *Novelle* does not have the usual pattern of Goethe's own stories; and its influence is seen less in Novellen of the nineteenth century than in a work of different dimensions like Stifter's novel *Der Nachsommer*, with its insistence on a common harmony governing both nature and human passions, its interrelation of nature and art, and its overcoming of discord through pedagogic reasonableness. Indeed Goethe's publication of *Novelle* in 1828 and of the completed *Wanderjahre* in 1829 might suggest two different intentions. The Novellen in the *Wanderjahre* involve the refined, sophisticated, balanced, ironical affirmation of the older modes of narration. In *Novelle*, Goethe wished to move out into a work that was remoter from such traditions but which summed up the special urges and concerns of the last years of his life, unworried about others' practice: the awareness that the inconstant and even destructive form a necessary part of existence (an insight of *Faust*) yet only as they relate to a sense of organic growth and order (the 'Entsagung' of *Wilhelm Meisters Wanderjahre*). The paradox lies in the fact that the conversation with Eckermann seems to herald some kind of new approach to the narrative conventions of the Novelle, but on examination fails to do this. The statement attributed to Eckermann does not do full justice to the aspirations of *Novelle*, in that it seems to relate it to the old 'or avenne che' and nothing much else. And Goethe, by excluding any reference to any stories by himself except *Die wunderlichen Nachbarskinder* and *Novelle*, seems to imply that all his other Novellen conform to some other patterns than the one adumbrated, which they demonstrably do not. For in its form and subject *Die wunderlichen Nachbarskinder* is one that would not be out of place either in *Unterhaltungen deutscher*

Definitions in their context 97

Ausgewanderten or the *Wanderjahre*. At most, therefore, Goethe's statement of 1827 restates the well-known at a moment when the obvious needed reaffirming, but confuses the issue by its restricted application to only two works.

Ludwig Tieck in 1829 went further. This was in the preface to the eleventh volume of his *Schriften*, the edition of his works being issued under his supervision from 1828 onwards. In this preface Tieck uses his now famous words about the 'Wendepunkt'. Before we examine that rather elusive term, it may be useful to recall the context in which it was formulated. Goethe was not associated in most people's minds with the Novelle; Tieck now was.[17] Tieck, in issuing his works during his own lifetime, was engaged in an act of self-assertion, and to some extent self-advertisement. The prefaces to his edition, often his only statements on certain aspects of his work, are therefore all the more significant as tokens of personal justification and as a poetic credo. They seem to speak with authority, to give a certain system to an *œuvre* which is, to say the least, diverse. They are also disarming, and slightly deceptive. Already between 1826 and 1828, Tieck had had other opportunities of reminding people that he had not disappeared and that, as the senior surviving Romantic, he had a position on various matters that was different from, say, Goethe's. His editions of Kleist, Lenz and Solger, with their prefaces (in Solger's case, with their published correspondence) had underlined his position of authority as an arbiter of poetic talent and taste. This might make Tieck seem to be doctrinaire or dominating. Far from it: his prefaces are concerned to engage in debate, to put various sides of problems, to show benevolent tolerance, to chide gently, if need be, but never over-assertively or with raised voice. His statements are less systematic than conversational, drawing the reader into discussion rather than hectoring him with raised forefinger. There is a wealth of interesting statements but no 'doctrine' or standards of aesthetic faith.

Not only had Tieck been asserting himself in the fashion described; he had also been writing Novellen for almanacs. In short, roughly since 1817, he had, apart from prefaces and editions, turned entirely to the writing of prose fiction, and in particular, the Novelle. Given the general debasement of this currency in the hands of popular writers, Tieck's espousal of the mode may seem like an act of condescension. In a way it was. But it also afforded, like Goethe's *Wanderjahre*, an opportunity for raising standards, for rising above the merely sensational and trivial and producing something that was both a popular form and also a work of art. And Tieck was not doing anything that Arnim or Hoffmann or Brentano had not already done; his name, however, carried more authority than theirs. His Novellen are nevertheless a very mixed bag, some lasting works of art, others bearing too much the stamp of having been written for money. And so we must bear in mind all these factors when examining the preface containing the statement about the 'Wendepunkt'.

Boccaz, Cervantes und Göthe sind die Muster in dieser Gattung geblieben, und wir sollten billig nach den Vorbildern, die in dieser Art für vollendet gelten können, das Wort Novelle nicht mit Begebenheit, Geschichte, Erzählung, Vorfall, oder gar Anecdote als gleichbedeutend brauchen. Das Wort Humor entstand gegen 1600 bei den Engländern zufällig, und jetzt können wir es in unsern Kunstlehren nicht mehr entbehren, um Productionen und eine Eigenschaft des Geistes zu bezeichnen, die weder mit Laune, Geist noch Witz charakterisirt sind. Eine Begebenheit sollte anders vorgetragen werden, als eine Erzählung; diese sich von Geschichte unterscheiden, und die Novelle nach jenen Mustern sich dadurch aus allen andern Aufgaben hervorheben, daß sie einen großen oder kleinern Vorfall in's hellste Licht stelle, der, so leicht er sich ereignen kann, doch wunderbar, vielleicht einzig ist. Diese Wendung der Geschichte, dieser Punkt, von welchem aus sie sich unerwartet völlig umkehrt, und doch natürlich, dem Charakter und den Umständen angemessen, die Folge entwickelt, wird sich der Phantasie des Lesers um so fester einprägen, als die Sache, selbst im Wunderbaren, unter andern Umständen wieder alltäglich sein könnte. So erfahren wir es im Leben selbst, so sind die Begebenheiten, die [,] uns von Bekannten aus ihrer Erfahrung mitgetheilt, den tiefsten und bleibendsten Eindruck machen [. . .]

Bizarr, eigensinnig, phantastisch, leicht witzig, geschwätzig und sich ganz in Darstellung auch von Nebensachen verlierend, tragisch wie komisch, tiefsinnig und neckisch, alle diese Farben und Charaktere läßt die ächte Novelle zu, nur wird sie immer jenen sonderbaren auffallenden Wendepunkt haben, der sie von allen andern Gattungen der Erzählung unterscheidet. Aber alle Stände, alle Verhältnisse der neuen Zeit, ihre Bedingungen und Eigenthümlichkeiten sind dem klaren dichterischen Auge gewiß nicht minder zur Poesie und edlen Darstellung geeignet, als es dem Cervantes seine Zeit und Umgebung war, und es ist wohl nur Verwöhnung einiger vorzüglichen Critiker, in der Zeit selbst einen unbedingten Gegensatz vom Poetischen und Unpoetischen anzunehmen. Gewinnt jene Vorzeit für uns an romantischem Interesse, so können wir dagegen die Bedingungen unsers Lebens und der Zustände desselben um so klarer erfassen.[18]

This comes at the end of a nearly ninety-page introduction, almost as if tacked on to a longer discussion of his own poetic career and self-awareness. But that should not diminish its significance. For the *Schriften* were to continue with volumes of Novellen, and Tieck was here taking the opportunity of stating his position and justifying it. He begins by tracing the history of the word back to the tradition of 'jede Erzählung, jeden Vorfall [. . .] die neu noch nicht bekannt waren'.[19] His stated preference is for Cervantes over Boccaccio, but these, with Goethe, must remain the models for the genre we designate as Novelle. Not any mere 'Begebenheit, Geschichte, Erzählung, Vorfall, oder gar Anecdote' will fall into this category, any more than, by analogy, we can use the blanket term 'Humor' for 'Laune', 'Geist' or 'Witz'. Instead, Tieck insists, the Novelle will give sudden illumination ('in's hellste Licht stellen') to an event which may be everyday or unremarkable in itself, an unexpected turning in the story which will raise it from the sphere of the quotidian into something unique, leaving a lasting impression on the mind and imagination. We notice from the examples which Tieck cites—one from Goethe's *Unterhaltungen deutscher Ausgewanderten* and one from *Wilhelm Meisters Lehrjahre*—that he has less a sudden or chance occurrence in mind, the sort of event which characterizes so many of Boccaccio's and quite a number of Cervantes's stories, than some focal point, some incident or set of circumstances which is unexceptional, or even natural, in itself, but which in the story will be invested with a higher meaning. This all would seem to suggest that Tieck's 'sonderbarer auffallender Wendepunkt' is not quite the same as the 'cas étrange' or 'caso estraño' of the older tradition. Nor is he using it in the way that August Wilhelm Schlegel draws an analogy with the drama in his as yet unpublished lecture of 1803. It is rather that an event may change its tenor, quality, or appearance as it opens up for the reader some kind of intimation of a higher order or a glimpse of a truth hitherto inaccessible to the finite mind. It is not some kind of structural principle by which the story suddenly changes its course and gives new initiatives to chance or fate or good fortune. It is in the mind of the reader, it is an *effect* that the true Novelle will produce.

The Novelle should and can affirm the world around it, not merely be concerned with extraordinary and inexplicable interventions. It is in this sense that we must read Tieck's real definition of the Novelle, if such it is. It is not merely the kind of story that has us on the edge of our chairs and excites the imagination, the sort that is so easily debased in popular fiction and gives the Novelle a bad name—the sort of ghost story that Grillparzer could turn out in *Das Kloster bei Sendomir*. No, the Novelle must allow for reflection, for discourse, for sidetracks and byways; it should not disdain the portrayal of its own age, not dismiss subjects that are arbitrarily deemed 'unpoetic', and here Cervantes's novelas are the model to be emulated; through 'Räsonnement, Urtheil und verschiedenartige Ansicht',[20] it can solve and reconcile the contradictions, the irrationalities, even the tragic occurrences of life. It is a forum of criticism, but also of resolution and consensus. Its function and effect will be, if through different means, not inferior to that achieved by the tragedy or the novel. This is a very significant manifesto in favour of prose, let alone just the Novelle. It is heterodox and undogmatic and refuses to lay down the law except on one point, the 'Wendepunkt', which, as we saw, was not a formal feature, but an inner attitude produced in the reader. Tieck is, in historical terms, turning away from the trivial sensationalism of the early Biedermeier Novelle while placing greater emphasis on its capacity for being 'geschwätzig und sich ganz in Darstellung auch von Nebensachen verlierend'.

We saw that Goethe's words to Eckermann might have caused him to exclude one of his own Novellen through his strict definition. Do Tieck's Novellen in their turn conform in any way to his preface and are they a useful guide to his production? The answer is: they do not and they are not, if we use the 'Wendepunkt' alone as our criterion. Some writers on the Novelle have made their lives difficult by looking hard for 'Wendepunkte' in Tieck and finding few;[21] the corollary being that, having seized on only one word of Tieck's preface, they have declared a good deal of his production not to be genuine Novellen at all. For the older, doctrinaire historians of the Novelle will have nothing of 'geschwätzig und sich ganz in Darstellung auch von Nebensachen verlierend' and find the vast *œuvre* of this writer rather much of a nuisance. The fact of the matter is that Tieck could turn his hand very adequately to almost any kind of prose writing; sometimes the results were better than others. Sometimes he makes shameless use of conventional material and stock situations; what is certain is that the stories were not written to any predetermined scheme or plan. There is even one Novelle, *Das Zauberschloss* of 1830,[22] that ought to be better known, which might be seen as a kind of self-parody, a 'Spaß aus einem Nichts',[23] as he himself called it. The main part of the story, with young lovers parted by parental intransigence, and stratagems to bring them together, using a 'haunted' castle as the main precinct, seems dashed off with much wit and jaunty conversation—and absolute control of the comic situation. But Tieck can also do, if on a smaller scale and with different emphasis, what Goethe does in *Unterhaltungen deutscher Ausgewanderten* and *Wilhelm Meisters Wanderjahre*: a story within a story. A seemingly gratuitous situation is arranged for one of the characters to take out of his pocket a Novelle:

Es rührt, was ich mittheile, von jenem Verfasser her, von dem schon manche Erzählungen bekannt geworden sind. Er scheint sich bei dem Titel Novelle etwas Bestimmtes, Eigenthümliches zu denken, welches diese Dichtungen charakterisiren und von allen andern erzählenden scharf absondern soll. Doch ist es nicht mein Beruf, ihn zu kommentiren, ich theile Ihnen die Geschichte selber mit, die überdies für eine wahre Anekdote ausgegeben wird.[24]

The author of the 'Wendepunkt' is quite clearly not above playing with his own categories, as 'Erzählung', 'Novelle', 'Geschichte', 'Anekdote', are interchanged with considerable insouciance. Yet the story itself, *Die wilde Engländerin*, shows what Tieck can do as a prose writer if he sets his mind to it. All is condensed, without a superfluous detail, with every incident planned; the style exudes mastery and elegant ease of presentation. It is one of those old subjects, with modern refinements: the lady who cannot express her love in conventional terms. It is not unlike Goethe's *Die wunderlichen Nachbarskinder*, in that the situations in the main story and the Novelle are reversed. For we have here, not lovers thwarted in their common design, but a young woman spurning the wooings of a lord, older than she, but of great dignity and worthiness. He tries one last time to open his heart to her: the moment is when they are out riding. She responds—with even greater vehemence—and the narrator proceeds:

Sterben eher! rief sie mit dem heftigsten Ausdruck des Widerwillens. Sie

selbst wollen mir es recht leicht machen, Ihre Abwesenheit zu ertragen. So leben Sie denn wohl!
   Sie trieb das Pferd an, und Beide waren im höchsten Unmuth bald vor dem Schlosse angelangt. Er stieg ab, um ihr zu helfen, sie wendete sich mit dem Ausdruck des höchsten Unwillens, sie wollte sich eilig vom Pferde schwingen, und das Reitkleid blieb fest am Sattelbogen, ein Moment, und sie stand halb nackt vor dem Erstaunten. Mit einer Schnelligkeit, die unmöglich schien, rannte sie ins Haus und der Lord gab die Pferde ab und begab sich nachdenkend träumend in den Park.[25]

For those who want a 'Wendepunkt', Tieck is here producing one to end them all. It leads, as in Goethe's story, to matrimony, children, grandchildren, and living happily ever after, but all with delicacy, worldly wisdom and gentle wit. Then the garrulous and highly improbable main story is resumed. And there, all similarity with *Die Wahlverwandtschaften* ends abruptly.

   Tieck's other statements on the Novelle are ambivalent. He can in one place speak of Kleist's stories as 'klassisch'[26] (by which he probably means Cervantian), but in another also unashamedly put in a good word for all kinds of popular fiction. He can write a preface for Eduard von Bülow's *Novellenbuch*, but spends most of his time discussing novels and seems to be unmindful of any hard-and-fast distinctions between one prose genre and the other.[27] He is much more concerned with reminding his readers that prose-writing has a good pedigree, has been practised for centuries, has no need to be ashamed of itself, from Cervantes to Fielding to Goethe, even to Balzac. It is Tieck reviving the Romantic emphasis on prose but also adding a word of encouragement to younger writers not to feel that they have become untrue to their calling if they espouse prose narrative. And Tieck is, in his own practice, as careless about distinctions in length between Novelle and novel. His *Der junge Tischlermeister* of 1836 has 350 pages as originally printed; he only decides at the last moment to call *Vittoria Accorombona* (similarly long) a novel. In the same way, he reprints some of his youthful stories, adaptations from French 'contes' or 'nouvelles', as 'Arabesken' or 'Erzählungen'—without advancing any reason for this interesting distinction.[28]

   Tieck's 'Wendepunkt', therefore, is not the dramatic turning-point, or the sudden intervention, that it may seem to be. It is, as has been seen, something which we must find ourselves as readers, not something imposed on us from outside by tricks of narrative or precipitate changes of fate. It is that by which we recognize a story to be not only entertaining or gripping, but also true. That had also been Cervantes's aim, although Tieck is tantalizingly unspecific about what constitutes a 'Wendepunkt' in Cervantes's stories. The clue may lie in 'alle Stände, alle Verhältnisse der neuen Zeit, ihre Bedingungen und Eigenthümlichkeiten'. For as Cervantes, avers Tieck, did not scruple to portray 'seine Zeit und Umgebung' in poetic fashion, so too the modern writer may find poetry and 'edle Darstellung' in his own times and circumstances. And it will be in those very 'Verhältnisse der neuen Zeit' that an opening will be found for the transcendent, the higher intimation, the divine, to invest everyday life with new, and deeper, meaning. One might go so far as to say that Tieck's preface of 1829 draws its real significance from its uncompromising acceptance of the real world as the surroundings for poetic endeavour and imagination (Mundt's 'schildert Alles'); that in the real world, not in a flight from it, we find the symbols that hint beyond this existence to another sense of being and the hope of continuing beyond flesh and matter. In that sense, it points towards the 'poetic realism' of the later century.

From Tieck's ironic loquacity and love of reflection to Paul Heyse's 'falcon' or 'silhouette' seems a long way, longer even than the forty-two years that separate the prefaces to Tieck's *Schriften* and Heyse's and Kurz's *Deutscher Novellenschatz*. The distance is made even greater when Heyse in 1900, in his *Jugenderinnerungen und Bekenntnisse*, while recognizing Tieck's historical position as the 'Schöpfer der modernen Novelle', goes on to condemn the 'störende Zutaten, witzige oder lehrhafte Gespräche'[29] that are so typical of Tieck and of so many Biedermeier Novellen. It reminds us that we are not far from the purism of a Paul Ernst, writing in 1901 of the 'moderne Auflösung der Novelle'.[30] Yet Heyse's statement of 1871, seen together with his others, is different only in specific emphasis from those of Goethe and Tieck. It, too, is complaining of a heterodoxy in matters of definition and standards of practice; it, too, is looking back to the models set by the Renaissance (and by Goethe); it, too, is seeking for that specific quality that gives the Novelle its special justification over other art forms and sets it apart with a mark of distinction. But unlike Goethe and Tieck, Heyse is not speaking all the time of his own production or stating his position in relation to it. The preface of the *Novellenschatz*, which seems to be formally prescriptive, is talking about others' works, those examples of the genre that may be held up to the reading public as being among the 'gediegensten deutschen Novellen',[31] as Heyse's assiduous publisher states in the endpapers. A more personal position on the Novelle is to be found in Heyse's preface to his *Moralische Novellen* of 1869, his eighth collection, in the address 'An Frau Toutlemonde in Berlin'. Significantly, Heyse has little or nothing to say about the formal qualities of the Novelle. Rather he is concerned with establishing what its competence and terms of reference are. And here Heyse has recourse to the traditional: 'Grenzgebiet', 'Ausnahmsfälle', 'das Problematische'.[32] He does add some psychological depth to the old 'cas étrange' by suggesting that the problematical situations, the extreme cases which veer towards the limits of accepted values, are caused by those who follow the urges of inner feeling rather than the dictates of society. And the Novelle still retains in Heyse's eyes some of its traditional moral worth when he states that this form of fiction may help to redefine or to widen the accepted bounds of morality and be useful to some persons in their search for inner freedom from social constraints. That had not been the particular burden of Tieck's preface, but the emphasis on the moral standards of society and their portrayal is common to both writers. It is taken up again in the foreword to the *Novellenschatz* in the statement that the Novelle has progressed from being a mere freakish or extraordinary occurrence to a forum where 'die tiefsten und wichtigsten sittlichen Fragen zur Sprache kommen'.[33]

Tieck's preface of 1829 had made a passing reference to the respective functions and expectations of drama, novel and Novelle. Not surprisingly—considering that similar considerations had arisen in the writings of Prutz and Vischer and Spielhagen, and were in the mind of Theodor Storm—Heyse's statements seek to draw distinctions between the genres: 'Frau Toutlemonde' will be told that the Novelle relates to the 'Ausnahmefall' as the drama does to 'das Gültige', a point repeated in the foreword to the *Novellenschatz*.[34] There, too, Heyse distinguishes Novelle from novel in terms of 'ein einzelner Conflict' as opposed to a 'Cultur- und Gesellschaftsbild im Großen'.[35] If this is reminiscent of Vischer's 'Strahl' and 'Lichtmasse', it is also essentially the point made by Edgar Allen Poe (see p. 3).

It can be seen, then, that Heyse is taking most of the major points of discussion surrounding the genre which we have examined in detail in Goethe and Tieck. What, then, of the 'Falke', that creature with whom Heyse is generally associated? Heyse is not merely drawing a distinction between Novelle and novel, but actually stating the acknowledged advantages and qualities of the *shorter genre*. Brevity need not be a disadvantage; that is the main message of the foreword. The popularity of the Novelle need not imply a lowering of artistic standards. And Heyse, taking advantage of his position later in the century, can point to examples outside German literature, to the French and above all to the 'russischen Meister der Seelenkunde',[36] Turgenev. This—rarely quoted—section of his introduction makes it clear that Heyse is not merely concerned with brevity as such but also with the fact that 'die geheimnißvollsten Gemüthstiefen',[37] psychological depth and perception, are well within the range of the Novelle for a great master.

Heyse's suggestion that Boccaccio's story of the falcon, or rather his summary of it, could be taken as a guideline for the well-constructed Novelle, is an appealing reminder that brevity of form, 'Ausnahmefall', 'etwas Eigenartiges, Specifisches schon in der bloßen Anlage'[38] are interrelated.

Im Allgemeinen aber halten wir auch bei der Auswahl für unsern Novellenschatz an der Regel fest, *der* Novelle den Vorzug zu geben, deren Grundmotiv sich am deutlichsten abrundet und—mehr oder weniger gehaltvoll—etwas Eigenartiges, Specifisches schon in der bloßen Anlage verräth. Eine *starke Silhouette*—um nochmals einen Ausdruck der Malersprache zu Hülfe zu nehmen—dürfte dem, was wir im eigentlichen Sinne *Novelle* nennen, nicht fehlen, ja wir glauben, die Probe auf die Trefflichkeit eines novellistischen Motivs werde in den meisten Fällen darin bestehen, ob der Versuch gelingt, den Inhalt in wenige Zeilen zusammenzufassen, in der Weise, wie die alten Italiener ihren Novellen kurze Überschriften gaben, die dem Kundigen schon im Keim den specifischen Werth des Thema's verrathen. Wer, der im Boccaz die Inhaltsangabe der 9ten Novelle des 5ten Tages lies't:
  'Federigo degli Alberighi liebt, ohne Gegenliebe zu finden; in ritterlicher Werbung verschwendet er all seine Habe und behält nur noch einen einzigen Falken; diesen, da die von ihm geliebte Dame zufällig sein Haus besucht und er sonst nichts hat, ihr ein Mahl zu bereiten, setzt er ihr bei Tische vor. Sie erfährt, was er gethan, ändert plötzlich ihren Sinn und belohnt seine Liebe, indem sie ihn zum Herrn ihrer Hand und ihres Vermögens macht'—wer erkennt nicht in diesen wenigen Zeilen alle Elemente einer rührenden und erfreulichen Novelle, in der das Schicksal

zweier Menschen durch eine äußere Zufallswendung, die aber die Charaktere tiefer entwickelt, aufs Liebenswürdigste sich vollendet? Wer, der diese einfachen Grundzüge einmal überblickt hat, wird die kleine Fabel je wieder vergessen, zumal wenn er sie nun mit der ganzen Anmuth jenes im Ernst wie in der Schalkheit unvergleichlichen Meisters vorgetragen findet.

Wir wiederholen es: eine so einfache Form wird sich nicht für jedes Thema unseres vielbrüchigen modernen Kulturlebens finden lassen. Gleichwohl aber könnte es nicht schaden, wenn der Erzähler auch bei dem innerlichsten oder reichsten Stoff sich zuerst fragen wollte, wo 'der Falke' sei, das Specifische, das diese Geschichte von tausend anderen unterscheidet.[39]

He could, of course, have chosen almost any story by Boccaccio, for the *Decameron* conveniently produces a synopsis each time before launching into the narrative itself. And that summary is a mere bald statement of happenings: the main point of the story—*chance*—is not discussed. Heyse also makes it clear that this brief précis is to be the guideline for his particular collection: it need not be, indeed cannot be, the measure of the genre itself: 'eine so einfache Form wird sich nicht für jedes Thema unseres vielbrüchigen modernen Kulturlebens finden lassen'; it is, nevertheless, worth reminding his readers of the wealth of fine—and short—fiction that this genre has produced in German (it is not called 'Novellenschatz' for nothing).

The relationship between Heyse's theoretical foreword and his actual selective practice is, however, not without its strains. For, in his concern to find stories that might fit his criteria, or which for other reasons might be suitable, Heyse has needed to go out into the highways and hedges of the nineteenth century to find sufficient guests for his pages. A less charitable view might be that Heyse's collection represents very much of nineteenth-century taste that has now sunk without trace. (It is interesting to recall that Theodor Storm in letters confirms Heyse's judgement in so many cases of now-forgotten authors.) When we examine those stories from the *Deutscher Novellenschatz* that have survived in our esteem today, we notice that relatively few would fit Heyse's 'Falke' criterion and indeed, if we were to apply it as a yardstick, we should be doing a gross injustice to the temper and texture of the original story. It might do for Kleist's *Die Verlobung in St. Domingo* or still for *Romeo und Julia auf dem Dorfe*, both of which Heyse includes. But would it suit *Die Judenbuche* or *Mozart auf der Reise nach Prag* or even *Kasperl und Annerl*, Novellen which are involved or discursive or finely-textured as the case may be and do not respond to this kind of Boccaccian reduction? It is against the context of the twenty-four volumes of the *Deutscher Novellenschatz* that we are to see Heyse's statement, and not in any abstract or purely theoretical light.

His later collections, *Neuer deutscher Novellenschatz* and *Novellenschatz des Auslandes*, almost completely invalidate the 'Falke', and Heyse must have known it. When in 1900 he returns in his *Jugenderinnerungen und Bekenntnisse*, to what by then he calls the 'Falkentheorie', it is with some reservations: 'daß man sich fragen müsse, ob . . .'. The certitude has gone.

Our examination of Goethe, Tieck and Heyse shows that none of them produces anything approaching an 'improvement' on Renaissance practice, but at most restatements of older insights, in order to restore some kind of profile to the genre. Moreover there is something inadequate about all three sets of statements in respect of the works of the authors themselves: Goethe's would appear to be too exclusive for much of his best prose work; Tieck's does not apply to his own practice; Heyse's is scarcely appropriate for many of the Novellen represented in his published collection. We are left with the conclusion that the nineteenth century in Germany produces at most a few modifications of what Italian, Spanish and French literatures had earlier established, and that, like them, the paramount concern was writing stories effective in their own terms, rather than deliberating on the reasons for so doing. The scope of the Novelle had not changed. At most, there might be a need to rescue it from debasement, or to demonstrate that it had its independent validity alongside more expansive genres like the novel and the drama.

Chapter Nine

'VON ZIEMLICH GLEICHEM WERTHE' THE CASE OF THEODOR STORM

Ich glaube, daß eigentlich meine Sachen
von ziemlich gleichem Werthe sind.[1]

Why Theodor Storm, and not Stifter, or Keller, Saar or Conrad Ferdinand Meyer? And why a 'case'? I have chosen Storm because he is in many ways more typical of the development of the genre between 1850 and 1890 than those others named, and because he illustrates its strengths and weaknesses rather more markedly than they do. He does not revise carefully like Stifter; he has less humour than Keller, less economy than Saar, and less stylistic uniformity than Meyer. Yet he lends himself to special study also because few writers of his generation produced anything as masterly as *Der Schimmelreiter*, but by the same token nothing as weak as some of the stories written more to alleviate material hardship than to gratify any aesthetic urge.

Did Storm, the writer of over fifty Novellen, really believe that his works were more or less of the same quality? Would it not be more appropriate to quote the letter written to Theodor Mommsen in 1884 accompanying the consignment of *Eekenhof, Beim Vetter Christian, Viola tricolor, Ein stiller Musikant, Aquis submersus* and *Die drei Märchen*?

Es sind das ziemlich verschiedene Töne, ein paar auch was man bei Goethe oder was er selbst Befreiungen nannte; und Alles ist kurz und ohne Ueberfluß.[2]

These two seemingly conflicting statements can perhaps be reconciled if we see in them an account of the two disparate sides of Storm's character as a writer: on the one hand, the man for whom the constraint to write was often a necessity demanded by physical circumstances; and the conscious artist, proudly linking himself with Goethe's poetry and declaring 'Meine Novellistik ist aus meiner Lyrik erwachsen'[3] or the Novelle to be 'die Schwester des Dramas'.[4]

Let us consider the first aspect. Storm, like Heyse, like Keller, Raabe, Fontane or Meyer, spans in his literary production the years immediately following the 1848 revolution up to the heyday of the 'Gründerjahre'. These are years in which the Novelle begins to fulfil the function accorded it by Heyse in 1871 as registering 'die tiefsten und wichtigsten sittlichen Fragen', working in easy cooperation with the more expansive novel and, for a time at least, supplanting the drama in actual quality of poetic utterance and organization. There is no abatement in production: Heyse's *Novellenschatz* and its preface make this very clear. But the old *Taschenbuch* of the 1820s, 1830s and 1840s is more or less a thing of the past. Shorter fiction finds that it can be more easily accommodated in the new magazines which document literary, social and political events and provide a forum for the discussion of those 'Fragen unserer Zeit'. The Novelle can in such a context demonstrate its adequacy in all respects: as a reflection of the cultural and poetical ambitions of its age, its formal self-awareness, its wish to record through symbol and not straight documentation, its love of lyrical atmosphere, or merely its wish that 'etwas soll geschehen'.

It may not do to over-generalize: but many of the significant writers of Novellen in the period find their way to mastery in this form through trial and error, accepting or rejecting a coexistence with other literary forms, or proceeding beyond the Novelle to excellence elsewhere: as with Keller, the youthful would-be dramatist and only partially successful novelist of maturity; or Saar, the failed dramatist and indifferent poet; or Ludwig, the dramatist and Shakespeare critic; or Raabe, finding a balance between shorter and longer fiction; or Fontane, gradually moving into the full-length novel; or Meyer, regarding his lyrical poetry as the real object of his attention and concern. Storm, by contrast, never indulged in flirtations or even *affaires du cœur* with other literary genres like the drama. There is, of course, his poetry, of which he was justifiably proud and which is certainly among the best written by his generation. It springs—in general—from the personal and intimate, familiar, sphere of life, is, as he says, truly 'Gelegenheitsdichtung',[5] an expression of the momentary movements and emotions of the soul, the longing, fulfilment, or deprivation of lover, husband, father or friend. It is in respect of his poetry that we have from

Storm the most important statements that amount to an aesthetic credo: his love of the lyrical atmosphere that he calls 'das echte "Tirili" der Seele';[6] his love of simplicity, essentials and 'klangvolle, wuchtige Verse, starke Herzenstöne'[7] as opposed to 'Phrase' and the indirect apparatus of imagery;[8] the 'richtiges Weglassen des Unwesentlichen',[9] the words of the nineteenth-century painter Anselm Feuerbach which express his aesthetic and much that is so important for the Realist generation; the proper balance of 'Geist', 'Phantasie' and 'Gemüth';[10] a rejection of coldness but also of extravagance and self-indulgence, yet an affirmation of the heart as it reaches out to others.

All of this we will find in Storm's Novellen as well. The personal note will be veiled behind the greater objectivity of the Novelle form, but will manifest itself in 'Herzenstöne', somewhat more than is compatible with 'richtiges Weglassen'. Certain of Storm's most deeply felt concerns—his love of 'die Perle aller deutschen Länder',[11] Schleswig-Holstein, his political indignation, his sense of social injustice, his professional observation of crime and punishment and their causes—find their due expression in his Novellen. Two of his very best stories, *Draussen im Heidedorf* and *Im Nachbarhause links* draw directly on his own role as *Stadtvogt* and uninvolved objective recorder of events. His stories will revolve time and again around what might appear the narrow base of one small region in what seems to be a remote corner of North Germany. They will do so not, one assumes, because Storm is incapable of situating his creative imagination elsewhere, but because the love of 'Heimat', 'Vaterland' and native roots is as one with the deepest commitments of the heart. As he writes from exile in 1857:

> Nun horch ich oft schlaflos in tiefer Nacht,
> Ob nicht der Wind zur Rückfahrt möge wehen.
> Wer in der Heimat erst sein Haus gebaut,
> Der sollte nicht mehr in die Fremde gehen.
> Nach drüben ist sein Auge stets gewandt;
> Doch eines blieb,—wir gehen Hand in Hand.[12]

And this poem is written within a year of arguably his finest story of youthful reminiscence, renunciation and loss, *Auf dem Staatshof* (1858).

Would all this not merely confirm all we have heard and know about Storm, as the poet associated with the 'graue Stadt am Meer', Husum, a writer of regionalism, poetic realism, insularity, achieving mastery only in the small form and limited scope of lyrical poem and Novelle, yet without any association with the wider world? These are factors which anyone attempting to discuss nineteenth-century German literature cannot dismiss as irrelevant. For, not only is there Storm in Schleswig-Holstein, but there is Droste associated with Westphalia; Stifter, Saar and Marie von Ebner-Eschenbach with Austria, Gotthelf and Keller with Switzerland, or Mörike with Swabia. It seems to fit in with an image of preindustrial rural, feudal Germany before 1871, a kind of idyllic, pre-established harmony undisturbed by political disruptions:

—Kein Klang der aufgeregten Zeit
Drang noch in diese Einsamkeit.[13]

as Storm's poem 'Abseits' seems to be saying. It is a world which, if we were to use the conventions of French or English nineteenth-century literature, would be that of the 'provincial' as opposed to the 'urban' (see p. 5f.). To the extent that Germany was without *one* major centre of culture, a capital like London or Paris, it is true. But that would be to overlook the fact that 'regionalism' or whatever else one may wish to call it, is not the same as mere provincialism, with all its associations of narrowness and parochialism. It would disregard what the Germans call 'Kulturlandschaften', regional pockets of culture and intellectual excellence which flourish perfectly well without the appeal of a major capital and are nurtured by local traditions and institutions. It means that, in the case of Germany, we must not assume the pattern that undoubtedly holds for France and England, with Paris or London meaning *grand monde* and all the richness that implies, whereas the provinces mean cultural deprivation. A Swabia, for instance, that had produced Hegel, Schelling and Hölderlin, and was to continue with Mörike, David Friedrich Strauss and Friedrich Theodor Vischer— even if only a few of these remained in their 'native land'—could hardly be aligned with the merely provincial.

The same applies to some extent to Schleswig-Holstein. A region that produces in one generation Hebbel, Theodor Mommsen, Storm, and—but for the accident of birth in Hamburg—Johannes Brahms, not to speak of lesser figures like Klaus Groth or Karl Müllenhoff, is not suffering from cultural impoverishment. Even then, these names subdivide into two groups: those who stay in Schleswig-Holstein and those who do not. Hebbel and Brahms move eventually to Vienna, the for them cultural centre of gravity of the German-speaking world; Mommsen to Berlin and Germany's most illustrious university. That leaves two figures less known outside the confines of their own region (although there are many readers outside North Germany who know Klaus Groth's poetry in Plattdeutsch)—and Storm.

Storm the writer lived in limited, even straitened, circumstances, for the most part in small towns and reduced to the cultural offerings they rose to—because he wished to do so. His family ties are too close, his emotional attachments too compelling, his political awareness too consuming, for him to live by choice anywhere else. The years spent in Berlin and Heiligenstadt, when the Danish regime in Husum made it impossible for him to exercise his profession, were ones of exile. So deep are these roots that there is scarcely a story that cannot be traced in its origins in one way or another back to Storm's native North Frisia. Yet we will also note that references to local forms and traditions are not so overt as to detract from their general or universal import. Storm's words on the classical in poetry (from which he modestly excluded himself) apply equally to his Novellen: 'der wesentliche geistige Gehalt seiner Zeit in künstlerisch vollendeter Form'.[14] On the one hand, 'Ein Dichter [. . .] darf gerade sein Heiligstes seinem Volke nicht vorenthalten';[15] but on the other, one cannot deny the poet 'Wirksamkeit auf die Gemüter [. . .] und auf die Taten der Menschen':[16] 'Bin ich ein Dichter, so habe ich mit dem aus meinem Innersten Ausgeprägten auch eine Wirkung auf mein Volk'.[17] When Eduard Mörike wrote to him in 1855 asking why he did not put any reflection of the Schleswig-Holstein tragedy into his prose work, Storm replied:

Sobald ich recht bewegt werde, bedarf ich der gebundenen Form. Daher ging von allem, was an Leidenschaftlichem und Herbem, an Charakter und Humor in mir ist, die Spur meist nur in die Gedichte hinein. In der Prosa ruhte ich mich aus von den Erregungen des Tages; dort suchte ich grüne stille Sommereinsamkeit.[18]

That might indeed have been a valid answer for 1855, where the lyrical poetry bears the main force of the pain of exile and the injustice of nations. But 'grüne stille Sommereinsamkeit' was hardly the theme of the stories written but a few years later, *Im Schloss* (1861) and *Auf der Universität* (1862). Rather we should interpret Storm's words to Mörike as meaning that his stories do indeed retreat behind symbol or reminiscence, while at the same time holding on to the essential norms and values of his own times which are worthy of preservation, a humanism, an avoidance of extremes of emotion or individual commitment, a reassertion of the worth of certain institutions like family and possessions—in the interest of the common weal—and a rejection of political solutions which flout these values. In this sense, Storm, without ever being an adherent of any literary school or concerned with literary politics, reflects the best ideals of 'programmatischer Realismus'.

This is not a man who is starved of intellectual debate, nor a man in the age of railways physically isolated from the rest of the world. He is the friend and correspondent of Mörike, Keller, Heyse, Turgenev, Fontane and Mommsen—not a bad list internationally—and of a Turgenev who moved between Paris and Baden-Baden but set very many of his best stories in rural and provincial Russia. Storm's dealings with publishers follow a similar pattern. He begins with journals that have a local association—*Immensee* (1849) is published in Biernatzki's *Volksbuch*—or are representative of small circles (*Argo* in Berlin), branching out very soon to *Über Land und Meer* in Stuttgart, the Leipzig *Illustrierte Zeitung*, *Westermanns illustrierte Monatshefte* and *Deutsche Rundschau*. In doing this he was also following patterns well established earlier in the century. Droste's story with marked local associations, *Die Judenbuche*, was entrusted to the leading publisher of the day, Cotta in Stuttgart; and Gotthelf's name was made by his Berlin publisher, Julius Springer. For all that, one will find in Storm far less detail of a purely folkloristic nature than in Gotthelf and even in Droste; and, like Keller, he rejects the sustained use of dialect[19] in order to place the universal validity of human endeavour in the forefront.

Yet Storm's association with the history of the nineteenth century Novelle would not be complete without the recognition that he did not merely write to rest 'von den Erregungen des Tages', but also for money. For a great deal of his significant work was done under the most adverse circumstances, with professional uncertainty, the needs of a growing family, and an inadequate salary. Poetic ideals seem remote when we hear him admitting to 'Verleger-Zerrissenheit',[20] being torn between publishers and the uncertainty of their payments. He writes to his wife in 1862:

> Die Schreiberei in dieser Sache, die Spannung auf die zu erwartenden Antworten, das Ruhigabwartenmüssen und der Mißmut, das Geld, was uns vollständig durchgeholfen hätte, unbedacht aus der Hand gegeben zu haben, machen mich geistig völlig stumpf. Ich habe die Lehre empfangen, daß der industriellen Welt gegenüber man nicht zu sehr auf den künstlerischen Wert eines Werkes pochen darf.[21]

These are the words of a man who has learned the hard way that the writer is in 'eine industrielle Welt' and must market his wares accordingly. If indeed we are sometimes dismayed at the lapses of which Storm can occasionally be capable, we should not forget the 'hit-or-miss' nature of his working conditions and the need to produce works against his better inclinations.

But it would surely be one-sided to reduce Storm's variety of output to such urges and constraints. The Novelle of the later nineteenth century had not cast off its traditions and conventions overnight, and Storm's work reflects in its variety—on a small scale—the mass of possibilities open to the writer of this genre, as volume after volume of Heyse's own work demonstrates and the *Novellenschatz* enshrines. The ever publicity-conscious and facilely assiduous Heyse might indeed issue his own Novellen in collections with titles like: 'Helldunkles Leben', 'Menschen und Schicksale', 'Originale', 'Märchen und Spukgeschichten', 'Dorfgeschichten', 'Moralische Novellen', in order to reinforce the multifarious options available to the writer in the second half of the century. In the case of Storm, we have to make the subdivisions for ourselves—or as nearly as we can. For we find him returning at all stages of his forty years as an active writer to different 'tones' of narrative. There is the pattern of reminiscence, for which *Immensee* is the precedent. There are stories involving the family and its structure. There are idylls, and there are 'Märchen' proper and some stories that have a touch of both of these modes. We see an emergent pattern of Novellen dealing with significant moral and social issues of the times. In all of these, Storm may excel or he may fall flat. There is no period of his active career in which this cannot be observed: near-kitsch alongside sheer mastery. For that reason, too, there is a surprising lack of unanimity among critics and literary historians as to which of the over fifty Novellen are the best. And so the remarks which follow inevitably represent a kind of 'personal' Storm and one inviting dissent.

When Storm made his observation to Mörike in 1855 about the respective functions of his lyrical poetry and his prose, he was right in one important respect. In his lyrical poetry, we do indeed have a unity of inner and outer world, experience and 'gebundene Form', personal character and restrained passion. Compared with Heine, or Droste, or Mörike, or Lenau, Storm is notable for the directness of his expression, his avoidance of rhetorical sophistication, of what he calls 'einzelne unzusammenhängende Bilder' or 'sogenannte bilderreiche Sprache'.[22] The directness only rarely comes over into his stories. There is a hesitation to commit himself, to go straight to the heart of the action, to use clear and unmistakable motivation. Storm was aware of the dangers: some of his worst stories—one could apply Heyse's teasing Plattdeutsch 'man swack' (weak stuff) to them[23]—like *Ein Fest auf Haderslevhuus* (1885), try to pack in as much event as possible. When Klaus Groth praised the story *Hans und Heinz Kirch* (1882) for having no 'Raffinement Turgeneffs',[24] he was doubtless glad not to have yet another situation where a narrator introduces a character and is constantly intervening in the story to guide it in a certain direction. Theodor Mommsen, on the other hand, had hoped to find in this archetypal father–son conflict 'die grimme Faust des Schicksals',[25] suggesting a more robust kind of motivation and narrative. Storm's reply is interesting:

Was ist das große Schicksal? Mir scheint es auch dort zu sein, wo zwei solche Naturen als Vater und Sohn sich gegenüber in die Welt gesetzt sind, und der Schlag infolge ihrer Eigenart erfolgt.[26]

Human fate is for Storm not a matter of some guiding force in man's destiny but of individual moments of confrontation between humans. That would be fully acceptable in the case of *Hans und Heinz Kirch* if the characters were in themselves more credible, or at least better motivated, and the situations less stereotyped. A story written one year earlier, *Der Herr Etatsrat*, with a narrator, and a hero of monstrous proportions, comes over much more powerfully because Storm had used that very 'Raffinement Turgeneffs' to good effect. The larger-than-life, scarcely credible Etatsrat who crushes and destroys both of his children between bouts of colossal dipsomania, has somewhat more than an edge over a Hans Kirch. Again, on occasions when Storm does not seem to be trying very hard, he does succeed in producing a story which is convincing or seizes our imagination because there is something improbable about it. The story *Im Nachbarhause links* (1875) is an example. It begins:

'Wenn du es hören willst', sagte mein Freund und streifte mit dem kleinen Finger die Asche von seiner Zigarre. 'Aber die Heldin meiner Geschichte ist nicht gar zu anziehend; auch ist es eigentlich keine Geschichte, sondern nur etwa der Schluß einer solchen.'
'Danke es', versetzte ich, 'unserer heurigen Novellistik, daß mir das letzte jedenfalls besonders angenehm erscheint.'[27]

And ends:

'Und daß es noch dergleichen in der Welt gibt'—so schloß mein Freund seine Erzählung, indem er sich statt der längst in Rauch aufgegangenen eine neue Zigarre anzündete—'das und den Dampf einer guten Importierten, beides finde ich unter Umständen außerordentlich tröstlich.'[28]

It is the ironic rejection of conventional narrative in favour of a reconstruction of a miserly recluse's fantasy world. The ending—a marriage, and a haunted house—parodies further well-tried techniques; but in the process the author has shown his artistic economy by telling this story in a little more than the time needed for a good cigar.

Storm's first major story, *Immensee* (1849/1851), and his last, *Der Schimmelreiter* (1888), apart from being among his very best known, are useful illustrations of the pattern which persisted, evolved or changed in the course of his work. It may even be possible to trace lines of development which lead from one story to the other.

Storm was conscious that in *Immensee* he had written a masterpiece. This work in fact seems to have brought home to him that his prose works need not be regarded as a mere adjunct to his lyrical poetry, but could stand in their own right and in their own terms. Writing to his wife in 1858 from Heiligenstadt, he admits this:

Wir kamen zuletzt auf den Poeten Th. Storm zu sprechen; mit meiner Ansicht, die Gedichte seien das bedeutendste, konnte ich aber nicht durchdringen. Er [Landrat von Wussow] meinte, es ginge mir wie fast allen, daß ich gerade auf mein Bestes den geringsten Wert lege. Immensee, das sei etwas, das den Stempel der Klassizität trage, und das dauern werde, eben wie Fouqués Undine.—Erinnerst Du noch, daß ich neulich gerade dasselbe zu Dir sagte in betreff Immensee, als ich es bei Schlüters vorgelesen hatte?[29]

Storm is right on both counts: that his story has the lineaments of the 'classical', and that it has lasted. The comparison with Fouqué's *Undine*, a 'Taschenbuchnovelle' of 1811, is only true in the sense that that rather trivial and charming little Romantic story has proved a notable survivor. The letter's reference to the relationship between Storm's poetry and his Novelle is interesting in view of his later confession to Erich Schmidt: 'Meine Novellistik ist aus meiner Lyrik erwachsen.'

What makes *Immensee* a classic? Certainly no Kleistian constraints of 'etwas soll geschehen' or Biedermeier claims of 'schildert Alles'. This is a story remarkable in what it manages to *leave out* in terms of event or social comment. Above all, it is the only story which Storm subjected to a major process of revision, between its first being issued in 1849 and its reprinting in 1851. The details of the revision have been discussed very adequately elsewhere,[30] their implications less. We might speculate as to whether Storm, in more favourable circumstances, might not have done the same to advantage with a number of stories. For *Immensee* seems to be of its times in the sense of 'richtiges Weglassen des Unwesentlichen' as an artistic principle of the later nineteenth century.

Generally one can assume that Storm wished the story to consist of incidents, snatches of memory or fragments of the past, linked only by congruent symbols, rather than of a continuous and detailed narrative. Much is therefore left unsaid, and we are left to work out the links and connections. It is a story that works on the level of suggestion rather than of overprinted sign. The interrelation of framework (Reinhard reminiscing) and the lyrical, sentimental, love atmosphere, is not a clear one; there is a fluidity, an associative ease of movement.

For his revised version, Storm has cut down several elements: the student scenes, the Christmas atmosphere, the discussion of folk-song, the reminiscences of Italy, and the motif of Reinhard's later marriage and widowhood. On the one hand, he has excised much that the Biedermeier Novelle throws in by way of extra sentiment, or employs to stress certain social or moral conventions (marriage). On the other, he does not want this story to proceed inexorably, stripped down to essentials, according to an obtrusively strict narrative pattern. It is unlike many later stories in that respect (for instance, *Im Schloss*, *Auf der Universität*); there, the first-person narrator is often able to provide the connections between that which is otherwise incomplete or not wholly congruous. Even some poems by Storm which have similarities with *Immensee* ('Hüben, drüben', 'Ein Sterbender') follow a stricter sequence of events in reminiscence.

One is therefore surprised at what seems to be an almost total, and mannered, commitment to memory, and a narrative style that refuses to be forced into the mere recounting of events but is also sparing of reflection. But then again neither Mörike's *Mozart* nor Grillparzer's *Der arme Spielmann*—written within a few years of this story—wish to be constrained into a straight sequence and deliberately reverse the usual order of happenings. Storm's espousal of reminiscence in *Immensee* is not merely to give some stamp of authenticity, as in some older patterns of the Novelle; it is to keep the narrator, and thus the reader, at several removes from the events. They are no longer left to speak for themselves, but become part of a development now past or overcome, stored only in the subjective area of personal recollection. Nor does Storm stand entirely alone in this. The major European exponent of this technique is Turgenev, whose *Huntsman's Sketches* were already taking shape in the 1840s. Usually, however, Turgenev allows a character to engage the narrator in conversation, out of which the portrayal of incident and character emerges. A writer who does use techniques similar to *Immensee*, in the sense that there are wide gaps between separate areas of reminiscence, is the Dane Steen Steensen Blicher (notably *En Landsbydegns Dagbog* (The Journal of a Parish Clerk), 1824, *Skytten paa Aunsbjerg* (The Gamekeeper at Aunsbjerg), 1839 and *Eneste Barn* (An Only Child), 1842). And there is no reason to suppose that Storm's attitude to Denmark excluded his knowledge of one of its great prose writers.

Like Blicher, and like Turgenev, Storm too has resisted the temptation of casting his story entirely in the language and style of sentiment; nor has he tried to make the lyrical sections of the story the main bearers of sentiment (they are reduced to essentials). Instead, a fairly precise nature description emerges as the symbolic accompaniment of inward, emotional processes: notably the search for the strawberries, and the attempt to secure the waterlily—the elusive flowers and fruits of erotic fulfilment, which the more active and resilient seize and enjoy. Yet in neither of the cases cited from *Immensee* do we notice a complete integration of emotional state and nature depiction. Storm seems, consciously or unconsciously, to introduce atmospheric elements that are not essential parts of the description but which are allusions to an old 'empfindsam' tradition, and to the book of all books in that mode: Goethe's *Werther*.

It is not the *Werther* of madness and death, but of renunciation and parting, that Storm chooses to heighten the atmosphere of his story: as Werther remarks the figure of Lotte disappearing along the avenue of limes, so Reinhard observes at a distance how Elisabeth slips from his view into 'Seitengänge' or 'Laubgänge';[31] and as Werther and Lotte exchange sentiments of 'Wiedersehn', so Elisabeth plays on the words 'Du kommst nicht wieder.'[32] It is sentimentality held in check, at one with the half-lit observations and fleeting glimpses of a beloved who is slipping from Reinhard's grasp. It is a technique that Turgenev's story *First Love* (1860) exploits brilliantly, as figures seen through trees and fleetingly at windows bring home to the hero that his youthful infatuations have been so cruelly deceived.

It is not a sentimentality such as often mars Storm's less successful stories; where potentially tragic situations are averted by means of last-minute conventional devices: reunions, recognitions or reconciliations (as in, for instance, *In St. Jürgen* or *Die Söhne des Senators*); or where the author goes on longer than narrative economy seems to require. One thinks of the otherwise fine story, *Eine Halligfahrt* (1877); the adequacy of symbol, narrative reminiscence and regretful distance is spoiled by the addition of only two or three pages. This lyrical and sentimental tailpiece seems out of place after a story in which the meeting of narrator and Susanne on the trip to the island, the insular intensity of their passion, the flock of seagulls which encircle Susanne as the couple seem to be enmeshed by sexual attraction, achieve an impressive unity in a careful economy of narrative. Storm was, nevertheless, concerned that his stories should not merely conform to a pattern, however successful or 'classical' *Immensee* should have proved. Writing to his wife in 1862 about Berthold Auerbach, the popular writer of 'Dorfgeschichten', he says:

Mitunter ist es einem freilich, als wenn namentlich die beiden Hauptpersonen zu sehr nach einem ausgearbeiteten Plan gemacht wären, als sei dabei der Gedanke und nicht die Anschauung das erste gewesen, man sieht zu sehr das Gerippe unter dem Fleisch [. . .] Auerbach ist vorwiegend Reflexionsmensch; der Gedanke an sich ist aber nicht zeugungsfähig; geistige wie leibliche Kinder können nur im Rausch der Phantasie entstehen; nur bei ihrer Ausbildung kann und muß der Verstand sein Werk verrichten.[33]

But there are occasions when Storm does seem to have chosen a device that is either gratuitous or inappropriate, in order not to give the impression of 'nach einem ausgearbeiteten Plan gemacht'. The well-known *Aquis submersus* of 1876, of which Storm was so proud, is an example. The technique involves the now familiar reminiscence, with a particularly striking introduction: the Bonnix epitaph in the church at Drelsdorf near Husum[34] becomes stylized into something of grim fatality and uncompromising bleakness; the double narrator—the story at two removes—points forward to *Der Schimmelreiter*. But was there any need to interlard the story with archaisms, as if one were supposed actually to be reading a seventeenth-century chronicle? Quite manifestly the story and its implications are not those of the century in which it is cast, and no amount of baroque fustian will make up for that fact. This 'altteutsch' element also detracts from the starkness of the tragedy and introduces something that is almost fairy-tale—and as such, in this context, spurious. This would apply equally to another archaicizing story, *Renate* (1878). It is the negative side of the century's desire for historical authenticity; it comes perilously close to the *faux-ancien* in some of Meyer's stories, and is not the strong point of Fontane's *Grete Minde*.

Another, earlier, story, *Auf dem Staatshof* (1858) seems a much more artistically pleasing resolution of the theme of reminiscence and renunciation, while not following slavishly in the patterns of *Immensee*. Above all, the nature descriptions are better integrated into the general atmosphere of inevitable tragedy and loss than in the early work. Here is an example:

Es war eine laue Nacht; über unsern Köpfen surrten die Nachtschmetterlinge, die den erleuchteten Fenstern des oberen Stockwerks zuflogen; die Luft war ganz von jenem süßen Duft durchwürzt, den in der warmen Sommerzeit die wolligen Blütenkapseln der roten Himbeere auszuströmen pflegen. Anne Lene knüpfte ihr Schnupftuch um den Kopf; dann gingen wir, wie wir es oft getan, um die Ecke des Hauses und über die Werfte nach dem Baumgarten zu. Wir sprachen nicht; ich wollte Anne Lene bitten, ihre Augen wieder nach der Welt zurück zu wenden und nicht mehr in den

Schatten der Vergangenheit zu leben; aber das beunruhigende Bewußtsein einer eigennützigeren Bitte, die ich für günstigere Zeiten im Grunde meines Herzens zurückbehielt, raubte mir den Atem und ließ kein Wort über meine Lippen kommen. Das Herz klopfte mir so laut, daß ich immer fürchtete, es werde auch ohne Worte meine innersten Gedanken kundmachen. Wir gingen durch die kleine Pforte in den Baumgarten hinein, zwischen die schimmernden Stämme der ungeheuren Silberpappeln, deren Laubkronen keinen Lichtstrahl durchließen. Die dürren Zweige, welche überall den Boden bedeckten, knickten unter unsern Füßen; und über uns, von dem Geräusche aufgestört, flogen die Raben von ihren Nestern und rauschten mit den Flügeln in den Blättern. Anne Lene ging schweigend und in sich verschlossen neben mir; ihre Gedanken mochten dort sein, von wo ich sie so sehnlich zurückzurufen wünschte.—So waren wir bis zur Graft hinabgekommen, welche auch hier die Grenze des eigentlichen Hofes bildete.[35]

The former childhood friends, Marx and Anne Lene, try to return to the lost idyll of childhood in the old farmstead, the 'Staatshof', and its romantic, overgrown garden. They are struck by tragedy, as the floor of a garden pavilion at the edge of a 'Graft', a small watercourse, gives way, and Anne Lene is drowned. The passage quoted is not free of convention or cliché: 'laue Nacht', 'Nachtschmetterlinge', 'süßen Duft'. But we soon see how an inner process and the outward manifestations of nature become one in the description: the beautiful summer's night emerges as a world of shades and shadows which hangs over their relationship, the 'Schatten der Vergangenheit'. The features of nature crowd in to create a sense of constriction and threat ('Silberpappeln, deren Laubkronen keinen Lichtstrahl durchließen', 'dürre Zweige', 'Raben'). It has affinities with the passage in Fontane's *Effi Briest* where the restricted space, the loss of light and air, produce the right atmosphere for Effi's moral endangerment and the predatory instincts of Crampas. The inability to communicate, the failure to find words, are all part of one process in *Auf dem Staatshof*; the 'set-piece' romantic nocturne merges into a process where outward nature image and inner uncertainty are one. It is interesting to observe that Storm underlines the total loss of youth, and innocent, but fragile, love, by avoiding the idyllic silver lining of *Immensee*:

Der jetzige Besitzer des Staatshofes ist Claus Peters. Er hat die alte Hauberg niederreißen lassen und ein modernes Wohnhaus an die Stelle gesetzt. Die Wirtschaftsgebäude liegen getrennt daneben.—Er hat recht gehabt, es geht ihm wohl; er liefert die größten Mastochsen zum Transport nach England, in seinen Zimmern stehen die kostbarsten Möbel, und er und seine Juliane glänzen von Gesundheit und Wohlbehagen. Ich aber bin niemals wieder dort gewesen.[36]

It is a step into the modern world, into economic realities, cutting any lingering sentiment brutally short.

A number of stories follow this pattern in extended fashion, making more than a passing reference to socio-economic issues, and now actually integrating them into narration of past event. *Im Schloss* (1861) is a good example. The technique is reminiscent of *Immensee*: sections of remembered happenings, without a continuous narrative structure. But Storm allows an interesting variation that gives the story a unity which the earlier one lacks. The theme is the love of the young heiress and 'gnädige Frau' for her son's tutor, their parting, her lonely penance in the country house, and their eventual reunion. The perspectives shift constantly between the different scenes of childhood: her upbringing amid corridors and mirrors and family portraits, his in the low-ceilinged cottage of the peasantry. Childhood is not an idyll to which one returns in sunny recollection, but a stage of development to be overcome amid the harsher realities of later life. And so there is a rhythm of evocation and the sober, if regretful, awareness of the implications of what one remembers: deprivation, solitariness, denial of one's deepest and most heartfelt wishes. The narrative accordingly moves from the framework to the written reminiscence of the Schlossdame, and back. Music and lyricism are counterbalanced by the return to the coldness of reality and parting.

From the social point of view, Storm makes it clear that for him the old, comfortable notions of 'the rich man in his castle, the poor man at his gate', their estates ordered by heavenly decree, are a deception and a falsehood. Interestingly enough, Storm chose *Die Gartenlaube*, a liberal magazine, for the publication of this story; he was aware, as he wrote to his mother in 1862, that he might well lose such readers from the 'Junkerpartei' as he might have had.[37] This is not the world of Eichendorff's *Das Schloss Dürande* of 1837, where, behind the criticism of pre-revolutionary society, the true and self-evident justification of aristocratic privilege shines through; or Droste's *Die Judenbuche*, where the respective social roles of 'Schlossherr' and forest-dwellers are immutably foreordained, or even the amiable and convivial condescension to genius on the part of the noble family in *Mozart*. Storm's story points rather more in the direction of Ferdinand von Saar's *Schloss Kostenitz* of 1892, where the feudal role of the aristocracy is unsentimentally relegated to the past.

We find Storm in fact turning more and more to the moral and social issues which troubled and disturbed him. *Auf der Universität* (1862), borne along by 'verhaltene Leidenschaft' and a hatred of student 'Korpswirtschaft',[38] succeeds in integrating social concern into the reminiscence of unfulfilled love. This time the narrator is the member of the 'Honoratioren' who recalls his unhappy relationship with a girl from the lower orders, how her aggrieved pride reaches its climax in a magnificent scene on the ice, and how she drifts into raffish student company and into eventual degradation and death. Again, one is impressed by the balance of nature symbolism and social reality, the fleetingly sentimental and the brutally unsentimental. But Storm can also go badly astray when dealing with burning issues of his times. The stories *Schweigen* (1883), with its theme of heredity, and *Ein Bekenntnis* (1887), with euthanasia, while seeming almost to enter into the world of Ibsen or Naturalism, are ruined by the worst recourse to cliché. One feels that *Schweigen* fails because it really contains the material for a novel: its scope suggests the larger form, but its execution rewards us with ill-motivated situations and perfunctory characterization. This may explain Storm's failure to execute the plan for a story *Im Korn*, communicated in some detail in a letter of 1862: 'Ein junger Gutsherr hat die Tochter des Schullehrers verführt unter Eheversprechen . . . '. Again, one feels that the story—it culminates in the landowner finding his dead child among his own cornfields—might well need expansion beyond the scope of a Novelle if its proposed ending in 'Große Erschütterungen, Versöhnung, eine stille Hochzeit'[39] were not to fulfil our worst expectations.

Storm is also capable of great coolness and almost harshness as a narrator. The notable example is *Draussen im Heidedorf* (1871), the story which some commentators take as marking the beginning of Storm's true greatness as a writer.[40] This time the narrator is not called upon so much to recall, as to record. He is the 'Stadtvogt' carrying out his professional duty. It reminds us of the other Storm, writing, in his official capacity, of 'Brandstiftung', 'Moorbrände, Holzdiebstähle', 'Südermarsch-Schafdiebe', 'Leichen, die das Meer aufgeworfen',[41] who could see the justice official and the writer as being 'in gutem Einvernehmen'.[42] In *Draussen im Heidedorf*, the observant town-dweller moves out among the peasantry, taking down evidence, collating his own recollections of persons in the face of new circumstances: the disappearance of a young husband and father from his farm after a history of fatal attraction for a young woman from the village. It is a hard, uncompromising, passionate and bitter world. The bleakness of the landscape prepares us for the tragic inevitability of the story and the bringing home of the man's corpse at nightfall:

> Aber die Gegend wurde anders; die bewachsenen Wälle mit den bebauten Feldern dahinter hörten auf. Statt dessen fuhren wir hart am Rande des sogenannten 'wilden Moors' entlang, das sich derzeit, so weit der Blick reichte, nach Norden hinauszog. Es schien hier, als sei plötzlich der letzte Sonnenschein, der noch auf Erden war, von dieser düsteren Steppe eingeschluckt worden. Zwischen dem schwarzbraunen Heidekraut, oft neben größeren oder kleineren Wassertümpeln, ragten einzelne Torfhaufen aus der öden Fläche; mitunter aus der Luft herab kam der melancholische Schrei des großen Regenpfeifers, der einsam darüber hinflog. Das war alles, was man sah und hörte.[43]

Storm has avoided two extremes, or pitfalls: the peasant idyll, but also the uniformly cruel world of animal-like passion that his Austrian contemporary Ludwig Anzengruber was capable of in his stories of peasant life. We rely on the dispassionate observer from outside to keep us free of both these conventions; there is in his mind a chain of inevitability between the realities of the peasant world, inheritance and property, careful husbanding of land, but also its neglect and loss, as fatal attraction and blind passion enter a man's life.

All these strands which we have traced find their culmination in Storm's last work, and crowning masterpiece, *Der Schimmelreiter* of 1888. There is firstly the expansion of scope almost into the lineaments of a short novel; it is a feature we find in Meyer's *Jürg Jenatsch* (1876) before he finds his 'ideal length', or, conversely and on a smaller scale, in Fontane's *Schach von Wuthenow* as it forms a stage towards the novel *Effi Briest*. But there are several features in *Der Schimmelreiter* that show it to be the result of Storm's own, peculiar preoccupations over a period of twenty-five and more years. There is the local subject, authenticated by personal memory. Nevertheless, although the story was told to the narrator, he is not willing to guarantee its veracity. Mere reminiscence or observation is now not enough. The fact that the story was current 'im Hause meiner Urgroßmutter'—and her name, Feddersen, belongs to Storm's own family—is not enough; for we are at several removes from the events. There is the 'damaliger Erzähler' whose brush with the Schimmelreiter's apparition leads over to the narrative of the schoolmaster, itself a highly selective account and subject to interspersed commentary. The notions of the old 'Aufklärer' who tells the story do not necessarily square with the 'damaliger Erzähler' whose own eyes lead him to be less sceptical about the supernatural. There is no absolute reliability; we are left to put together our own image from various accounts. And—more importantly—the story does not end on a note of 'Spoekenkiekerei' but on the solid ground of Hauke Haien's achievement, the 'Hauke-Haien-Deich'.

The story relies on other techniques for its sense of conviction. Nature—not some kind of preternatural influence—is superior to man, despite his intelligent and energetic attempt to tame the inconstant force of the sea. The sea is the inimical element, associated with threat and loss and death—and also superstition. Hauke Haien's achievement is to win back land from the sea. His whole existence as Deichgraf has to do with his being on a 'Werfte', a raised piece of ground, and while there immune to the ravages of tide and weather. But he is never free from less practical awareness: the old cottager Trin' Jans is also part of his existence and later forms part of his household, referring beyond pragmatic reality to the world of folk belief. Yet Storm refers this superstition, and the apparition of a 'disbelieving' Hauke Haien, to the reliability of the several, contradictory, witnesses. Like other contemporaries, he plays on people's imagination of the uncanny and visionary, their penchant to clothe their inmost doubts and fears in supernatural beliefs: the revenant cat in Leskov's brutal *Lady Macbeth of the Mtsensk District*, the haunted bed in Zola's *Thérèse Raquin*, the fatally vivid imagination of the dead come alive in Fontane's *Unterm Birnbaum* (for even the Naturalist generation could not resist the attractions of a ghost story). The real achievement of Storm's story does not merely lie in its treatment of the supernatural; rather it rests on the mastery of indirect feeling, where no sentimentality, in fact no extraneous feeling of any kind, is admitted; on the lapidary and concentrated style which has no place for relaxed and dreamy reminiscence but relates its description strictly to main character and main plot; on the ability to intersperse a fair amount of technical detail—almost on a Naturalist scale—without detracting from the reader's interest.

Some modern commentators are, however, less apt to link *Der Schimmelreiter* with Naturalism than with the so-called 'Gründerjahre', the years of the foundation of the German nation after 1871.[44] These years, characterized by their brash assertiveness, vulgarity, monumentality, pseudo-classical grandioseness (so it is claimed) find their reflection in Hauke Haien, the know-all *macho*, who ruthlessly manipulates all around him, and is only defeated—but in a grand heroic gesture of almost Bismarckian defiance—by the force of nature itself.[45] A kind of Invictus, 'bloody, but unbow'd', 'I am the master of my fate; I am the captain of my soul'. Even that phrase, 'richtiges Weglassen des Unwesentlichen', which sums up much of the aesthetic of German Realism, was after all coined by a monumentally self-aware painter in the grand Renaissance style, Anselm Feuerbach. There might be an element of truth in all this—but an element at most. For this story can refer, too, to those features of 'programmatischer Realismus' that affirm human values, that see man at work for the benefit of his fellows, as the expression of a humanist ethos and aesthetic, that deplores extremes of religious commitment or political engagement, but that can write more confidently as it feels the benefits of political stability. Above all, such a view would do but little justice to Storm's own agnosticism and melancholy, that saw little lasting in human affairs, but affirmed human values—in marriage, family and friends—for as long as they lasted on earth, until swallowed up by 'de Dod, de allens fritt'. Hauke Haien is not some kind of superman whose Nietzschean will to power leaves its mark in a dike, but a character who can affirm both physical and emotional values, who seizes opportunities (unlike the characters from *Immensee* and *Aquis submersus*) to exploit their potential for himself—and others.

If in Storm's hands the Novelle was no longer the slightly garrulous and commodious genre that it once had been ('schildert Alles'), it could still uphold the claim made earlier in the century that it was 'die berufenste Kunstform, das Höchste darzustellen' and more recently by Heyse, as treating 'die tiefsten und wichtigsten sittlichen Fragen'. Storm, never much given to theoretical statements about others' work or his own, allowed himself to be drawn just once, in 1881, on the subject of the Novelle. It is, however, a statement that he declined to publish in his lifetime (the main points also went into a letter to Gottfried Keller from the same year):

> Die Novelle, wie sie sich in neuerer Zeit, besonders in den letzten Jahrhunderten, ausgebildet hat und jetzt in einzelnen Dichtungen in mehr oder minder vollendeter Durchführung vorliegt, eignet sich zur Aufnahme auch des bedeutendsten Inhalts, und es wird nur auf den Dichter ankommen, auch in dieser Form das Höchste der Poesie zu leisten. Sie ist nicht mehr, wie einst, 'die kurzgehaltene Darstellung einer durch ihre Ungewöhnlichkeit fesselnden und einen überraschenden Wendepunkt darbietenden Begebenheit'; die heutige Novelle ist die Schwester des Dramas und die strengste Form der Prosadichtung. Gleich dem Drama behandelt sie die tiefsten Probleme des Menschenlebens; gleich diesem verlangt sie zu ihrer Vollendung einen im Mittelpunkt stehenden Konflikt, von welchem aus das Ganze sich organisiert, und demzufolge die geschlossenste Form und die Ausscheidung alles Unwesentlichen; sie duldet nicht nur, sie stellt auch die höchsten Forderungen der Kunst.[46]

Storm's 'definition' has never quite achieved the canonicity ascribed to Goethe's, Tieck's and Heyse's. It has, however, been seized on by those who place stress on event, fate, and economy in this kind of narrative prose. And some of Storm's work—but by no means all of it—would seem to bear out what he is saying. Yet we should not entirely forget his unrepentant love of undramatic idylls or his tendency to use the most unfortunate clichés of salon drama to round off his less successful stories. Storm is nevertheless saying that the Novelle may take on the lineaments of dramatic writing because it is 'streng' and 'geschlossen', not self-indulgent like the novel. But, with 'Aufnahme auch des bedeutendsten Inhalts' and 'das Höchste', he is saying that prose writing, not the writing of dramas, can now receive the accolade of the highest form of poetry, with the greatest dignity of subject, not just the old 'caso' or 'Begebenheit'. He is saying what Mundt had already said in 1834: 'die berufenste Kunstform, das Höchste darzustellen'; but that the monopoly, indeed domination, from Schiller to Richard Wagner, of the grand themes, symbolic statements and universal insights, by the drama, is now a thing of the past; that mere attempts to wax Shakespearean or Schillerian—the 1870s and 1880s are full of them—are no guarantee in themselves of potential artistry. It is a proud assertion that prose, in its more economical form, has now achieved full maturity. There is no need to be apologetic when the major issues of the day are being treated with both adequacy and artistry in this medium. It is not a definition of the Novelle as such, but a statement that, in 1881, if not perhaps in 1795, or 1826, or even 1850, the Novelle stands on its own as one of the major achievements of German literature.

Appendix

SELECTED STATEMENTS ON THE THEORY AND PRACTICE OF THE NOVELLE

I. Goethe: *Unterhaltungen deutscher Ausgewanderten* (1795)

Wo sind die schönen und zierlichen Gedichte geblieben, die sonst so oft aus den Brieftaschen unsrer jungen Frauenzimmer zur Freude der Gesellschaft hervorkamen? Wohin haben sich die unbefangenen philosophischen Betrachtungen verloren? Ist die Lust gänzlich verschwunden, mit der ihr von euren Spaziergängen einen merkwürdigen Stein, eine uns wenigstens unbekannte Pflanze, ein seltsames Insekt zurückbrachtet und dadurch Gelegenheit gabt, über den großen Zusammenhang aller vorhandenen Geschöpfe wenigstens angenehm zu träumen? Laßt alle diese Unterhaltungen, die sich sonst so freiwillig darboten, durch eine Verabredung, durch Vorsatz, durch ein Gesetz wieder bei uns eintreten! Bietet alle eure Kräfte auf, lehrreich, nützlich und besonders gesellig zu sein! . . . . . .

'Ich habe nie', fuhr der Alte fort, 'auf das, was ich tue, viel Wert gelegt, denn ich weiß, daß ich gegen andere Menschen ein großer Faulenzer bin; indessen hab ich doch eine Sammlung gemacht, die vielleicht eben jetzt dieser Gesellschaft, wie sie gestimmt ist, manche angenehme Stunde verschaffen könnte.'

'Was ist es für eine Sammlung?' fragte die Baronesse.

'Gewiß nichts weiter als eine skandalöse Chronik,' setzte Luise hinzu.

'Sie irren sich,' sagte der Alte.

'Wir werden sehen,' versetzte Luise.

'Laß ihn ausreden,' sagte die Baronesse; 'und überhaupt gewöhne dir nicht an, einem, der es auch zum Scherze leiden mag, hart und unfreundlich zu begegnen! Wir haben nicht Ursache, den Unarten, die in uns stecken, auch nur im Scherze Nahrung zu geben. Sagen Sie mir, mein Freund, worin besteht Ihre Sammlung? Wird sie zu unsrer Unterhaltung dienlich und schicklich sein? Ist sie schon lange angefangen? Warum haben wir noch nichts davon gehört?'

'Ich will Ihnen hierüber Rechenschaft geben,' versetzte der Alte. 'Ich lebe schon lange in der Welt und habe immer gern auf das achtgegeben, was diesem oder jenem Menschen begegnet. Zur Übersicht der großen Geschichte fühl ich weder Kraft noch Mut, und die einzelnen Weltbegebenheiten verwirren mich; aber unter den vielen Privatgeschichten, wahren und falschen, mit denen man sich im Publikum trägt, die man sich insgeheim einander erzählt, gibt es manche, die noch einen reineren, schönern Reiz haben als den Reiz der Neuheit, manche, die durch eine geistreiche Wendung uns immer zu erheitern Anspruch machen, manche, die uns die menschliche Natur und ihre inneren Verborgenheiten auf einen Augenblick eröffnen, andere wieder, deren sonderbare Albernheiten uns ergetzen. Aus der großen Menge, die im gemeinen Leben unsere Aufmerksamkeit und unsere Bosheit beschäftigen und die ebenso gemein sind als die Menschen, denen sie begegnen oder die sie erzählen, habe ich diejenigen gesammelt, die mir nur irgendeinen Charakter zu haben schienen, die meinen Verstand, die mein Gemüt berührten und beschäftigten und die mir, wenn ich wieder daran dachte, einen Augenblick reiner und ruhiger Heiterkeit gewährten.'

'Ich bin sehr neugierig', sagte die Baronesse, 'zu hören, von welcher Art Ihre Geschichten sind und was sie eigentlich behandeln.'

'Sie können leicht denken,' versetzte der Alte, 'daß von Prozessen und Familienangelegenheiten nicht öfters die Rede sein wird. Diese haben meistenteils nur ein Interesse für die, welche damit geplagt sind.'

Luise. 'Und was enthalten sie denn?'

Der Alte. 'Sie behandeln, ich will es nicht leugnen, gewöhnlich die Empfindungen, wodurch Männer und Frauen verbunden oder entzweit, glücklich oder unglücklich gemacht, öfter aber verwirrt als aufgeklärt werden.'

Luise. 'So? Also wahrscheinlich eine Sammlung lüsterner Späße geben Sie uns für eine feine Unterhaltung? Sie verzeihen mir, Mama, daß ich diese Bemerkung mache; sie liegt so ganz nahe, und die Wahrheit wird man doch sagen dürfen.'

Der Alte. 'Sie sollen, hoffe ich, nichts, was ich lüstern nennen würde, in der ganzen Sammlung finden.' . . .

... durch einige Wendung des Gesprächs kam man auf die entschiedene Neigung unsrer Natur, das Wunderbare zu glauben.

Man redete vom Romanhaften, vom Geisterhaften, und als der Alte einige gute Geschichten dieser Art künftig zu erzählen versprach, versetzte Fräulein Luise: 'Sie wären recht artig und würden vielen Dank verdienen, wenn Sie uns gleich, da wir eben in der rechten Stimmung beisammen sind, eine solche Geschichte vortrügen; wir würden aufmerksam zuhören und Ihnen dankbar sein.'

Ohne sich lange bitten zu lassen, fing der Geistliche darauf mit folgenden Worten an:

'Als ich mich in Neapel aufhielt, begegnete daselbst eine Geschichte, die großes Aufsehen erregte und worüber die Urteile sehr verschieden waren. Die einen behaupteten, sie sei völlig ersonnen, die andern, sie sei wahr, aber es stecke ein Betrug dahinter. Diese Partei war wieder untereinander selbst uneinig; sie stritten, wer dabei betrogen haben könnte. Noch andere behaupteten, es sei keineswegs ausgemacht, daß geistige Naturen nicht sollten auf Elemente und Körper wirken können, und man müsse nicht jede wunderbare Begebenheit ausschließlich entweder für Lüge oder Trug erklären. Nun zur Geschichte selbst!'...

'Doch wenn Sie uns eine Geschichte zur Probe geben wollen, so muß ich Ihnen sagen, welche Art ich nicht liebe. Jene Erzählungen machen mir keine Freude, bei welchen nach Weise der 'Tausendundeinen Nacht' eine Begebenheit in die andere eingeschachtelt, ein Interesse durch das andere verdrängt wird, wo sich der Erzähler genötigt sieht, die Neugierde, die er auf eine leichtsinnige Weise erregt hat, durch Unterbrechung zu reizen und die Aufmerksamkeit, anstatt sie durch eine vernünftige Folge zu befriedigen, nur durch seltsame und keineswegs lobenswürdige Kunstgriffe aufzuspannen. Ich tadle das Bestreben, aus Geschichten, die sich der Einheit des Gedichts nähern sollen, rhapsodische Rätsel zu machen und den Geschmack immer tiefer zu verderben. Die Gegenstände Ihrer Erzählungen gebe ich Ihnen ganz frei; aber lassen Sie uns wenigstens an der Form sehen, daß wir in guter Gesellschaft sind. Geben Sie uns zum Anfang eine Geschichte von wenig Personen und Begebenheiten, die gut erfunden und gedacht ist, wahr, natürlich und nicht gemein, soviel Handlung als unentbehrlich und soviel Gesinnung als nötig, die nicht still steht, sich nicht auf einem Flecke zu langsam bewegt, sich aber auch nicht übereilt, in der die Menschen erscheinen, wie man sie gern mag, nicht vollkommen, aber gut, nicht außerordentlich, aber interessant und liebenswürdig. Ihre Geschichte sei unterhaltend, solange wir sie hören, befriedigend, wenn sie zu Ende ist, und hinterlasse uns einen stillen Reiz, weiter nachzudenken.'

II. Friedrich Schlegel: *Nachricht von den poetischen Werken des Johannes Boccaccio* (1801)

Die subjektive Beschaffenheit oder Beziehung fast aller Werke des Boccaz fällt in die Augen. Nehmen wir nun an, daß dies an sich nicht fehlerhaft, daß es vielmehr die eigentliche, also richtige Tendenz seiner Kunst war, das Subjektive mit tiefster Wahrheit und Innigkeit rein ans Licht zu stellen, oder in klaren Sinnbildern heimlich anzudeuten, so wird es begreiflich, daß sie gerade in der FIAMMETTA in ihrem höchsten Glanze erscheint; und wenn es uns gelingt, den Charakter der Novelle mit diesem Begriff von der Tendenz des Künstlers in Beziehung zu setzen, so werden wir einen Mittelpunkt und gemeinschaftlichen Gesichtspunkt für alle seine Werke gefunden haben, die man ganz richtig nur als Annäherungen und Vorbereitungen zur FIAMMETTA oder zur Novelle, oder als unwillkürliche Verbindungsversuche und zwischen beiden schwankende und schwebende Mittelglieder betrachten würde.

Ich behaupte, die Novelle ist sehr geeignet, eine subjektive Stimmung und Ansicht, und zwar die tiefsten und eigentümlichsten derselben indirekt und gleichsam sinnbildlich darzustellen. Ich könnte mich auf Beispiele berufen und könnte fragen: Warum sind denn unter den Novellen des Cervantes, obgleich alle schön sind, einige dennoch so entschieden schöner? Durch welchen Zauber erregen sie unser Innerstes und ergreifen es mit göttlicher Schönheit, als durch den, daß überall das Gefühl des Dichters, und zwar die innerste Tiefe seiner eigensten Eigentümlichkeit sichtbar unsichtbar durchschimmert, oder weil er wie im CURIOSO IMPERTINENTE Ansichten darin ausgedrückt hat, die eben ihrer Eigentümlichkeit und Tiefe wegen entweder gar nicht oder nur so ausgesprochen werden konnten? Warum steht der ROMEO auf einer höhern Stufe als andre dramatisierte Novellen desselben Dichters, als weil er in jugendliche Begeisterung ergossen in ihm mehr als in jeder andern ein schönes Gefäß für diese fand, so daß er ganz davon angefüllt und durchdrungen werden konnte?—Auch bedarf es keiner Auseinandersetzung, um zu zeigen, daß diese indirekte Darstellung des Subjektiven für manche Fälle angemessener und schicklicher sein kann, als die unmittelbare lyrische, ja daß gerade das Indirekte und Verhüllte in dieser Art der Mitteilung ihr einen höhern Reiz leihen mag. Auf ähnliche Weise ist die Novelle selbst zu dieser indirekten und verborgenen Subjektivität vielleicht eben darum besonders geschickt, weil sie übrigens sich sehr zum Objektiven neigt, und wiewohl sie das Lokale und das Costum gerne mit Genauigkeit bestimmt, es dennoch gern im allgemeinen hält, den Gesetzen und Gesinnungen der feinen Gesellschaft gemäß, wo sie ihren Ursprung und ihre Heimat hat; weshalb sie auch in jenem Zeitalter vorzüglich blühend gefunden wird, wo Rittertum, Religion und Sitten den edlern Teil von Europa vereinigten.

Aber es läßt sich diese Eigenschaft der Novelle auch aus ihrem ursprünglichen Charakter unmittelbar deduzieren. Es ist die Novelle eine Anekdote, eine noch unbekannte Geschichte, so erzählt, wie man sie in Gesellschaft erzählen würde, eine Geschichte, die an und für sich schon einzeln interessieren können muß, ohne irgend auf den Zusammenhang der Nationen, oder der Zeiten, oder auch auf die Fortschritte der Menschheit und das Verhältnis zur Bildung derselben zu sehen. Eine Geschichte also, die streng genommen, nicht zur Geschichte gehört, und die Anlage zur Ironie schon in der Geburtsstunde mit auf die Welt bringt. Da sie interessieren soll, so muß sie in ihrer Form irgendetwas enthalten, was vielen merkwürdig oder lieb sein zu können verspricht. Die Kunst des Erzählens darf nur etwas höher steigen, so wird der Erzähler sie entweder dadurch zu zeigen suchen, daß er mit einem angenehmen Nichts, mit einer Anekdote, die, genaugenommen, auch nicht einmal eine Anekdote wäre, täuschend zu unterhalten und das, was im Ganzen ein Nichts ist, dennoch durch die Fülle seiner Kunst so reichlich zu schmücken weiß, daß wir uns willig täuschen, ja wohl gar ernstlich dafür interessieren lassen. Manche Novellen im DECAMERONE, die bloß Späße und Einfälle sind, besonders in dem letzten provinziell-florentinischen Teile desselben gehören zu dieser Gattung, deren schönste und geistreichste der LICENCIADO VIDRIERA von Cervantes sein dürfte. Aber da man es selbst in der besten feinen Gesellschaft mit dem was erzählt wird, wenn nur die Art anständig, fein und bedeutend ist, nicht eben so genau zu nehmen pflegt, so liegt der Keim zu diesem Auswuchs schon in dem Ursprunge der Novelle überhaupt. Doch kann es eigentlich nie allgemeine Gattung werden, so reizend es auch als einzelne Laune des Künstlers sein mag, denn diese würde, wenn sie förmlich konstituiert und häufig wiederholt würde, eben dadurch ihren eigentümlichen Reiz verlieren müssen. Der andre Weg, der sich dem künstlichern Erzähler, dem vielleicht schon die ersten Blüten vorweggenommen sind, zeigt, ist der, daß er auch bekannte Geschichten durch die Art, wie er sie erzählt und vielleicht umbildet, in neue zu verwandeln scheine. Es werden sich ihm eine große Menge darbieten, die etwas objektiv Merkwürdiges und mehr oder weniger allgemein Interessantes haben. Was anders soll die Auswahl aus der Menge bestimmen, als die subjektive Anneigung, die sich allemal auf einen mehr oder minder vollkommnen Ausdruck einer eignen Ansicht, eines eignen Gefühles gründen wird? Und welchem Erzähler einzelner Geschichten ohne innern, weder historischen noch mythischen Zusammenhang, würden wir wohl lange mit Interesse zuhören, wenn wir uns nicht für ihn selbst zu interessieren anfingen? Man isoliere diese natürliche Eigenheit der Novelle, man gebe ihr die höchste Kraft und Ausbildung, und so entsteht jene oben erwähnte Art derselben, die ich die allegorische nennen möchte, und die wenigstens, mag man sie so oder anders bezeichnen sollen, sich immer als der Gipfel und die eigentliche Blüte der ganzen Gattung bewähren wird. . . .

Da die Poesie bei den Neuern anfangs nur wild wachsen konnte, weil die ursprüngliche und natürlichste Quelle derselben, die Natur und der Enthusiasmus für die unmittelbare Idee derselben in der Anschauung göttlicher Wirksamkeit, entweder gewaltsam verschlossen war, oder doch nur sparsam sich ergoß: so mußte, den Trennungen der Stände und des Lebens gemäß, neben der Romanze, die Helden- und Kriegsgeschichten für alle, und der Legende, die Heiligengeschichten für das Volk sang oder erzählte, auch die Novelle in der modernen Poesie notwendiger Weise entstehen mit und für die feine Gesellschaft der edlern Stände.

Da die Novelle ursprünglich Geschichte ist, wenn auch keine politische oder Kulturgeschichte, und wenn sie es nicht ist, dieses nur als erlaubte, vielleicht notwendige, aber immer doch nur einzelne Ausnahme angesehen werden muß: so ist auch die historische Behandlung derselben in Prosa mit dem Styl eines Boccaz die ursprünglichste; welches gar nicht gegen die mögliche Dramatisierung vielleicht aller Novellen streiten soll; aber doch demjenigen, der der Gegenstand dieses Versuchs war, den Ruhm vindizieren kann, als Vater und Meister der Gattung zu gelten.

III. August Wilhelm Schlegel: *Geschichte der romantischen Litteratur* (1803)

Deswegen muß es nun auch in der modernen Poesie eine eigenthümlich historische Gattung geben, deren Verdienst darin besteht, etwas zu erzählen, was in der eigentlichen Historie keinen Platz findet, und dennoch allgemein interessant ist. Der Gegenstand der Historie ist das fortschreitende Wirken des Menschengeschlechts; der jener wird also dasjenige seyn, was immerfort geschieht, der tägliche Weltlauf, aber freylich damit er verdiene aufgezeichnet zu werden. Die Gattung, welche sich dieß vornimmt, ist die Novelle, und hieraus läßt sich einsehen, daß sie, um ächt zu seyn, von der einen Seite durch seltsame Einzigkeit auffallen, von der andern Seite eine gewisse allgemeine Gültigkeit haben muß, wie man denn leicht bemerken kann, daß viele der besten und wahrhaft unsterbliche Geschichten in allen Ländern und Zeiten erzählt werden, als gerade dort und dann geschehen, worin man auch in einem gewissen Sinne unstreitig Recht hat. Da nun die Novelle Erfahrung von wirklich geschehenen Dingen mittheilen soll, so ist die ihr ursprünglich und wesentlich eigne Form die Prosa. . . .

Etwas anders ist es mit der Dramatisirung von Novellen. Dieß ist von den größten Meistern, namentlich Shakspeare, vielfältig geschehen, und zwar theils so, daß er sie durchgehends unverändert gelassen, wie z.B. Romeo und Julie, theils daß er sie nach eignen und tiefern Absichten fast in allen Umständen umgebildet. Es kann das Drama dadurch einen eignen geheimnißvollen Reiz gewinnen, daß der Dichter seine Erfindung begränzt und eine bedingte Aufgabe sich zur Lösung vorsetzt. Möglich mag es vielleicht seyn, alle Novellen zu dramatisiren, und dieß könnte vielleicht, bey der Nothwendigkeit im Dramatischen gründlicher und detaillirter zu motiviren, eine Probe der Richtigkeit abgeben. Keinesweges aber möchte ich behaupten, daß jede Novelle die bequeme Empfänglichkeit für die Dramatische Form sogleich solle ansehen lassen; denn es könnten zufällige Äußerlichkeiten im Wege stehn. So viel ist gewiß: die Novelle bedarf entscheidender Wendepunkte, so daß die Hauptmassen der Geschichte deutlich in die Augen fallen, und dieß Bedürfniß hat auch das Drama. Mit leisen und allmähligen Fortschritten und Veränderungen bloß in den innern Verhältnissen der Personen zu einander ist es nicht gethan, diese bleiben der ausführlichen Darstellung des Romans billig vorbehalten, denn sie fodern eine graduelle Entwickelung: und hiebey ist keine andre Wahl als die höchste Feinheit zu erreichen, wie es z.b. im Don Quixote geschehen, oder gänzlich insipide und langweilig zu werden. In der Novelle muß etwas geschehen; ein dreister energischer Charakter der Sitten ist ihr daher vortheilhaft und es läßt sich mehr als bezweifeln, ob es in unsern Zeiten, wo das Leben sich in lauter Kleinlichkeiten zerbröckelt, und fast niemand eigentlich das Herz hat unbekümmert nach seinem Sinne zu leben, möglich seyn dürfte, eine solche Masse von Novellen aufzubringen, die in unsern Sitten gegründet und der Denkart des Zeitalters angemessen wären, als die unter den Boccazischen sind, welche einen historischen Grund haben und das damalige Zeitalter schildern. Man wird vielleicht, bey der Anstößigkeit der meisten dieser Geschichten, hievon Gelegenheit nehmen, die Fortschritte unsers Zeitalters in der geselligen Ordnung, Sittlichkeit und Anständigkeit zu rühmen; allein es ist weiter nichts als daß jenes derber, rüstiger, gesunder ist, und daß heut zu Tage sogar die Verderbniß ins Kränkeln gekommen und keine Energie mehr hat. . . .

   Um eine Novelle gut zu erzählen, muß man das alltägliche, was in die Geschichte mit eintritt, so kurz als möglich abfertigen, und nicht unternehmen es auf ungehörige Art aufstutzen zu wollen, nur bey dem Außerordentlichen und Einzigen verweilen, aber auch dieses nicht motivirend zergliedern, sondern es eben positiv hinstellen, und Glauben dafür fodern. Das Unwahrscheinlichste darf dabey nicht vermieden werden, vielmehr ist es oft gerade das Wahrste, und also ganz an seiner Stelle. An die materielle Wahrscheinlichkeit d.h. die Bedingungen der Wirklichkeit eines Vorfalls, muß sich der Erzähler durchaus binden, hier erfodert sein Zweck die größte Genauigkeit.

   Die politische Historie ist ein sehr ernstes Studium, welches Anstrengung des Geistes fodert; die Novelle, als ein poetisches Gegenbild derselben, ist vielmehr der Erhohlung gewidmet, die Unterhaltung muß in der Erscheinung oben auf seyn, und die Belehrung sich nur von selbst einstellen. Die Erfahrungen des geselligen Lebens sind eine der beliebtesten und angemessensten Unterhaltungen in der Gesellschaft; deswegen ist das eigentliche

Muster für den Vortrag der Novelle der gebildete gesellige Erzähler, natürlich mit derjenigen Freyheit der Erhöhung des natürlichen Urbildes, welche der Poesie überall zugestanden wird. Schon die *Trouveres*, als Dichter der *Fabliaux*, waren gesellige Erzähler, aber freylich bezahlte Lustigmacher. Boccaz hat die Novelle gleich zusammen mit ihrer gebührenden Umgebung, nämlich einem anmuthigen geselligen Zirkel, und als den Gipfel der Unterhaltung dargestellt.

Die Novelle kann von ernsten Begebenheiten mit tragischer Katastrophe bis zur bloßen Posse alle Töne durchlaufen, aber immer soll sie in der wirklichen Welt zu Hause seyn, deswegen liebt sie auch die ganz bestimmten Angaben von Ort, Zeit und Namen der Personen. Daher muß sie den Menschen in der Regel nach seinem Naturstande nehmen, d.h. mit allen den Schwächen, Leidenschaften und selbstischen Trieben, welche der ungeläuterten Natur anhängen. Sie soll den Weltlauf schildern, wie er ist; sie darf also die Motive im allgemeinen nicht über Gebühr veredeln. Giebt sie dadurch Anstoß? Man kann erwiedern: die Welt ist durchaus anstößig für den, der ihr Treiben so geradehin für ein Muster der Nachfolge annehmen wollte. Es giebt dafür kein andres Gegenmittel als der verständige Blick und die überlegne Ansicht, und diese ist es eben, welche der Novellist hervorrufen will, indem er die Gemeinheit der Motive keinesweges verkleidet. Aber warum, könnte man wieder einwenden, muß denn die Sittsamkeit so häufig verletzt, warum die ganze scandalöse Chronik ausgekramt werden?—Ich weiß wohl, daß sich Cervantes bey seinen Novellen strengere Gesetze aufgelegt, und werde noch Gelegenheit haben von diesem preiswürdigen Streben zu reden. Allein wie meisterlich er auch die Schwierigkeit zu umgehen weiß, und sich in diesen Fesseln bewegt, so ist doch nicht zu läugnen, daß die Gattung dadurch sehr beschränkt worden, ja hier und da in der That ins manierirte gefallen ist, man nehme z.B. den *Zeloso Estremeno*.— Die Sache verhält sich so. Die Novelle ist eine Geschichte außer der Geschichte, sie erzählt folglich merkwürdige Begebenheiten, die gleichsam hinter dem Rücken der bürgerlichen Verfassungen und Anordnungen vorgefallen sind. Dazu gehören theils seltsame bald günstige bald ungünstige Abwechselungen des Glücks, theils schlaue Streiche, zur Befriedigung der Leidenschaften unternommen. Das erste giebt hauptsächlich die tragischen und ernsten, das letzte die komischen Novellen.

IV. Ludwig Tieck: preface to volume XI of *Ludwig Tieck's Schriften* (1829)

Im vierzehnten Bande befindet sich die Novelle *der Geheimnißvolle*, die, ob sie schon nach 1819 geschrieben wurde, doch in diese Sammlung aufgenommen ist. Der Kenner sieht vielleicht, daß der Gegenstand ursprünglich zu einer Comödie bestimmt war, die letzte Entwickelung nämlich. Nachher, als ich es zu einer Erzählung umschuf, mußte das dramatische Element zurücktreten, und die ersten zwei Drittheile, die mir im erzählenden Vortrage nothwendig schienen, wurden hinzugefügt.

Wir brauchen jetzt das Wort Novelle für alle, besonders kleineren Erzählungen; manche Schriftsteller scheinen sogar in diese Benennung eine Entschuldigung legen zu wollen, wenn ihnen selbst die Geschichte, die sie vortragen wollen, nicht bedeutend genug erscheint. Was wir mit dem Roman bezeichnen wollen, wissen wir jetzt so ziemlich; aber der Engländer nennt schon seit lange alle seine Romane Novellen. Als das Wort zuerst unter den Italiänern aufkam, sollte es wohl jede Erzählung, jeden Vorfall bezeichnen, die neu noch nicht bekannt waren. So wurde der Name fortgebraucht, und die Italiäner zeichneten sich dadurch aus, daß ihre meisten Geschichten, die sie gaben, anstößig, obscön oder lüstern waren. Unzucht, Ehebruch, Verführung, mit lustigem Geist, sehr oft ohne alles moralisches Gefühl vorgetragen, nicht selten bittre Satyre und Verhöhnung der Geistlichen, die seit Boccaz, um so mehr sie regieren wollten, um so mehr von den Witzigen verspottet wurden, ist der Inhalt der meisten dieser Novellen. Als Cervantes seinem züchtigern Volke, das unter einer strengen geistlichen Polizei stand, Novellen geben wollte, mußte er diesem ärgerlichen Titel das Beiwort moralisch hinzufügen, um anzuzeigen, daß sie nicht im Tone jener italiänischen seyn sollten.

Boccaz, Cervantes und Göthe sind die Muster in dieser Gattung geblieben, und wir sollten billig nach den Vorbildern, die in dieser Art für vollendet gelten können, das Wort Novelle nicht mit Begebenheit, Geschichte, Erzählung, Vorfall, oder gar Anecdote als gleichbedeutend brauchen. Das Wort Humor entstand gegen 1600 bei den Engländern zufällig, und jetzt können wir es in unsern Kunstlehren nicht mehr entbehren, um Productionen und eine Eigenschaft des Geistes zu bezeichnen, die weder mit Laune, Geist noch Witz charakterisirt sind. Eine Begebenheit sollte anders vorgetragen werden, als eine Erzählung; diese sich von Geschichte unterscheiden, und die Novelle nach jenen Mustern sich dadurch aus allen andern Aufgaben hervorheben, daß sie einen großen oder kleinern Vorfall in's hellste Licht stelle, der, so leicht er sich ereignen kann, doch wunderbar, vielleicht einzig ist. Diese Wendung der Geschichte, dieser Punkt, von welchem aus sie sich unerwartet völlig umkehrt, und doch natürlich, dem Charakter und den Umständen angemessen, die Folge entwickelt, wird sich der Phantasie des Lesers um so fester einprägen, als die Sache, selbst im Wunderbaren, unter andern Umständen wieder alltäglich sein könnte. So erfahren wir es im Leben selbst, so sind die Begebenheiten, die [,] uns von Bekannten aus ihrer Erfahrung mitgetheilt, den tiefsten und bleibendsten Eindruck machen.

Um uns an ein Beispiel zu erinnern. So ist in jener Göthischen Novelle in den Ausgewanderten, der sich aufhebende Ladentisch, der das Schloß überflüssig macht, welches der junge Mann eine Zeitlang benutzt, um sich mit Geld zu versehen, ein solcher alltäglicher und doch wunderbarer Vorfall, eben so wie die Reue und Besserung des Jünglings, die in eine Zeit fällt, daß sie fast unnütz wird. Das sonderbare Verhältniß der Sperata im Meister, ist wunderbar und doch natürlich, wie dessen Folgen; in jeder Novelle des Cervantes ist ein solcher Mittelpunkt.

Bizarr, eigensinnig, phantastisch, leicht witzig, geschwätzig und sich ganz in Darstellung auch von Nebensachen verlierend, tragisch wie komisch, tiefsinnig und neckisch, alle diese Farben und Charaktere läßt die ächte Novelle zu, nur wird sie immer jenen sonderbaren auffallenden Wendepunkt haben, der sie von allen andern Gattungen der Erzählung unterscheidet. Aber alle Stände, alle Verhältnisse der neuen Zeit, ihre Bedingungen und Eigenthümlichkeiten sind dem klaren dichterischen Auge gewiß nicht minder zur Poesie und edlen Darstellung geeignet, als es dem Cervantes seine Zeit und Umgebung war, und es ist wohl nur Verwöhnung einiger vorzüglichen Critiker, in der Zeit selbst einen unbedingten Gegensatz vom Poetischen und Unpoetischen anzunehmen. Gewinnt jene Vorzeit für uns an romantischem Interesse, so können wir dagegen die Bedingungen unsers Lebens und der Zustände desselben um so klarer erfassen.

Es wird sich auch anbieten, daß Gesinnung, Beruf und Meinung, im Contrast, im Kampf der handelnden Personen sich entwickeln, und dadurch selbst in Handlung übergehen. Dies scheint mir der ächten Novelle vorzüglich geeignet, wodurch sie ein individuelles Leben erhält. Eröffnet sich hier für Räsonnement, Urtheil und verschiedenartige Ansicht eine Bahn, auf welcher durch poetische Bedingungen das klar und heiter in beschränktem Rahmen anregen und überzeugen kann, was so oft unbeschränkt und unbedingt im Leben als Leidenschaft und Einseitigkeit verletzt, weil es durch die Unbestimmtheit nicht überzeugt und dennoch lehren und bekehren will, so kann auch die Form der Novelle jene sonderbare Casuistik in ein eigenes Gebiet spielen, jenen Zwiespalt des Lebens, der schon die frühesten Dichter und die griechische tragische Bühne in ihrem Beginn begeisterte. So hat man wohl dasjenige, was sich vor dem Auge des Geistes und Gewissens, noch weniger vor der Satzung der Moral und des Staates nicht ausgleichen läßt, Schicksal genannt, um die Streitfrage vermittelst der Phantasie und der religiösen Weihe in einen höhern Standpunkt hinaufzurücken; Orest vom Gott der Weissagung begeistert, wird Muttermörder, und als solcher vom ältesten und einfachsten Naturgefühl in der Gestalt der Erynnien verfolgt, bis Gott und Mensch ihn frei sprechen. Und wie der Dichter hier das Geheimnißvolle zwar klar, menschlich und göttlich zugleich, aber doch wieder durch ein Geheimniß ausgleichen will: so ist in allen Richtungen des Lebens und Gefühls ein Unauflösbares, dessen sich immer wieder die Dichtkunst, wie sie sich auch in Nachahmung und Darstellung zu ersättigen scheint, bemächtigt, um den todten Buchstaben der gewöhnlichen Wahrheit neu zu beleben und zu erklären. Strebt die Tragödie durch Mitleid, Furcht, Leidenschaft und Begeistrung uns in himmlischer Trunkenheit auf den Gipfel des Olymp zu heben, um von klarer Höhe das Treiben der Menschen und den Irrgang ihres Schicksals mit erhabenem Mitleid zu sehn und zu verstehn; führt uns der Roman der Wahlverwandtschaften in die Labyrinthe des Herzens, als Tragödie des Familienlebens und der neuesten Zeit; so kann die Novelle zuweilen auf ihrem Standpunkt die Widersprüche des Lebens lösen, die Launen des Schicksals erklären, den Wahnsinn der Leidenschaft verspotten, und manche Räthsel des Herzens, der Menschenthorheit in ihre künstlichen Gewebe hinein bilden, daß der lichter gewordene Blick auch hier im Lachen oder in Wehmuth, das Menschliche, und im Verwerflichen eine höhere ausgleichende Wahrheit erkennt. Darum ist es dieser Form der Novelle auch vergönnt, über das gesetzliche Maas hinweg zu schreiten, und Seltsamkeiten unpartheiisch und ohne

Bitterkeit darzustellen, die nicht mit dem moralischen Sinn, mit Convenienz oder Sitte unmittelbar in Harmonie stehn. Es läßt sich ohne Zweifel das Meiste und Beste im Boccaz nicht nur entschuldigen, sondern auch rechtfertigen, was niemand wohl mit den spätern italiänischen Novellisten versuchen möchte.

Ich habe hiermit nur andeuten wollen, warum ich im Gegensatz früherer Erzählungen verschiedene meiner neueren Arbeiten *Novellen* genannt habe.

V. Theodor Mundt: *Moderne Lebenswirren* (1834)

Ich für mein Theil wende daher die Frage wieder auf das Zeitgemäße hin, und frage, welche poetische Kunstform am meisten in der Richtung der Zeit begründet liege? Es ist die Novelle. Das Drama ist einer kunstgerechteren Form fähig, es ist vielleicht der schönste Gipfel eines künstlerisch gefügten Organismus, der Triumph einer vollendeten Architektonik der Poesie. Aber darauf kommt es in diesem Augenblick nicht an, es kommt auf die Lebensperspectiven an, welche die Poesie vor den Augen der Zeit aufthun soll. Und dafür ist die Novelle biegsamer, weil sie unbegränzter ist, und mit einer großen Keckheit der Darstellung in alle Gebiete des innern und äußern Lebens übergreifen kann. Das Drama ist zu feierlich gemessen, zu thatenmuthig und unmittelbar heraustretend für den heutigen Tag; man muß die Deutschen mit der Novelle fangen. Die Novelle nistet sich noch am meisten in Stuben und Familien ein, sitzt mit zu Tische und belauscht das Abendgespräch, und man kann da dem Herrn Papa zur guten Stunde etwas unter die Nachtmütze schieben oder dem Herrn Sohn bei gemächlicher Pfeife eine Richtung einflüstern, die vielleicht einmal für die ganze Nation Folgen haben mag. Die Novelle ist ein herrliches Ährenfeld für die politische Allegorie, wozu sie noch viel zu wenig angebaut ist. Man muß große Lebensgebilde erträumen und sie in Novellenform den Deutschen auf's Zimmer schicken. Sie sind zu faul, sich anzuziehn, und selbst hinauszugehn zum Drama; sie können im Drama nur Kotzebue vertragen, der ihnen ihre eigene Deutsche Misère jeden Abend lustig einrührte. Man kann auch auf die Deutschen nicht wirken, wenn sie in Schauspielhäusern sitzen. Sie sind da entweder nur modisch aufgelegt, denn sie fühlen sich im Zusammensein nie als eine Nation, oder es graut sie heimlich untereinander vor der Öffentlichkeit, in der sie sich da gegenübersehen, und man darf ihnen in diesem Zustande kein erregendes Wort sagen, weil sie es gleich von wegen der offenbaren Öffentlichkeit als gefahrbringend einsehn. Draußen vor dem Schauspielhause ist auch Gensdarmerie und Polizei aufgestellt, und behüten das Drama. Die Novelle steht sich mit der Polizei besser, und sie flüchtet sich auf die Stube, wo es keine Gensdarmerie gibt. In seiner Stube ist der Deutsche auch ein ganz anderer Mensch, da kann man mit ihm reden. Hier sitzt er still und läßt sich gern für Alles begeistern, er glaubt an die Freiheit, und schwört auf ein höheres Nationalleben. Er sieht ein, wo ihm Unrecht geschieht und Recht widerfahren muß. Er ist ein vorzüglicher Mensch. Er schaut fast so aus, als könnte ihn die Weltgeschichte noch einmal brauchen. Er nimmt sich wirklich wie ein Mann aus, der Augen, Ohren, Mund und Nase hat. In dieser seiner glücklichen Stimmung muß ihn die Novelle zu Hause zu treffen suchen, sie muß sich in diese einschleichen oder sie aufrufen in ihm. Mitten in der Trägheit der Novellenleserei, wo er recht zu faullenzen glaubt, muß sie ihm einen Floh in's Ohr setzen, und muß ihn allmählig durch Gebilde eines glückseeligeren, kräftigeren, hochherzigeren Lebens überraschen, daß er vor Ungeduld und Sehnsucht ganz unbändig wird. So fasse ich die Novelle als Deutsches Hausthier auf, und als solches ist sie mir jetzt die berufenste Kunstform, das Höchste darzustellen. Ich säe und ärnte auf ihrem Acker meine schönsten Hoffnungen.

VI. Paul Heyse: *An Frau Toutlemonde in Berlin* (1869)

Sie werden mich nicht so mißverstehen, verehrte Frau, als wollte ich aus der Poesie einen idealen Bagno machen, der alle causes célèbres, alle pikanten Verbrecher versammelte. Die Zeit der Räuberromane, der 'Geheimnisse' von Paris, London und Philadelphia ist Gottlob vorüber. Eben so wenig dürfen Sie mir die Meinung unterschieben, als ob ich nur das für poesiefähig hielte, was sich außerhalb der guten Gesellschaft gestellt hat [. . .]. Das Bild des Friedens, der schlichten Treue, der idyllischen Beschränktheit hat so viel Recht, einen Maler zu finden, als die heroischesten Kämpfe tragischer Naturen. Das braucht Ihnen ein so warmer Verehrer Fritz Reuter's, wie Schreiber dieses seit der *Franzosentid* gewesen ist, nicht erst zu versichern. Nur daß man, weil dies schlichte 'Ja Ja und Nein Nein' gut und erfreulich ist, nicht glaube, was darüber ist, sei vom Uebel. Der Kreis der sittlichen Aufgaben ist mit den zehn Geboten nicht abgeschlossen; Vieles ist, was nicht geschrieben steht, wofür die Pfundwage der alltäglichen Moral nicht ausreicht, und wo ein Komödiant einen Pfarrer lehren könnte.

Fälle dieser Art darzustellen ist von jeher die Aufgabe der Novelle gewesen, die in der unscheinbaren Form, in der sie zunächst bei den romanischen Völkern auftrat, sehr geeignet war, theils wirklich Geschehenes, theils Erfundenes mitzutheilen, was nur als Ausnahme gelten wollte, während für die höheren Formen der Poesie, zumal das Drama, das auf den sympathischen Wiederhall der großen Menge angewiesen ist, alles Problematische, nur relativ Gültige bedenklich schien. Aber auch die künstlerisch anspruchsvollere *moderne* Novelle hat es sich immer herausgenommen, bedeutsame Ausnahmsfälle zu verzeichnen, um so mehr, da ja auch die große Poesie in ihren erhabensten Schöpfungen häufig den Gegensatz des Einzelnen gegen das Allgemeine betont, das den Alten als Schicksal, den Modernen als sociale Weltordnung erscheint.

Sämmtliche Geschichten [. . .], die mein übelberufener siebenter Band enthält, haben mit jenen tragischen Problemen den aristokratischen Familienzug gemein, daß die handelnden Personen es anders machen, als unter denselben Umständen die große Mehrheit der Menschen es gemacht haben würde.

VII. Paul Heyse: preface to *Deutscher Novellenschatz* (1871)

Aber—trotz der glänzenden Nachfolge Heinrich's von Kleist—erst seit 1822, in welchem Jahre Tieck mit seiner ersten Novelle hervortrat, datirt der Aufschwung dieser Gattung bei uns. Die große Wirkung, welche Tieck's Novellen auf ihre Mitwelt ausgeübt haben, ist der heutigen Nachwelt kaum noch begreiflich; so viel man aber auch mit allem Recht an ihnen aussetzen mag: zu ihrer Zeit waren sie eine That; ein offener Bruch mit der falschen Kunst, zwei für sich gleichberechtigte Erzählungsgebiete, das Wunderbare und das Natürliche, das Märchen und die Wirklichkeit, zu beiderseitigem Schaden mit einander zu vermengen. Goethe's recht ausdrücklich *Novelle* überschriebene phantastisch-mystische Erzählung von dem Knaben, der den Löwen mit Gesang bezähmt, schien diesen Mißbrauch zu rechtfertigen, und Tieck selbst hatte ihm, besonders in einigen Erzählungen seines *Phantasus*, nur allzu sehr gehuldigt. Jetzt führte er die Novelle aus der Zaubernacht und Dämmerung der Romantik in das helle Tageslicht heraus. Er selbst hat Boccaz, Cervantes und Goethe als seine Muster und Vorbilder in dieser Gattung bezeichnet, und zumal mit Begeisterung spricht er von den 'leuchtenden' Novellen des Cervantes. So sind es denn hauptsächlich die beiden Deutschen und der Spanier, deren Standbilder wir am Eingang unseres Novellenhaines aufzustellen haben.

Allein die neue Richtung, welche Tieck angegeben, wurde den alten Sauerteig so bald nicht los. Der Meister selbst erlitt gewisse Rückfälle; und was von der Natur gesagt ist, daß sie mit keiner Gewalt ganz auszutreiben sei, das läßt sich zu Zeiten auch von der Unnatur sagen. Die falsche Romantik war in der alten Gestalt überwunden; aber sie wechselte proteïsch ihre Formen und Farben, und noch eine geraume Zeit sollte es dauern, bis ihr wunderlicher Rocken bis auf den letzten Faden abgesponnen war.

Denn nicht viele Jahrzehnte sind zu zählen, seit die Novelle das von Tieck gegebene Versprechen, daß sie auch im Wunderbaren stets natürlich sein werde, in gutem Ernste zu erfüllen begann. Damit dies geschehen konnte, mußte erst der sociale und künstlerische Geist im Allgemeinen die große Wandlung erfahren, die mit den letzten Regungen der Romantik entschieden brach, und die wir mit dem landläufigen Schulwort die Wendung zum Realismus nennen wollen. Eine Zeit, die in Politik und Philosophie sich zunächst wieder auf den Boden des Thatsächlichen stellte, in der Geschichtschreibung die Quellenforschung, in Physik und Chemie das Experiment ihrer Methode zu Grunde legte, mußte auch einer Dichtungsart günstig sein, in der die Begebenheit, das Ereigniß, der einzelne Fall so vielfach ohne alle höheren Ansprüche auf absoluten sittlichen und dichterischen Werth zu ihrem Rechte kommen. War es doch auch in Goethe's weltumfassendem Naturell der Respect vor dem Thatsächlichen, das epische Geltenlassen der Wirklichkeit, die Freude am überraschenden Phänomen gewesen, was ihn zum Begründer des deutschen Romans gemacht hatte. Nach dem verwirrenden Um- und Abweg durch den verkehrten und nur scheinbaren Idealismus der Romantik fand sich der poetische Geist der Nation wieder zu ihrem großen Führer zurück, um die von diesem eingeschlagene Bahn, allerdings oft ins Breite und Flache sich verlierend, mit klarem Selbstbewußtsein bis an die äußersten Grenzen zu verfolgen.

Bei dem unverkennbaren Einfluß, den diese allgemeinen Zustände insbesondere auch auf die Entwicklung der Novelle ausübten, hat noch ein ganz äußerlicher Umstand aufs Entscheidenste mitgewirkt: das Aufblühen des Journalismus; denn die von Jahr zu Jahr wachsende Menge der Tages- und Wochenblätter begünstigte in früher ungeahntem Maße die Prosaformen der Dichtung und machte durch den breiten Spielraum, den sie in ihren Spalten dem Roman und der Novelle öffnete, zugleich mit der Lockung rasch zu gewinnender Popularität selbst Talente sich dienstbar, die in der klassischen Periode unzweifelhaft höheren Formen sich zugewandt hätten.

So wurde zunächst mit einem Nachtheil für die sogenannte 'hohe Poesie', die der rhythmischen Form nicht entbehren kann, der Gewinn für die Ausbildung einer künstlerischen Prosa bezahlt; aber auch für die Novelle selbst lagen in dem Hausrecht, das ihr der Journalismus einräumte, sehr erhebliche Gefahren. Denn es konnte nicht ausbleiben, daß man in der Nachbarschaft anderer Tagesneuigkeiten auch ihren Namen, der ja im Grunde nichts Anderes bedeutet, allzu wörtlich nehmen und die Novelle von gestern schon heute veraltet finden mußte. Von dem künstlerischen Rang, den sie in den Händen ihrer Meister erhalten, drohte sie zu bloßer Unterhaltungswaare herabzusinken und somit die schnelle und allgemeine Gunst, die sie erfuhr, durch die Flüchtigkeit dieser Gunst mehr als aufzuwiegen. Dazu machte sich auch ein künstlerischer Nachtheil nur allzu rasch fühlbar.

Die abgerissene Form des Erscheinens nämlich entwöhnte die Leser bald genug, auch eine Novelle als ein kleines Kunstwerk, ein abgerundetes Ganzes zu genießen und selbst an diese bescheidenste dichterische Form die Ansprüche der möglichsten Vollendung zu machen. Diese Genügsamkeit hatte die natürliche Folge, daß auch die Schaffenden Fähigkeit und Bedürfniß, es auf ein künstlerisch organisirtes Ganzes abzusehen, mehr und mehr verloren und dafür die Fertigkeit ausbildeten, was im Großen und Ganzen eingebüßt war, im Kleinen und Einzelnen wieder einzubringen. Es galt, den flüchtigen Leser, wie jene geistreiche Märchenerzählerin ihren grillenhaften Sultan, um jeden Preis von heut auf morgen festzuhalten, ihn, wenn er etwa nur ein mitten herausgerissenes Fragment in die Hände bekam, durch den reizenden Geschmack dieses Brockens nach der 'Fortsetzung' lüstern zu machen und so von der Hand in den Mund lebend die tausend und einen Werkeltage des literarischen Handwerks hinzubringen. Daher das Übergewicht des Vortrags über den Stoff, der geistreichen Ausführung über die Gediegenheit der Composition, und das Umsichgreifen jener Zwittergattungen, die als Reisenovellen, Feuilletonphantasieen, Capriccio's u.s.w. so lange Jahre gewuchert und den gesunden Wuchs der echten Novelle verkümmert haben.

In noch höherem Grade hat der Romanstil unter der heillosen Zerstückelung der Tagesblätter zu leiden gehabt, und die Klage darüber ist selbst in jenen Kreisen laut geworden, von denen das Übel ausging. George Sand, im Vorwort zu ihrer *Jeanne* vom Jahre 1852, bezeichnet sogar ein bestimmtes Datum, auf das sich der Beginn dieser hastig dramatisirenden, in musivisch aneinandergereihten Effectscenen sich fortbewegenden Manier zurückführen lasse. 'Es war', sagt sie, im Jahre 1844, als der alte *Constitutionnel* sich verjüngte, indem er zum großen Format überging. Seitdem besaßen Alexander Dumas und Eugène Sue im höchsten Grade die Kunst, jedes Kapitel mit einer spannenden Peripetie zu schließen, die den Leser beständig in Athem erhalten und zur ungeduldigsten Neugier stacheln sollte. Das war nicht das Talent Balzac's und noch weniger das meine. Balzac, dessen Geist mehr von einem Mittelpunkt aus zu entwickeln liebte, ich, mehr von einem langsamen und träumerischen Charakter, wir konnten nicht daran denken, mit dieser an Erfindung von Begebenheiten und Häufung von Intriguen unerschöpflichen Phantasie zu wetteifern.'—

Sagen wir es mit Einem Wort: dem Roman wie der Novelle ist heutzutage die epische Ruhe des Stils mehr oder weniger verloren gegangen, die in den Mustern der Gattung bei den romanischen Völkern so großen Reiz übt und dem, was unser deutscher Großmeister der Erzählungskunst geschaffen, unvergänglichen Werth verleiht.

Aber wenn wir diese Thatsache mit unverhohlenem Bedauern erkennen, sind wir doch von der Meinung fern, als ob die Novelle nothwendig 'umkehren' und um jeden Preis die edle Einfalt und classische Mäßigung zurückgewinnen müsse, die sie in ihrer Jugend besaß. Jeder Zeitgeschmack ist eine Macht, die zwar nicht vor Recht geht, der aber ein doctrinärer Eigensinn sich nicht in den Weg stellen darf. So wenig wir von Robert Schumann's durchgeistigt subjectiver Form und dem problematisch leidenschaftlichen Charakter seiner Kunst zu der durchsichtigen Objektivität

Vater Haydn's zurückkönnen, weil die Stimmungen und Strömungen unseres heutigen Lebens über den Rand dieser krystallklaren Formen hinausschwellen, eben so wenig wird es uns einfallen dürfen, mit archaistischer Willkür die Novelle zu freiwilliger Armuth, zur Beschränkung an Stoffen und Darstellungsmitteln zu verpflichten. Nil humani a me alienum puto—Alles, was eine Menschenbrust bewegt, gehört in meinen Kreis—dieser Loosung wird die Novelle mit vollster Unumschränktheit treu bleiben müssen. Haben doch auch gerade in der neueren Zeit bedeutende Talente im verschiedensten Sinne mit diesem Wahlspruch Ernst gemacht. Von dem einfachen Bericht eines merkwürdigen Ereignisses oder einer sinnreich erfundenen abenteuerlichen Geschichte hat sich die Novelle nach und nach zu der Form entwickelt, in welcher gerade die tiefsten und wichtigsten sittlichen Fragen zur Sprache kommen, weil in dieser bescheidenen dichterischen Gattung auch der Ausnahmsfall, das höchst individuelle und allerpersönlichste Recht im Kampf der Pflichten, seine Geltung findet. Fälle, die sich durch den Eigensinn der Umstände und Charaktere und eine durchaus nicht allgemein gültige Lösung der dramatischen Behandlung entziehen, sittliche Zartheit oder Größe, die zu ihrem Verständniß der sorgfältigsten Einzelzüge bedarf, alles Einzige und Eigenartige, selbst Grillige und bis an die Grenze des Häßlichen sich Verirrende ist von der Novelle dichterisch zu verwerthen. Denn es bleibt ihr von ihrem Ursprung her ein gewisses Schutzrecht für das bloß Thatsächliche, das schlechthin Erlebte, und für den oft nicht ganz reinlichen Erdenrest der Wirklichkeit kann sie vollauf entschädigen, theils durch die harmlose Lebendigkeit des Tons, indem sie Stoffe von geringerem dichterischen Gehalt auch in anspruchsloserer Form, ohne den vollen Nachdruck ihrer Kunstmittel überliefert, theils durch die unerschöpfliche Bedeutsamkeit des Stoffes selbst, da der Mensch auch in seinen Unzulänglichkeiten dem Menschen doch immer das Interessanteste bleibt.

Thöricht wäre daher die Forderung, auch Probleme der oben bezeichneten Art, die oft nur durch die zartesten Schattirungen, reizendes Helldunkel oder eine photographische Deutlichkeit unser Interesse gewinnen, in jener naiven Holzschnittmanier der alten Italiener oder mit den ungebrochenen Farben des großen Spaniers zu behandeln. Hier sind alle jene Mittel höchst individueller Vortragsweise nicht nur erlaubt, sondern sogar gefordert, wie sie einigen der französischen Erzähler und in noch höherem Grade dem russischen Meister der Seelenkunde, Iwan Turgenjew, in so bewundernswerthem Maße zu Gebote stehen. Der Dichter, der uns in die geheimnißvollsten Gemüthstiefen seltener oder doch sehr entschieden ausgeprägter Individuen blicken läßt, wird, um uns in volle Illusion zu bringen, andere Töne anschlagen müssen, als wer uns von einem geraubten und unter Zigeunern wiedergefundenen Kinde erzählt, in dessen Geschick die abenteuerliche Verwicklung und Lösung äußerer Umstände das Hauptinteresse bildet. Bei jenen höchst modernen Aufgaben ist eine dramatische Unmittelbarkeit berechtigt, eine gesteigerte Schärfe der Naturlaute, ein gewisser nervöser, herzklopfender Stil, die mit der oben gerühmten epischen Ruhe im äußersten Gegensatz stehen.

Und freilich ist diese, wie jede Virtuosität, auch sehr der Gefahr ausgesetzt, die Mittel zum Zweck zu machen und über dem Reiz, mit der Schwierigkeit der Form zu spielen, den Sinn für den Werth des Ganzen einzubüßen. Auch der Erzähler dürfte nie vergessen, daß, wie bloße Farbeneffecte noch kein Bild machen, ein noch so geistreiches Spiel mit zerflatternden Motiven keine Geschichte ergiebt, die unserer Phantasie eingegraben bleibt, und daß auch in diesem Gebiet 'groß sein heißt, nicht ohne großen Gegenstand sich regen.'

Denn wie sehr auch die kleinste Form großer Wirkungen fähig sei, beweist unseres Erachtens gerade die Novelle, die im Gegensatz zum Roman den Eindruck eben so verdichtet, auf Einen Punkt sammelt und dadurch zur höchsten Gewalt zu steigern vermag, wie es der Ballade, dem Epos gegenüber, vergönnt ist, mit einem raschen Schlage uns das innerste Herz zu treffen. Es kann hier nicht unsere Aufgabe sein, das Kapitel der Ästhetik über Roman und Novelle zu schreiben, so wenig wir mit den einleitenden Notizen eine Geschichte der deutschen Novellistik zu geben dachten. So viel aber muß doch zu vorläufiger Verständigung gesagt werden, daß wir allerdings den Unterschied beider Gattungen nicht in das Längenmaß setzen, wonach ein Roman eine mehrbändige Novelle, eine Novelle ein kleiner Roman wäre. Da lang und kurz relative Begriffe sind und man bekanntlich die simpelste Liebesgeschichte für den Liebhaber nicht lang genug ausspinnen, dagegen den Inhalt der *Odyssee* 'zum Gebrauch des Dauphin' auf eine Quartseite bringen kann, so muß, wenn es sich um mehr als Namen handeln soll, schon im Thema, im Problem, im unentwickelten Keim etwas liegen, das mit Nothwendigkeit zu der einen oder andern Form hindrängt. Und dies scheint, wenn man auf das Wesentliche sieht, in Folgendem zu beruhen. Wenn der Roman ein Cultur- und Gesellschaftsbild im Großen, ein Weltbild im Kleinen entfaltet, bei dem es auf ein gruppenweises Ineinandergreifen oder ein concentrisches Sichumschlingen verschiedener Lebenskreise recht eigentlich abgesehen ist, so hat die Novelle in einem einzigen Kreise einen einzelnen Conflict, eine sittliche oder Schicksals-Idee oder ein entschieden abgegrenztes Charakterbild darzustellen und die Beziehungen der darin handelnden Menschen zu dem großen Ganzen des Weltlebens nur in andeutender Abbreviatur durchschimmern zu lassen. Die Geschichte, nicht die Zustände, das Ereigniß, nicht die sich in ihm spiegelnde Weltanschauung, sind hier die Hauptsache; denn selbst der tiefste ideelle Gehalt des einzelnen Falles wird wegen seiner Einseitigkeit und Abgetrenntheit—der Isolirung des Experiments, wie die Naturforscher sagen—nur einen relativen Werth behalten, während es in der Breite des Romans möglich wird, eine Lebens- oder Gewissensfrage der Menschheit erschöpfend von allen Seiten zu beleuchten. Freilich wird es auch hier an Übergangsformen nicht fehlen. Hat doch unser größter Erzähler in seinen *Wahlverwandtschaften* ein echt novellistisches Thema mit vollem Recht zum Roman sich auswachsen lassen, indem er das bedeutende Problem mitten in ein reich gegliedertes sociales Leben hineinsetzte, obwohl vier Menschen auf einer wüsten Insel eben so gut in die Lage kommen konnten, die Gewalt dieses Naturgesetzes an sich zu erfahren.

Im Allgemeinen aber halten wir auch bei der Auswahl für unsern Novellenschatz an der Regel fest, der Novelle den Vorzug zu geben, deren Grundmotiv sich am deutlichsten abrundet und— mehr oder weniger gehaltvoll—etwas Eigenartiges, Specifisches schon in der bloßen Anlage verräth. Eine starke Silhouette—um nochmals einen Ausdruck der Malersprache zu Hülfe zu nehmen— dürfte dem, was wir im eigentlichen Sinne Novelle nennen, nicht fehlen, ja wir glauben, die Probe auf die Trefflichkeit eines novellistischen Motivs werde in den meisten Fällen darin bestehen, ob der Versuch gelingt, den Inhalt in wenige Zeilen zusammenzufassen, in der Weise, wie die alten Italiener ihren Novellen kurze Überschriften gaben, die dem Kundigen schon im Keim den speci-

fischen Werth des Thema's verrathen. Wer, der im Boccaz die Inhaltsangabe der 9ten Novelle des 5ten Tages lies't:
'Federigo degli Alberighi liebt, ohne Gegenliebe zu finden; in ritterlicher Werbung verschwendet er all seine Habe und behält nur noch einen einzigen Falken; diesen, da die von ihm geliebte Dame zufällig sein Haus besucht und er sonst nichts hat, ihr ein Mahl zu bereiten, setzt er ihr bei Tische vor. Sie erfährt, was er gethan, ändert plötzlich ihren Sinn und belohnt seine Liebe, indem sie ihn zum Herrn ihrer Hand und ihres Vermögens macht'—wer erkennt nicht in diesen wenigen Zeilen alle Elemente einer rührenden und erfreulichen Novelle, in der das Schicksal zweier Menschen durch eine äußere Zufallswendung, die aber die Charaktere tiefer entwickelt, aufs Liebenswürdigste sich vollendet? Wer, der diese einfachen Grundzüge einmal überblickt hat, wird die kleine Fabel je wieder vergessen, zumal wenn er sie nun mit der ganzen Anmuth jenes im Ernst wie in der Schalkheit unvergleichlichen Meisters vorgetragen findet.

Wir wiederholen es: eine so einfache Form wird sich nicht für jedes Thema unseres vielbrüchigen modernen Culturlebens finden lassen. Gleichwohl aber könnte es nicht schaden, wenn der Erzähler auch bei dem innerlichsten oder reichsten Stoff sich zuerst fragen wollte, wo 'der Falke' sei, das Specifische, das diese Geschichte von tausend anderen unterscheidet. [. . .]

VIII. Wilhelm Heinrich Riehl: *Novelle und Sonate* (1885)

Ein Novellist muß vor allen Dingen zweierlei können, erfinden und erzählen. Wem nicht stets neue Erfindungen und Geschichten von selber zuströmen, wer mühsam nach Stoffen sucht, der ist kein Novellist. Schildern und ausmalen soll man in der Novelle so knapp wie möglich, man soll erzählen. Die vorherrschende Situations- und Stimmungs-Novelle ist der Anfang vom Ende der Novellistik. Lange Gespräche der handelnden Personen stören den novellistischen Grundton; man soll die Leute nur ausnahmsweise selber sprechen lassen, in der Regel aber bündig erzählen, was sie gedacht und gesagt haben. Durch die Dialoge werden die Novellen zu lang, und das ist ein großer Fehler. Die Novelle ist kein Drama; dramatische Novellen und dramatische Sonaten sind immer bedenklich. Beim Erzählen ist der Plan, der Aufbau die Hauptkunst; eine Thatsache, ein Motiv muß notwendig aus dem andern hervorgehn.

Zum breiten Schildern hat der gute Erzähler gar keine Zeit. Wer eine eben erlebte spannende Geschichte frischweg berichtet, der wird sich bei Schilderungen gewiß nicht über Not aufhalten, und der Novellist soll erzählen, als berichte er eine 'Neuigkeit', die er soeben selbst erlebt habe. Die besten Novellen sind darum relativ kurz. Aber es ist schwer, eine kurze und gute Novelle zu schreiben, weit schwerer als eine ellenlange.

Sources

I. *Goethes Werke.* Hamburger Ausgabe, 14 vols, ed. Erich Trunz, VI (Romane und Novellen I) (Munich 1973), 139, 142–3, 146, 166–7.

II. *Kritische Friedrich-Schlegel-Ausgabe*, ed. Ernst Behler, Jean-Jacques Anstett and Hans Eichner, part 1, vol. 2, ed. Hans Eichner (Munich–Paderborn–Vienna–Zurich 1967), 393–6.

III. August Wilhelm Schlegel, *Vorlesungen über schöne Litteratur und Kunst*, part 3, ed. J. Minor, Deutsche Litteraturdenkmale des 18. und 19. Jahrhunderts 19 (Heilbronn 1884), 242–3, 244–6, 247–8.

IV. *Ludwig Tieck's Schriften*, XI (Berlin 1829), lxxxiv–xc.

V. Theodor Mundt, *Moderne Lebenswirren. Briefe und Zeitabenteuer eines Salzschreibers* (Leipzig 1834), 155–7.

VI. Paul Heyse, *Moralische Novellen. Achte Sammlung* (Berlin 1869), xvi–xxiii.

VII. Paul Heyse, *Deutscher Novellenschatz*, ed. Paul Heyse and Hermann Kurz, 1 (Munich [1871]), vii–xx.

VIII. Wilhelm Heinrich Riehl, *Freie Vorträge. Zweite Sammlung* (Stuttgart 1885), 453–4.

NOTES

Some preliminary remarks pp. 1–10

1 *Novelle*, 73.
2 *Theorie und Kritik*, 71.
3 Edgar Allen Poe, *Tales, Poems, Essays*, with an Introduction by Lawrence Meynell (London–Glasgow 1952), 520 f.
4 J. M. Ritchie, 'Die Ambivalenz des "Realismus" in der deutschen Literatur 1830–1880', in *Begriffsbestimmung des literarischen Realismus*, ed. Richard Brinkmann, Wege der Forschung CCXII (Darmstadt 1969), 376–99, ref. 384–9.
5 Georg Hirzel, 'Ungedruckte Briefe an Georg Andreas Reimer', *Deutsche Revue* 18, vol. 4 (Oct.–Dec. 1893), 98–114, 238–53, ref. 249.
6 *The Edinburgh Review*, Oct. 1827, no. XCII, 334.
7 Roy Pascal, *The German Novel. Studies* (Manchester 1956), 32.
8 Ibid. vii. This has to some extent been rectified by Eric A. Blackall, *The Novels of the German Romantics* (Ithaca–London 1983).
9 *Realismus und Gründerzeit*, II, 73.
10 Friedrich Sengle, 'Der Romanbegriff in der ersten Hälfte des 19. Jahrhunderts', in *Arbeiten zur deutschen Literatur 1750–1850* (Stuttgart 1965), 175–96.
11 Goethe to Eckermann, 9 Mar. 1831.
12 *Novelle*, 72. In slightly different form, in a letter to Keller, *Theorie und Kritik*, 120.
13 Maurice Parturier, *Une amitié littéraire. Prosper Mérimée et Ivan Tourguéniev* (Paris 1952), 124–5.
14 *Novelle*, 87.
15 Ibid. 88.
16 Set out in *Novelle*, 95–245.
17 Cf. *Novelle*, 79–86.
18 Ibid. 135 (Bernhard Bruch).
19 Ibid. 167 (André Jolles).
20 Ibid. 164 (Adolf von Grolmann).
21 Ibid. 163 (Adolf von Grolmann).
22 Ibid. 219 (Johannes Klein).
23 Ibid. 195–221.
24 This is the especial merit of two very different studies, Schröder, and Hellmuth Himmel, *Geschichte der deutschen Novelle*, Sammlung Dalp 94 (Berne and Munich 1963).

Chapter One pp. 11-19

1 Bernhard von Arx, *Novellistisches Dasein. Spielraum einer Gattung in der Goethezeit*, Zürcher Beiträge zur deutschen Literatur- und Geistesgesch. 5 (Zurich 1953), 7 ff.
2 Wolfram Krömer, *Die französische Novelle im 19. Jahrhundert* (Frankfurt a. M. 1972), 16.
3 Polheim, 217.
4 For an account of the various cognate forms in the main European literatures cf. Gerald Gillespie, 'Novella, Nouvelle, Novelle, Short Novel? A Review of Terms', *Neophilologus* 51 (1967), 117–27, 225–30.
5 *Novellenbuch*, Hausbücherei der Deutschen Dichter-Gedächtnis-Stiftung, 7 vols (Hamburg–Großborstel 1904–9), VII, 27–33.
6 Walter Pabst, *Novellentheorie und Novellendichtung. Zur Geschichte ihrer Antinomie in den romanischen Literaturen*, second edn (Heidelberg 1967), esp. 7–24.
7 Boccaccio, *The Decameron*, trans. G. H. McWilliam (Harmondsworth 1972), 47.
8 Pabst, op. cit. 35 f.
9 *Les Cent Nouvelles nouvelles*, Texte revu avec beaucoup de soin sur les meilleures éditions (Paris 1893), v.
10 Cf. Werner Krauss, 'Cervantes und der spanische Weg der Novelle', in *Studien und Aufsätze*, Neue Beiträge zur Literaturwissenschaft 8 (Berlin 1959), 93–138, ref. 95.
11 *Les Cent Nouvelles nouvelles*, vi.
12 Marguerite de Navarre, *L'Heptaméron*, ed. Michel François, Classiques Garnier (Paris 1960), 7.
13 Ibid. 10.
14 Erich Auerbach, *Zur Technik der Frührenaissancenovelle in Italien und Frankreich* (Heidelberg 1921) 24 ff.
15 Pabst, op. cit. 116 f.
16 *Theorie und Kritik*, 92.
17 On this cf. Hellmuth Himmel, *Geschichte der deutschen Novelle*, esp. 16–30.
18 Rudolf Fürst, *Die Vorläufer der modernen Novelle im achtzehnten Jahrhundert. Ein Beitrag zur vergleichenden Litteraturgeschichte* (Halle 1897), 1.
19 *Novelle*, 27.
20 Ibid.
21 Cf. Erich Loos, 'Die Gattung des *conte* und das Publikum im 18. Jahrhundert', *Romanische Forschungen* 71 (1959), 113–37.

Chapter Two pp. 20–4

1 The account of *Unterhaltungen deutscher Ausgewanderten* is much indebted to Erich Trunz's apparatus to vol. VI of the Hamburger Ausgabe of Goethe (referred to subsequently as HA for all Goethe quotations).
2 Cf. Schröder, 99 ff., 107.
3 HA,VI.125.
4 Ibid.
5 HA,VI.137.
6 HA,VI.138.
7 HA,VI.135.
8 HA,VI.167.
9 HA,VI.143.
10 HA,VI.145.
11 *Les Cent Nouvelles nouvelles*, 422 (Nouvelle C).
12 HA,VI.185.
13 HA,VI.208.
14 HA,VI.215.
15 HA,VI.238.
16 Most accessible in: Christoph Martin Wieland, *Ausgewählte Werke in drei Bänden*, ed. Friedrich Beißner (Munich 1964–5), 239–370. Cf. Hansjörg Schelle, 'Zu Entstehung und Gestalt von C. M. Wielands Erzählzyklus *Das Hexameron von Rosenhain*', *Neophilologus* 60 (1976) 107–23.
17 HA,VIII, 572.

Chapter Three pp. 25–36

1 *Ludwig Tieck's Schriften*, 28 vols (Berlin 1828–54), IV, 146.
2 Cf. Walter Bausch, *Theorien des epischen Erzählens in der deutschen Frühromantik*, Bonner Arbeiten z. dt. Lit. 8 (Bonn 1964), 9.
3 *Novelle*, 45.
4 Ibid. 43, cf. also 37.
5 Ibid. 49.
6 Ibid.
7 Ibid. 38.
8 Ibid. 47.
9 HA,VI.143.
10 *Novelle*, 35.
11 Ibid. 47.
12 Ibid. 36.
13 Ibid. 47.
14 Ibid.

15 Ibid.
16 *Kritische Friedrich-Schlegel-Ausgabe*, ed. Ernst Behler et al. (Munich–Paderborn–Vienna–Zurich 1958–), XI. 148.
17 *Novelle*, 41.
18 Ibid. 43.
19 Ibid. 38.
20 Ibid. 40.
21 Ibid. 41.
22 Ibid. 40.
23 Ibid. 44.
24 Ibid. 45.
25 Ibid. 47.
26 Ibid. 35.
27 Ibid. 50.
28 Cf. Ulrich Im Hof, *Das gesellige Jahrhundert. Gesellschaft und Gesellschaften im Zeitalter der Aufklärung* (Munich 1982).
29 Quoted in *Die romanische Novelle*, 256.
30 *Theorie und Kritik*, 145.
31 Polheim, 225 f.
32 *Tieck's Schriften*, IV. 104 f.
33 Ibid. 120, 128.
34 Ibid. 286 f.
35 Ibid. 360.
36 Cf. Hubert Ohl, 'Das zyklische Prinzip von Gottfried Kellers Novellensammlung *Die Leute von Seldwyla*', *Euphorion* 63 (1969) 216–26.

Chapter Four pp. 37–57

1 All references to Kleist taken from: Heinrich von Kleist, *Sämtliche Werke und Briefe*, ed. Helmut Sembdner, 2 vols (Munich 1961); here II. 893.
2 *Kritische Schriften. Zum erstenmale gesammelt und mit einer Vorrede herausgegeben von Ludwig Tieck*, 4 vols (Leipzig 1848–52) II. 46.
3 *Theorie und Kritik*, 92.
4 Cf. Schröder, 125 ff.
5 *Deutscher Novellenschatz herausgegeben von Paul Heyse und Hermann Kurz*, I (Munich 1871), viii.
6 Kleist, II. 250.
7 Ibid. 893.
8 Cf. J.-U. Fechner, 'Cervantes und Kleist—Ein Kapitel europäischer Novellistik', *Levende Talen* (1964), 711–23 (comes to conclusions rather different from mine). Cf. also Hans-Peter Herrmann, 'Zufall und Ich. Zum Begriff der Situation in den Novellen Heinrich von Kleists', *Germanisch–Romanische Monatsschrift* NF 11 (1961), 69–99, esp. 78–

80; Gerhard Dünnhaupt, 'Kleist's *Marquise von O* . . . and its Literary Debt to Cervantes', *Arcadia* 10 (1975), 147–57.
9 Werner Krauss, 'Cervantes und der spanische Weg der Novelle', 98 f.
10 Cf. Leo Spitzer, 'Das Gefüge einer cervantinischen Novelle: El celoso estrameño, *Die romanische Novelle*, 175–213, esp. 178 f., Walter Pabst, *Novellentheorie und Novellengattung*, 117–37.
11 My remarks are indebted to the most useful chapter by Hans-Jörg Neuschäfer, 'Regel und Ausnahme: Die unerhörte Begebenheit und die Auffassung des Zufalls in der Novelle', *Die romanische Novelle*, 61–77.
12 Kleist, II. 150.
13 In *Michael Kohlhaas*, ibid. 96, and the anecdote *Unwahrscheinliche Wahrhaftigkeiten*, ibid. 277 f.
14 Cf. Erich Loos, 'Die Gattung des *conte*', 125 f.
15 *Ludwig Tieck's Schriften*, IX. 97.
16 Pabst, op. cit. 119.
17 Cf. already the older source studies by Richard Maria Werner, 'Kleists Novelle "Die Marquise von O . . ."', *Vierteljahrsschrift für Litteraturgeschichte* 3 (1890), 483–500; Georg Minde-Pouet, 'Zur Marquise von O . . . ', *Euphorion* 4 (1897), 542–5.
18 Kleist, II. 161.
19 Voltaire, *Romans et contes*, ed. Henri Bénac, Classiques Garnier (Paris 1958), 220.
20 On this question cf. Wolfgang Wittkowski, 'Skepsis, Noblesse, Ironie. Formen des Als-ob in Kleists *Erdbeben*', *Euphorion* 63 (1969), 247–83.
21 Cf. Jacob Minor, 'Zum Stil der Kleistischen Erzählungen', *Euphorion* 1 (1894), 585–9, the basis of all subsequent studies of this aspect.
22 Chr. M. Wieland, *Ausgewählte Werke in drei Bänden*, III. 310.
23 Kleist, II. 229.
24 *Decameron*, 463 f.
25 Cf. Hans-Jörg Neuschäfer, 'Regel und Ausnahme', esp. 64 ff.
26 *Lehrreiche Erzählungen von Miguel de Cervantes Saavedra, übersetzt von D. W. Soltau*, 3 vols (Königsberg 1801), I. 343.
27 Kleist, II. 237.
28 Ibid. 253.
29 On affinities between these stories by Kleist and Hoffmann cf. Jean-F.-A. Ricci, *E. T. A. Hoffmann, L'homme et l'œuvre* (Paris 1947), 396–7; cf. *Das Gelübde* and *Der Findling*, in Elizabeth Wright, *E. T. A. Hoffmann and the Rhetoric of Terror. Aspects of Language Used for the Evocation of Fear*, Bithell Series of Dissertations 1 (London 1978), 116–45; Hermann Pongs, 'Grundlagen der deutschen Novelle des 19. Jahrhunderts', *Jb. d. Freien Deutschen Hochstifts* 1930, 151–231, ref. 159–65.
30 Kleist, II. 281.
31 Ibid. 108.

32 Ibid. 109.
33 Ibid. 117.
34 Ibid. 120 f.
35 Ibid. 123.
36 Ibid. 122.
37 Ibid. 124.
38 Ibid. 126.
39 Ibid. 132.
40 Ibid. 143.
41 Cf. Kurt Willimczik, *E. T. A. Hoffmann. Die drei Reiche seiner Gestaltenwelt*, Neue Deutsche Forschungen. Abt. Neuere Deutsche Literaturgeschichte 19 (Berlin 1939), 133.

Chapter Five pp. 58–75

1 *Theorie und Kritik*, 141 f.
2 Ibid. 146.
3 Ibid. 71.
4 Ibid. 56.
5 Ibid. 88.
6 Cf. for most of my subsequent remarks, Schröder, 53 ff.; Friedrich Sengle, 'Voraussetzungen und Erscheinungsformen der deutschen Restaurationsliteratur', in *Arbeiten zur deutschen Literatur 1750–1850* (Stuttgart 1965), 118–54, ref. 140 f., and *Biedermeierzeit. Deutsche Literatur im Spannungsfeld zwischen Restauration und Revolution 1815–1848*, 3 vols (Stuttgart 1971–80), II. 833 ff.
7 Diderot's phrase. Cf. Erich Loos, 'Die Gattung des *conte*', 112.
8 Cf. Werner Krauss, 'Cervantes und der spanische Weg der Novelle', 94.
9 Wilhelm Hauff, *Werke*, ed. Bernhard Zeller, 2 vols (Frankfurt a. M. 1969), II. 625. On the position of Tieck, cf. Schröder, 20–52; Ralf Stamm, *Ludwig Tiecks späte Novellen. Grundlage und Technik des Wunderbaren*, Studien zur Poetik und Geschichte der Literatur 31 (Stuttgart–Berlin–Cologne–Mainz 1973); Sengle, *Biedermeierzeit*, I. 246–8; Roger Paulin, *Ludwig Tieck: A literary biography* (Oxford 1985).
10 *Theorie und Kritik*, 63.
11 Ibid. 33.
12 Ibid. 44.
13 Ibid. 43.
14 Ibid. 96.
15 Ibid. 36.
16 Ibid. 37.
17 *Novelle*, 53 f.
18 *Theorie und Kritik*, 88.

19 Ibid. 36.
20 Ibid. 64.
21 Cf. Schröder, 214 ff.
22 Cf. Reinhard Wagner, 'Die theoretische Vorarbeit für den Aufstieg des deutschen Romans im 19. Jahrhundert', *Zs. f. dt. Philologie* 74 (1955), 353–63; Friedrich Sengle, 'Der Romanbegriff in der ersten Hälfte des 19. Jahrhunderts', in *Arbeiten zur deutschen Literatur 1750–1850*, 175–196, ref. 195 f.; 'Voraussetzungen und Erscheinungsformen', 150 ff.; Fritz Martini, 'Zur Theorie des Romans im deutschen "Realismus"', in *Deutsche Romantheorien. Beiträge zu einer historischen Poetik des Romans in Deutschland*, ed. Reinhold Grimm (Frankfurt a. M.–Bonn 1968), 142–64.
23 'Voraussetzungen und Erscheinungsformen', 120–6.
24 On various interpretations of this story, cf. Roger Paulin, 'Jeremias Gotthelf', in *Zur Literatur der Restaurationsepoche 1815–1848. Forschungsreferate und Aufsätze*, ed. Jost Hermand and Manfred Windfuhr (Stuttgart 1970), 273–5.
25 Quotations from the excellent edition by H. M. Waidson (Oxford 1955), 30.
26 Ibid. 68.
27 Ibid. 79.
28 Cf. Schröder, 127 ff.
29 *Theorie und Kritik*, 40.
30 Annette von Droste-Hülshoff, *Sämtliche Werke*, ed. Clemens Heselhaus (Munich 1962), 882.
31 Ibid.
32 Ibid. 936.
33 Cf. Schröder, 177 ff.
34 *Theorie und Kritik*, 64.
35 Wilhelm Hauff, *Werke*, I. 12.
36 E. T. A. Hoffmann, *Fantasie- und Nachtstücke*, ed. Walter Müller-Seidel (Munich 1962), 187.
37 Franz Grillparzer, *Sämtliche Werke*, ed. Peter Frank and Karl Pörnbacher, 4 vols (Munich 1960–5), III. 148, 150, 186.
38 *Theorie und Kritik*, 36.
39 Adalbert Stifter, *Erzählungen in der Urfassung*, III, ed. Max Stefl (Basle 1953), 209.
40 Adalbert Stifter, *Bunte Steine. Späte Erzählungen*, ed. Max Stefl (Augsburg 1960), 54.
41 My remarks on this subject are indebted to Ulrich Eisenbeiss, *Das Idyllische in der Novelle der Biedermeierzeit*, Studien zur Poetik und Geschichte der Literatur 36 (Stuttgart–Berlin–Cologne–Mainz 1973).
42 Of the many useful discussions in Eisenbeiss (op. cit.) cf. esp. that of *Bergkristall*, 102 ff.

Notes

43 *Deutscher Novellenschatz herausgegeben von Paul Heyse und Hermann Kurz*, I (Munich 1871), xxi.
44 *I. S. Turgenev und Deutschland. Materialien und Untersuchungen*, ed. Gerhard Ziegengeist, I, Deutsche Akad. d. Wiss. Veröff. d. Inst. f. Slawistik 34 (Berlin 1965), 83.
45 Droste-Hülshoff, op. cit., 900 f.
46 Theodor Storm, *Werke. Gesamtausgabe in drei Bänden*, ed. Hermann Engelhard (Stuttgart 1958), III. 314 f.
47 Ibid. 406 f.

Chapter Six pp. 76–81

1 Friedrich Hebbel, *Werke*, ed. Gerhard Fricke, Werner Keller and Karl Pörnbacher, 5 vols (Munich 1963–7), I. 809.
2 Cf. the discussion of the question of continuity in Werner Hahl, *Reflexion und Erzählung. Ein Problem der Romantheorie von der Spätaufklärung bis zum programmatischen Realismus*, Studien zur Poetik und Geschichte der Literatur 18 (Stuttgart–Berlin–Cologne–Mainz 1971), 202–5; Hermann Kinder, *Poesie als Synthese. Ausbreitung eines deutschen Realismus-Verständnisses in der Mitte des 19. Jahrhunderts*, Ars poetica 15 (Frankfurt a. M. 1973), esp. 50–8.
3 Fritz Martini, *Deutsche Literatur im bürgerlichen Realismus 1848–1898* (Stuttgart 1962), 58 ff.
4 *Realismus und Gründerzeit*, II. 170.
5 Ibid. 172.
6 Ibid. 174.
7 Gottfried Keller, *Sämtliche Werke und Ausgewählte Briefe*, ed. Clemens Heselhaus, 3 vols (Munich 1978–9), III. 342.
8 As set out in *Realismus und Gründerzeit*, I. 32–47, II. 64–145; Hans-Joachim Ruckhäberle and Helmuth Widhammer, *Roman und Romantheorie des deutschen Realismus. Darstellung und Dokumente*, Athenäum-Taschenbücher 2125: Literaturwiss. (Kronberg 1977), 37–98.
9 *Realismus und Gründerzeit*, II. 94.
10 Ibid. 105.
11 Ibid. 124 f.
12 Ibid. 397.
13 Ibid. 382.
14 Otto Ludwig, *Gesammelte Schriften*, ed. Adolf Stern and Erich Schmidt, 6 vols (Leipzig 1891), V. 265.
15 Martini, op. cit., esp. 612–15, and for much of the following.
16 *Theorie und Kritik*, 122.
17 Ibid. 128–30.
18 Ibid. 143.

19 Cf. the point made by Martini, *Bürgerlicher Realismus*, 611–15, and in his article: 'Wilhelm Raabes "Prinzessin Fisch"'. Wirklichkeit und Dichtung im erzählenden Realismus des 19. Jahrhunderts', in *Begriffsbestimmung des literarischen Realismus*, 301–36, esp. 326 f. Also Clemens Heselhaus, 'Das Realismusproblem', ibid. 337–64.
20 *Theorie und Kritik*, 143.
21 Ibid. 132.
22 *Novelle*, 74.
23 'Le Roman', Preface to *Pierre et Jean*, in Guy de Maupassant, *Romans*, ed. Albert-Marie Schmidt (Paris 1970), 835.
24 Julian Schmidt, 'Iwan Turgénjew', *Preußische Jahrbücher* 22 (1868) 432–61, ref. 450.
25 *I. S. Turgenev und Deutschland*, 85.
26 Cf. J. Eichholz, 'Turgenev in der deutschen Kritik bis zum Jahre 1883', *Germanoslavica* I (1931–2), 43–54, 557–93. *I. S. Turgenev und Deutschland*, loc. cit.
27 Oskar Walzel, *Gehalt und Gestalt im Kunstwerk des Dichters*, second edn (Darmstadt 1957), 337 f.
28 Iwan Turgenjew, *Briefe an Ludwig Pietsch* (Berlin and Weimar 1968), 104.

Chapter Seven pp. 82–9

1 Cf. Eberhard Lämmert, postscript to Friedrich von Blanckenburg, *Versuch über den Roman*, Sammlung Metzler 39 (Stuttgart 1965), 560 ff.
2 In the essay 'Der poetisch-tragische Gehalt', Ludwig, *Gesammelte Schriften*, v. 470.
3 Cf. Sengle, 'Der Romanbegriff', loc. cit. 194 f.
4 Cf. Helmut Schanze, 'Die Anschauung vom hohen Rang des Dramas in der zweiten Hälfte des 19. Jahrhunderts und seine tatsächliche "Schwäche"', in *Beiträge zur Theorie der Künste im 19. Jahrhundert*, I, ed. Helmut Koopmann and J. Adolf Schmoll gen. Eisenwerth, Studien zur Philosophie und Literatur des 19. Jahrhunderts 12/1 (Frankfurt a. M. 1971), 85–96.
5 A full analysis of this story by William J. Lillyman, *Otto Ludwig's Zwischen Himmel und Erde. A Study of its Artistic Structure*, Stanford Studies in Germanics and Slavics 3 (The Hague–Paris 1967).
6 *Theorie und Kritik*, 116.
7 Ibid. 165.
8 Cf. *L. Tieck's Schriften*, XI. lxxxiv.
9 Cf. Ohl, 'Das zyklische Prinzip von *Die Leute von Seldwyla*', op. cit. 216–26.
10 Keller, *Sämtliche Werke*, II. 61.
11 Cf. *Realismus und Gründerzeit*, I. 83.

12 'Realistische Motivierung'. Ludwig, v. 525.
13 *Realismus und Gründerzeit*, II. 107.
14 Tieck, *Kritische Schriften*, III. 188.
15 G. G. Gervinus, *Shakespeare*, 4 vols (Leipzig 1849–50), II. 2, 3, 22.
16 'Romeo und Julia'. Ludwig, v. 189.
17 Gervinus, II. 12.
18 Cf. Gerhard Kaiser, 'Sündenfall, Paradies und himmlisches Jerusalem in Kellers "Romeo und Julia auf dem Dorfe"', in *Wanderer und Idylle. Goethe und die Phänomenologie der Natur in der deutschen Dichtung von Geßner bis Gottfried Keller* (Göttingen 1977), 258–89; E. A. McCormick, 'The Idylls in Keller's Romeo und Julia', *German Quarterly* 35 (1962), 265–79.
19 Theodor Fontane, *Sämtliche Werke*, ed. Walter Keitel, Aufsätze, Kritiken, Erinnerungen, 1 (Munich 1969), 495.
20 *Realismus und Gründerzeit*, I. 59.
21 'Lear'. Ludwig, v. 209.

Chapter Eight pp. 90–107

1 *Theorie und Kritik*, 157–9.
2 HA, VI. 717; IX. 572–4.
3 The story *Freundschaft und Liebe auf der Probe*.
4 HA, IX. 602 f. Cf. also the edition of Eugen Wolff (Frankfurt a. M. 1916) in the original 'Novellenkranz' form.
5 HA, IX. 573.
6 HA, VI. 572.
7 Ibid.
8 Ibid.
9 HA, VI. 723.
10 *Novelle*, 34.
11 Johann Christoph Adelung, *Grammatisch–kritisches Wörterbuch der Hochdeutschen Mundart*, part 4 (Leipzig 1801), 845.
12 Goethe, *Sämtliche Werke*, Artemis-Gedenkausgabe (Zurich 1949), IX. 411.
13 HA, IX. 180.
14 Ibid. 181.
15 Ibid. 395.
16 HA, VI. 725.
17 For the following, cf. Roger Paulin, *Ludwig Tieck: a literary biography*.
18 *Novelle*, 53 f.
19 Ibid. 52.
20 Ibid. 54.
21 Recorded in Roger Paulin, 'Der alte Tieck', in *Zur Literatur der Restaurationsepoche*, 247–62, ref. 253–7. See on this whole subject the

eminently sensible article by Manfred Schunicht, 'Der "Falke" am "Wendepunkt". Zu den Novellentheorien Tiecks und Heyses', *Germanisch-Romanische Monatsschrift* 41 (1960), 44–65.
22 Cf. my account of this in *Ludwig Tieck: a literary biography*.
23 *Letters of Ludwig Tieck Hitherto Unpublished 1792–1853*. Collected and ed. by Edwin H. Zeydel, Percy Matenko and Robert Herndon Fife (New York–London 1937), 199.
24 *Ludwig Tieck's Schriften*, XXI. 225 f.
25 Ibid. 237 f.
26 Ludwig Tieck, *Kritische Schriften*, II. 46.
27 Ibid. II. 375–88.
28 These are in vols IX and XIV of *Tieck's Schriften*.
29 *Theorie und Kritik*, 150, 151.
30 *Novelle*, 85.
31 Endpapers to *Neuer Deutscher Novellenschatz*, ed. Paul Heyse and Ludwig Laistner, 24 vols (Munich and Leipzig 1884–1887), XXIV.
32 *Realismus und Gründerzeit*, 373 f.
33 *Theorie und Kritik*, 146.
34 *Realismus und Gründerzeit*, 374; *Theorie und Kritik*, 146.
35 *Theorie und Kritik*, 147 f.
36 Ibid. 146.
37 Ibid.
38 *Novelle*, 68.
39 Ibid.
40 Ibid. 75.

Chapter Nine pp. 108–28

1 Letter from Storm to Fontane, in *Theodor Storm–Theodor Fontane. Briefwechsel. Kritische Ausgabe*, ed. Jacob Steiner (Berlin 1981), 137.
2 *Theodor Storms Briefwechsel mit Theodor Mommsen*, ed. Hans-Erich Teitge (Weimar 1966), 124.
3 *Theodor Storm–Erich Schmidt. Briefwechsel. Kritische Ausgabe*, ed. Karl Ernst Laage, 2 vols (Berlin 1972–6), II. 57.
4 *Novelle*, 72.
5 Unless otherwise stated, references to Storm are taken from *Werke. Gesamtausgabe in drei Bänden*, ed. Hermann Engelhard (Stuttgart 1958); here III. 792.
6 *Theodor Storm–Paul Heyse. Briefwechsel. Kritische Ausgabe*, ed. Clifford Albrecht Bernd, 3 vols (Berlin 1969–74), III. 28.
7 Storm, III. 757.
8 *Theodor Storms Briefe an Friedrich Eggers*, ed. H. Wolfgang Seidel (Berlin 1911), 17.
9 Anselm Feuerbach, *Ein Vermächtniß* (Vienna 1882), 81.

10 *Briefe an Friedrich Eggers*, 16.
11 *Theodor Storm's Briefe in die Heimat aus den Jahren 1853–1864*, ed. G. Storm (Berlin 1907), 156.
12 Storm, I. 118 ('Gedenkst du noch?').
13 Ibid. 152.
14 Storm, III. 744.
15 Theodor Storm, *Briefe an seine Kinder*, ed. Gertrud Storm (Berlin–Brunswick–Hamburg 1916), 30.
16 Ibid. 52.
17 Ibid.
18 *Briefwechsel zwischen Theodor Storm und Eduard Mörike*, ed. Hanns Wolfgang Rath (Stuttgart [1919]), 95.
19 *Der Briefwechsel zwischen Theodor Storm und Gottfried Keller*, ed. Peter Goldammer (Berlin 1960), 41.
20 *Briefe an seine Kinder*, 41.
21 Theodor Storm, *Briefe an seine Frau*, ed. Gertrud Storm (Berlin–Brunswick–Hamburg 1915), 135.
22 *Briefe an Friedrich Eggers*, 17.
23 *Storm–Heyse*, I. 101.
24 Gertrud Storm, *Vergilbte Blätter aus der grauen Stadt* (Regensburg and Leipzig 1922), 69.
25 *Theodor Storms Briefwechsel mit Theodor Mommsen*, 126.
26 Ibid.
27 Storm, II. 198.
28 Ibid. 224.
29 *Briefe an seine Frau*, 55.
30 These changes recorded in: Theodor Storm, *Immensee*, ed. J. M. Ritchie (London–Toronto–Wellington–Sydney 1969), 76–84.
31 Storm, I. 272–4.
32 Ibid. 278.
33 *Briefe an seine Frau*, 118.
34 Cf. Karl Friedrich Boll, 'Das Bonnixsche Epitaph in Drelsdorf und die Kirchenbilder in Theodor Storms Erzählung "Aquis submersus"', *Schriften der Theodor-Storm-Gesellschaft* 14 (1965), 24–39.
35 Storm, II. 165.
36 Ibid. 168 f.
37 *Briefe in die Heimat*, 179.
38 Storm, III. 807.
39 *Briefe an seine Frau*, 124 f.
40 Cf. Franz Stuckert, *Theodor Storm. Sein Leben und seine Welt* (Bremen 1955), 305 ff.; Brian Coghlan, 'Dauer im Wechsel. Kontinuität und Entwicklung der Stormschen Erzählkunst', *Schriften der Theodor-Storm-Gesellschaft* 20 (1971), 9–22.
41 *Briefe an seine Kinder*, 6 f., 25, 57.

42 Storm, III. 750.
43 Ibid. II. 179.
44 Cf. Richard Hamann and Jost Hermand, *Gründerzeit*, Epochen deutscher Kultur von 1870 bis zur Gegenwart 1 (Munich 1971), 179.
45 Jost Hermand, 'Hauke Haien. Kritik oder Ideal des gründerzeitlichen Übermenschen?', in *Von Mainz nach Weimar (1793–1919). Studien zur deutschen Literatur* (Stuttgart 1969), 250–68.
46 *Novelle*, 72.

INDEX

The Novelle: terms and concepts

theory of, studies on 1f., 8–10, 28, 32, 37, 79, 82, 90, 100, 106, 126f.
terms cognate with ('Erzählung', 'conte', 'nouvelle', 'novela', 'novella', 'short story', etc.) 2f., 12f., 15f., 18f., 23–6, 28, 30, 43, 81, 91f., 99, 101f., 114, 138f.
renewals or adaptations of stock situations or traditions in 14–17, 22, 26, 32–4, 39, 41, 43–5, 48, 50f., 53, 56, 58, 60, 63, 66, 70, 77, 91–3, 95f., 98, 101–3, 107, 118, 134f., 138, 143, 147
status as prose work 6f., 20, 28f., 32, 100, 102, 127
high status of ('berufenste Kunstform, das Höchste darzustellen') 29f., 58, 60, 63, 79, 103, 109, 126–8, 132, 141, 143, 145
collections, mass production of 20, 23f., 29–32, 34–6, 39, 43, 58f., 62, 85f., 91–3, 95, 98, 136
in almanacs ('Taschenbuchnovelle') 58–60, 85, 92, 97f., 109
and novel 3–5, 7f., 17, 24, 31, 42f., 63f., 79, 91f., 96f., 100, 104f., 107, 109, 124, 136, 140, 145f., 148f.
analogies with drama ('Schwester des Dramas') 6f., 20, 30, 44f., 79, 82–9, 99f., 104, 107, 109, 127f., 134f., 138, 140f., 143, 148, 150
narrative economy of ('etwas muß geschehen', 'soll erzählen') 8f., 22, 30–2, 37f., 41f., 50f., 53, 78–80, 82, 96, 101, 109, 117–19, 125f., 131, 136, 145, 148, 151f.
scope and subject-matter of, reference to real life ('schildert Alles') 7, 15, 29, 58, 63f., 67f., 78, 80, 85, 92f., 103–5, 109, 122f., 126–8, 133, 137, 139, 141, 147
chance or the unexpected in ('es traf sich', 'Zufall', 'or avenne che') 8, 13, 26, 31, 39–42, 46f., 49–53, 66, 94, 96, 99f., 104, 106, 130, 137, 143, 147
unusual but real event of ('unerhörte Begebenheit', 'cas étrange', 'caso estraño') 1, 13f., 16, 21–3, 26f., 29, 31, 33, 37, 40–8, 50–4, 56f., 60, 62f., 66–9, 73, 78, 82, 84, 90f., 93f., 99f., 104, 131, 133–8, 141, 147
turning-point of ('geistreiche Wendung', 'Wendepunkt') 1, 22, 29, 49, 82, 84, 90, 97f., 100–3, 130, 135, 139
brevity of ('Falke') 1, 3, 8, 11f., 16, 22, 62f., 79f., 88, 90, 105f., 109f., 117, 119, 125, 131, 136, 140f., 145, 148–52
exemplary nature of ('moralische Erzählung', 'conte moral', 'novelas ejemplares') 14–16, 18, 22f., 39, 44, 50, 91, 104
framework narrative in ('Rahmenerzählung') 14f., 20f., 23, 33–6, 40, 65f., 68, 70, 81, 115, 125
pleasure and instruction in ('unterhaltend und befriedigend') 13–16, 18, 21f., 25, 29, 53, 104, 129f., 132, 136
discursive and reflective qualities of ('geschwätzig', 'bequem') 9, 21, 38, 47, 53, 60–2, 66, 78, 80f., 95f., 100, 102f., 117f., 126, 131, 139f.
convivial, sociable and conversational qualities of ('gesellig') 14, 21, 24, 29, 32–6, 60–2, 84, 95, 129, 133, 136f.

Names and titles

Adelung, Johann Christoph 94
Alexis, Willibald 7, 59, 63, 66f.
Anzengruber, Ludwig 124
Arnim, Ludwig Achim von 7, 28, 31f., 34, 37, 40, 59, 90, 92, 98
Auerbach, Berthold 78, 86, 119

Baculard d'Arnaud, François Thomas Marie 22, 44
Balzac, Honoré de 2, 5, 7, 64, 84, 102, 146
Baudelaire, Charles 61
Biernatzki, Johann Christoph 113
Blanckenburg, Friedrich von 82
Blicher, Steen Steensen 118
Boccaccio, Giovanni, *Decameron* 13–16, 18, 20f., 28f., 31–4, 40–2, 50, 59f., 63, 66, 68, 91f., 94, 96, 98f., 105–7, 132–5, 136f., 138, 141, 144, 149f.
Böcklin, Arnold 87
Brahms, Johannes 111f.
Brentano, Clemens 37f., 90, 98, 106
Brockhaus, publisher 59
Büchner, Georg 6f, 66f., 74, 77
Bülow, Eduard von 16, 35, 37, 102

Calderón de la Barca, Pedro 29
Cent Nouvelles nouvelles 14f., 20, 22, 41, 59
Cervantes Saavedra, Miguel de 10, 15, 18, 29–31, 39f., 42, 44f., 47, 50–7, 60, 63, 68, 91f., 98–100, 102f., 132f., 136–9, 144
  Don Quijote 18, 29, 31, 136, *Novelas ejemplares* 15, 29–31, 39f., 42, 44f., 47, 50–7, 60, 63, 68, 91f., 98–100, 102f., 132f., 136–9, 144, Soltau's translation of 29, 51, 'La Fuerza de la sangre' 45, 50–7
Chaucer, Geoffrey 16
Chesterfield, Lord 18
Clairon, La, Claire Leris called, 22

Clauren, H. 93
Cotta, publisher 59, 92, 113

Dante 29
Dickens, Charles 2, 5, 79
Diderot, Denis 12, 18f., 43
Dostoevsky, Fedor 3
Droste-Hülshoff, Annette von 38, 59f., 63–7, 69–74, 76, 90, 106, 111, 113, 115, 122, *Die Judenbuche* 38, 59f., 64–7, 69–74, 106, 122
Dumas, Alexandre 146

Ebner-Eschenbach, Marie von 111
Eckartshausen, Karl von 18
Eckermann, Johann Peter 7, 91–3, 95f., 100
Eichendorff, Joseph von 31, 59, 122
Ernst, Paul 9, 90, 103

Feuerbach, Anselm 110, 126
Fielding, Henry 17, 30f., 102
Flaubert, Gustave 3, 5, 79
Fontane, Theodor 7f., 12, 32, 38, 76, 79, 87f., 109, 113, 120f., 124f.
Fouqué, Friedrich de la Motte 117
Freytag, Gustav 5–7, 77–9
Friedländer, L. 70
Fürst, Rudolf 17

George, Stefan 9
Gervinus, Georg Gottfried 87
Giorgione 87
Goethe, Johann Wolfgang 2, 4, 6f., 10–12, 14, 17–19, 20–4, 25–33, 38, 40–4, 53, 58, 60, 62f., 82, 90–103, 105, 107, 108, 119, 127, 129–32, 138–40, 143f., 149
  Das Märchen 23, 27f., *Die guten Weiber* 21, 92, 94, *Die Wahlverwandtschaften* 12, 24, 91, 93f., 96, 101f., 140, 149, 'Die wunderlichen

Index

Nachbarskinder' story 24, 91, 93f., 96, 101f., *Hermann und Dorothea* 11, 20f., *Novelle* 21, 24, 91–7, 143, *Unterhaltungen deutscher Ausgewanderten* 11, 14, 20–4, 25–8, 32, 40–4, 53, 58, 60, 91, 94–7, 99, 101, 129–32, 139, 'Antonelli' story 22, 27, 53, 'Bassompierre' story 22, 27, 'Ferdinand' story 22, 'Prokurator' story 14, 20, 22, *Wilhelm Meisters Lehrjahre* 20, 28, 82, 99, 139, *Wilhelm Meisters Wanderjahre* 21, 24, 31, 91–8, 101, 'Der Mann von funfzig Jahren' 94f., 'Die neue Melusine' 24, 92, 'Die pilgernde Törin' 92, 'Nicht zu weit' 95
Gotthelf, Jeremias 59f., 65f., 69f., 74f., 76f., 83, 90, 111, 113
  Die schwarze Spinne 59f., 65f., 69f., 74f.
Grabbe, Christian Dietrich 7
Grillparzer, Franz 6, 59f., 63, 68–70, 100, 118
Grimm, Jacob and Wilhelm 28
Grolmann, Adolf von 9
Grosse, Karl 27
Groth, Klaus 111f., 115
Gutzkow, Karl 7, 59, 63

Hauff, Wilhelm 59f., 62, 67, 84f.
Hauptmann, Gerhart 7
Hawthorne, Nathaniel 3
Haydn, Josef 33, 147
Hebbel, Friedrich 6, 76, 111f.
Hegel, Georg Wilhelm Friedrich 111
Heine, Heinrich 77, 115
Hettner, Hermann 77, 84
Heyse, Paul 2, 10f., 33, 35, 38, 58, 70, 79f., 90f., 103–7, 109, 113–15, 126f., 142–50
  Deutscher Novellenschatz 35, 38, 58, 70, 80, 103–7, 109, 114, 143–50, *Novellenschatz des Auslandes* 2, 80, 107
Hobbes, Thomas 47
Hoffmann, Ernst Theodor Amadeus 4, 28, 32f., 35, 38, 52f., 56f., 59, 61f., 68, 82, 85, 90, 98
  Das Gelübde 52f., 56f., *Die Serapionsbrüder* 32, 35
Hofmannsthal, Hugo von 9, 35
Hölderlin, Friedrich 111
Humboldt, Wilhelm von 92f.

Ibsen, Henrik 123
Immermann, Karl 5, 63
Irving, Washington 35

James, Henry 2
Jean Paul 4f.

Keller, Gottfried 1, 5–7, 28, 32, 35f., 38, 73, 76f., 8of., 83–7, 90, 106, 108f., 111, 113, 127
  Die Leute von Seldwyla 35f., 76, 85f., *Romeo und Julia auf dem Dorfe* 35f., 85–7, 106
Klein, Johannes 9
Kleist, Heinrich von 6, 9, 12, 37–57, 58, 61f., 66, 82f., 90, 94, 97, 102, 106, 117, 143
  Das Bettelweib von Locarno 12, 38, 40, 42, *Das Erdbeben in Chili* 38–42, 45–8, 52, *Der Findling* 38, 40, 47f., *Der Zweikampf* 38–40, 42, 49, 51f., *Die heilige Cäcilie* 38, 40, 42, 47f., 61, *Die Marquise von O ...* 38–40, 42, 45, 48, 51–7, *Die Verlobung in St. Domingo* 38–40, 45f., 48, 106, *Michael Kohlhaas* 12, 38, 40, 42, 47
Kotzebue, August von 141
Krömer, Wolfram 11
Kunz, Josef 9, 37
Kurz, Hermann *see* Heyse, Paul, *Deutscher Novellenschatz*

La Bruyère, Jean de 18
Lafontaine, August 18
Laistner, Ludwig *see* Heyse, Paul, *Novellenschatz des Auslandes*
Langbein, August 18
Laube, Heinrich 7, 58f., 63, 90
Lenau, Nikolaus 115
Lenz, Johann Michael Reinhold 97
Lermontov, Mikhail 35
Leskov, Nikolai 85, 125
Ludwig, Otto 6f., 38, 73, 76–8, 81, 83f., 86–8, 109

Mann, Thomas 79
Manzoni, Alessandro 63
Marguerite de Navarre, *Heptaméron* 15, 20
Marmontel, Jean François 22
Martini, Fritz 79
Marx, Karl 77

Maupassant, Guy de 2, 33, 80, 88
Meissner, August Gottlieb 18
Melville, Herman 2, 35
Mérimée, Prosper 2, 7, 12, 80, 83
Metternich, prince 64, 77
Meyer, Conrad Ferdinand 12, 88, 108f., 120, 124
Molière, Jean-Baptiste 84
Mommsen, Theodor 108, 111–13, 115
Mörike, Eduard 32, 36, 59–63, 67f., 70, 90, 106, 111–13, 115, 118, 123
Mozart auf der Reise nach Prag 36, 59–62, 67f., 70, 106, 118, 123
Müllenhoff, Karl 111
Mundt, Theodor 2, 58, 63, 78, 103, 127, 141f.
Musäus, Johann Karl August 25
Musil, Robert 8f.

Nerval, Gérard de 4, 61
Nicolai, Friedrich 25
Nietzsche, Friedrich 6
Novalis 28

Ostade, Adriaen van 87

Pabst, Walter 13
Palma il Vecchio 87
Pascal, Roy 4f.
Piccolomini, Enea Silvio 16
Poe, Edgar Allen 2–4, 28, 61, 91, 104
Polheim, Karl Konrad 10, 12, 33
Pongs, Hermann 9, 37
Prutz, Robert 104
Pushkin, Alexander 2, 83
Pustkuchen, Johann Friedrich Wilhelm 93

Raabe, Wilhelm 5, 7, 76f., 79f., 109
Raynal, abbé 46
Reimer, publisher 59
Reinbeck, Georg 63, 68
Reuter, Fritz 142
Richardson, Samuel 18
Riehl, Wilhelm Heinrich 79f., 90, 150f.
Ritchie, J. M. 3
Rosenkranz, Karl 58
Rousseau, Jean-Jacques 47

Saar, Ferdinand von 76f., 79, 83, 88f., 108f., 111, 123
Sand, George 146
Sartre, Jean-Paul 33

Schelling, Friedrich Wilhelm Joseph 111
Schiller, Friedrich 4, 6f., 19–21, 25, 79, 85, 127
Schimmelmann, count 46
Schlegel, August Wilhelm 4, 28–32, 34, 41, 60, 79, 83f., 90, 99, 135–7
Schlegel, Friedrich 28–32, 60, 84, 90, 132–5
Schleiermacher, Friedrich 34
Schmidt, Erich 117
Schmidt, Julian 77f., 80
Schnabel, Johann Gottfried 17
Schumann, Robert 33, 146
Scott, Walter 7, 63, 67
Sealsfield, Charles 38, 59, 83
Shakespeare, William 17, 29f., 40, 79, 82–9, 109, 132, 135
Silz, Walter 37
Solger, Karl Wilhelm Ferdinand 97
Soltau, Diedrich Wilhelm *see also* Cervantes, *Novelas ejemplares*, Soltau's translation of 29, 51
Spielhagen, Friedrich 79, 84, 104
Spiess, Christian Heinrich 18
Springer, Julius, publisher 113
Staël, Germaine de 4
Staiger, Emil 11f.
Stendhal 7
Sterne, Lawrence 43
Stifter, Adalbert 5, 59f., 62f., 66, 68–70, 74, 76, 80, 90, 96, 108, 111
Bunte Steine 59f., 66, 68–70, 74
Storm, Theodor 1, 7, 12, 28, 32f., 71–5, 76f., 80f., 83, 90, 104–6, 108–28
Aquis submersus 108, 120, 126, *Auf dem Staatshof* 110, 120–2, *Der Schimmelreiter* 12, 33, 71–5, 108, 116, 120, 124–6, *Draussen im Heidedorf* 110, 123f., *Immensee* 113f., 116–19, 121f., 126
Strauss, David Friedrich 111
Sue, Eugène 146

Thackeray, William Makepeace 2, 5
Tieck, Ludwig 7, 10, 12, 17f., 25–9, 31–5, 37, 40, 43, 58–63, 67, 82, 84, 86, 90–2, 97–105, 107, 127, 138–41, 143f.
Das Zauberschloss 101f., *Der blonde Eckbert* 26f., 35, 43, *Phantasus* 27f., 32–5, 40, 58, 60, 143f.
Tolstoy, Leo 3, 5, 79
Turgenev, Ivan 2f., 7, 80f., 88, 105, 113, 115, 118f., 148

Velde, Carl Franz van der 93
Vischer, Friedrich Theodor 77, 79, 104, 111
Volksbuch 17, 26
Voltaire, François Marie Arouet de 18, 41f., 45f.

Wagner, Richard 2, 6, 127
Walpole, Horace 27

Walzel, Oskar 80
Wezel, Johann Karl 18
Wieland, Christoph Martin 17–19, 23f., 26f., 32, 44, 48–50, 91
 Das Hexameron von Rosenhain 23f., 26f., 32, 44, 48–50, 91

Wölfflin, Heinrich 9

Zola, Emile 84, 125